FINANCE

A Theoretical Introduction

DAVID E. ALLEN

Martin Robertson · Oxford

First published in 1983 by Martin Robertson &
Company Ltd., 108 Cowley Road, Oxford OX4 1JF.

British Library Cataloguing in Publication Data

Allen, David E
    Finance: a theoretical introduction
    1. Finance
    I. Title
    332   HG154

    ISBN 0-85520-539-3
    ISBN 0-85520-540-7 Pbk

Typeset by Santype International Ltd., Salisbury, Wilts.
Printed and bound in Great Britain by
T. J. Press Ltd., Padstow.

To Barbara, Corinne and Justine

Contents

Preface

This book is intended primarily for undergraduates in their second or later years of study, reading finance or business studies, economics, accountancy, or banking degrees, and first-year postgraduate students specializing in finance. It should also be of use to advanced professional students pursuing finance courses in preparation for careers in accountancy, investment analysis, or banking.

The book is the result of several years' experience in teaching finance on various undergraduate, postgraduate, and post-experience courses, in both the university and polytechnic sectors, during which I became convinced of the need for a more 'accessible' text on the theory of finance. There are a number of excellent, very advanced texts, but these tend to be extremely demanding for the reader. Whilst not intended for the complete beginner, the book should be readily intelligible to the readership described, or to anyone with a knowledge equivalent to foundation levels in the courses mentioned. Any more general reader with a grasp of basic calculus and simple algebra should have no difficulties in following the arguments. The material contained has been extensively used by the author on undergraduate courses in economics, business studies, and accounting, and on postgraduate business studies courses.

The aim throughout has been to provide a comprehensive yet concise review of the theory of finance. Unlike most texts on the subject this book also draws on representative selections from the relevant empirical work, since it is my view that the development of the subject cannot be readily comprehended without an appreciation of the progress and problems encountered in the empirical 'verification' of the theory. Admittedly only a representative sample can be provided, given the vast extent of the empirical literature, but this, surely, is preferable to the complete neglect of this literature. Suggestions for further reading are included in the notes and references at the end of each chapter.

The book reflects the fundamental 'revolution' that has taken place in financial theory since modern portfolio theory (in a mean–variance context), coupled with an economic-theory-based approach to the subject, fostered the development of a unified theory of finance. The sequence of topics covered reflects both that unity and the logical self-consistent structure of modern financial theory. The essence of the theory consists of a number of interrelated hypotheses, propositions and equilibrium pricing models which lend themselves to mathematical expression. Hence, descriptive institutional material is omitted from the book.

The book is divided into four parts. In Part I the basic concepts are introduced and explained. Chapter 1 establishes the scope, content, and issues covered in the theory of finance, plus some very basic concepts. Chapters 2 and 3 are concerned with the twin pillars which support the structure of the theory – the analysis of risk and the use of expected utility theory.

Part II is concerned with equilibrium market valuation models. Central to this are modern portfolio theory and the capital asset pricing model which feature in chapter 4. It is no accident that this is the longest chapter in the book since this material provides the linchpin of modern financial theory. The material included also covers the arbitrage pricing model, state preference theory, and the 'efficient markets' literature. Chapter 5 provides a comprehensive treatment of option theory, probably the most exciting theoretical development of the last decade, and a review of some of its multifarious potential applications. The establishment of the various equilibrium pricing models in this part is of central importance, in that the current theory of finance is largely developed in an 'equilibrium' framework.

Part III is concerned with both real investment decisions and financial decisions made by corporate bodies. Throughout, recourse is made to models developed in Part II. This is particularly apparent in chapter 6, in which there is fairly extensive consideration of the theoretical difficulties involved in the application of CAPM to multiperiod capital budgeting decisions, following a review of the more 'standard' capital investment decision criteria. Chapter 7 investigates the theory of dividend decisions and in the course of this establishes various valuation models of the corporation. Finally, chapter 8 examines the capital structure decision from various angles.

In the final part, chapter 9 attempts an evaluation of the current state of the art. Attention is drawn to the possible drawbacks associated with an equilibrium, economic-theory-based approach to the subject largely phrased in the context of perfect markets. These include the difficulty of rehabilitating institutions into such a theory and the problems encountered in assigning a positive role for liquidity. Thus it is no accident that topics such as the demand for liquidity and the management of short-term assets are not included, since the theory behind the treatment of these items is largely *ad hoc* and is not readily incorporated into the mainstream theory which is the concern of the book. Programming models dealing with maximization subject to constraints are largely neglected, since they too sit uneasily with the central thrust of the material considered.

The book includes a considerable amount of new material and unusual topics. As already noted, there is continual reference to the empirical literature where appropriate. Other 'novel' features include the treatment of arbitrage pricing theory and state preference theory in chapter 4. Option theory, introduced in chapter 5, is still so new that few texts give extensive coverage. Part III covers the latest developments and applications of concepts introduced in Part II.

Although the book is conceived and developed as a unified whole, the chapters are individually structured so that they 'stand on their own feet', and therefore use of the book can be tailored to the individual requirements of a course and to the preferences of the reader concerned. Thus, the book is not written with the requirements of a particular course – accountancy, economics, or business studies – or department in mind, but provides a general introduction to the theory of finance. This should meet the needs, in whole or in part, of courses in finance in all the areas mentioned previously, as well as being a useful reference text for all those readers wishing to keep abreast of developments in the theory of finance.

Acknowledgements

Thanks are due first and foremost to the various authorities in the field, who have all been my teachers vicariously via the literature. It is to be hoped that the compression, simplification, and condensation required in a text of this nature has not done injustice to the richness and complexity of their thought. I am indebted to my colleagues in the University of Edinburgh, in particular to Dr J. Kwiatkowski for help with some mathematical points, and, above all, to Dr I. R. C. Hirst who read and constructively commented on the entire manuscript, and who was unstintingly generous with his time. I would also like to thank Brian Goodale, freelance editor, for his meticulous editing. My thanks go to J. R. Franks and S. D. Hodges for permission to reproduce figures 6.3–6.6. Finally, I would like to thank my wife Barbara for her encouragement, and my daughters Corinne and Justine for providing 'light relief'. The usual caveat applies with respect to any errors.

DAVID E. ALLEN
1982

PART I

The Foundations

CHAPTER 1

Introduction and basic concepts

In the end all prices depend on someone's estimate of future income.[1]*

This statement, taken from John Burr Williams's 1938 text, pierces the very heart of the subject of finance. Yet his stance was atypical, and in general the economic-theory-based approach he adopted was remarkably 'modern'. To set the material which follows in some perspective, the manner in which the subject has historically evolved will be considered first.

1.1   THE EVOLUTION OF THE SUBJECT

One of the earliest books written on the subject was Greene's *Corporation Finance* which appeared around the turn of this century.[2] Over the next forty years major works appeared by Meade, Dewing, and Lyon.[3] These works shared a certain commonality of view and preoccupation for which Solomon has employed the phrase 'the "traditional" approach to finance'.[4] By this he meant that the popular approach was legalistic, descriptive, and concentrated on the major events in the life cycle of a corporation, such as the issuance of securities and mergers and combinations, as viewed from the outside. Nevertheless, further removed from the popular view, other work was under way which provided a base for modern theoretical developments.

Knight's work on *Risk, Uncertainty and Profit* was published in 1921; in the next decade Fisher developed further some of the foundations of modern interest rate theory, and Williams's work

---

* Notes and references will be found at the end of each chapter.

(mentioned previously) anticipated modern developments in a number of areas.[5]

In the immediate post-war period the popular general treatment switched in emphasis to internal financial managerial problems as exemplified by such topics as financial and budgetary control. The tremendously successful work by Hunt and Williams is representative of this approach.[6]

Although all these popular works were concerned with the central issues of the subject, they lacked analytical rigour and were predominantly descriptive. They could not undertake a positive analysis of the nature of financial decisions, and therefore normative prescriptive statements about how issues ought to be tackled were ruled out.

The first impetus towards an economic-theory-based approach which would provide an integrated methodological structure for dealing with all financial decision areas came in the fifties. A sophisticated treatment of the capital budgeting decision was provided by the Lutzes, though it was Joel Dean in his famous work, *Capital Budgeting*, who really popularized an economic-theory-based approach to this branch of the subject.[7] At the same time Markowitz was producing his work on portfolio theory, which was to father many subsequent developments and, not least, revolutionize the treatment of risk in finance.[8] His formal quantification of the benefits of risk diversification, and elucidation of the nature of the basic trade-off between risk and expected return, were insights whose repercussions were to continually reverberate through the development of the subject. The development of an explicit treatment of risk was extremely important; previously, rather like Banquo's ghost at the feast, it had existed but been formally unacknowledged.

Subsequent extension and generalization of this work, by Sharpe amongst others, was to lead to a general pricing or valuation model for assessing risky assets in financial markets.[9] This work has its origins in a theory of valuation developed in securities' markets from a perspective of individual portfolio investment management. Amongst the securities valued, a large proportion will be made up of corporate equity and debt; therefore financial policy and investment decisions on the part of corporate financial managers will play an important role in determining these values. There is thus a bridge between investment management and corporate financial decisions, previously regarded as separate branches of finance. The formal bridging of this theoretical divide was undertaken by Rubinstein.[10]

If corporate decisions are going to be effectively reflected in corporate security valuation, the dissemination and processing of information about corporate activities within financial markets will play a key role. If markets are fully informed they are said to be 'efficient'. Much empirical work has been done on the testing the 'market efficiency' hypothesis, in various forms, in the various markets around the world. Although, as will later be seen, the work had its origins outside mainstream financial literature, its popular adoption and main impetus stemmed from Cootner's book of readings, *The Random Character of Stock Market Prices.*[11]

The spirit of the new theory of finance, with its foundations in economic theory and its assumptions of fully informed 'perfect' capital markets is epitomized by the work of Modigliani and Miller in the late fifties and early sixties. Their original work on capital structure theory and dividend policy is still a source of inspiration and debate.[12]

All these developments, which have taken place since the beginning of the fifties, will be the central concern of this book. So too will the main development of the seventies – the option pricing model developed by Black and Scholes.[13] This work, although concerned with option pricing, was seen by them to have widespread implications for the valuation of corporate liabilities; however, its subsequent fecundity has probably outstripped what they first imagined.

The existence of a unified theory of finance, founded on economic theory, was demonstrated in the early seventies by the publication of Fama and Miller's standard work on the theory of finance.[14] This work was structured around the premise that the individual investor or company is concerned with the allocation of resources over time. This choice is made under conditions of uncertainty with a view to maximizing the expected utility of the outcomes. In the case of individual agents it was assumed that decisions are made with a view to an ultimate objective of maximizing the utility of lifetime consumption.

In the course of this book, all the developments mentioned and many more will be encountered. The rapid growth of the theory of finance is only matched by the expansion of its accompanying empirical literature. Yet the subject is still in its infancy. Many absolutely central issues, such as whether or not an optimal capital structure or dividend policy exists, and what is their precise nature, are still unresolved. There still exist doubts about the adequacy of the 'conventional' treatment of uncertainty and the robustness of techniques currently adopted for dealing with multiperiod decisions. All these factors will be considered. It will also be seen that, despite the evident strengths of and indisputably major advances in current knowledge, there are some possible associated weaknesses and draw-backs. These will be considered in the final chapter.

The developments accomplished so far are novel and exciting. This trend has perhaps accelerated over the last decade, and holds every promise of continuing to do so throughout the next.

1.2 THE TIME VALUE OF MONEY

At the beginning of this chapter it was mentioned that prices are dependent upon estimates of future income. This introduces two pivotal problems encountered in finance – uncertainty and time. Both can be regarded as aspects of the same fundamental problem. Hicks has recently commented that, 'What the past is to the historian, the present is to the economist. The work of each of them is in time, in historical time, as the work of most natural scientists is not.'[15] This is one of the central philosophical and 'scientific' methodological problems encountered throughout the social sciences. Anyone making a decision, if it is a rational decision, takes it with a view to its desired future effects. This is typically the case with financial decisions. Usually there is a time lag between cause (decision) and effect (desired result), and because of that lag, and of the nature of the 'economic' world, the consequence is not perfectly predictable. Time and uncertainty are at the heart of the matter, and the greater part of the next two chapters will attempt to build a theoretical framework capable of tackling the problem. For the moment the problem of uncertainty will be ignored in favour of that of time.

Throughout it will be assumed that decisions are made rationally with a view to maximizing the expected utility of their outcome (there will be a detailed analysis of this in chapter 3). Ultimately, it can be assumed that economic decisions are taken with a view to final consumption and its associated utility. If this is the case, at the outset it can be assumed that a decision is being made about the allocation of consumption in a two-period world in which there is no doubt about the value of second-period consumption.

To develop the argument a hypothetical case will be considered of the choice between two different amounts of wealth or values of consumption of £100 in the current period (period 0) and £105 in the next period (period 1). If the world is one which is characterized by complete certainty, there will exist a 'pure' rate of interest which reflects the 'time preference' or 'impatience' to consume on the part of individuals. It will always be positive, since it is assumed that

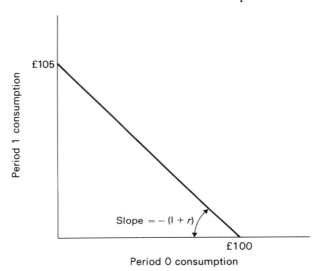

FIGURE 1.1   *The time value of money in a two-period model*

people typically prefer to consume income now rather than later. This pure rate of interest r will determine the translation of income now into income one year later, as shown in figure 1.1.

If the pure rate of interest is 5 per cent per period a rational individual would be indifferent between £100 now and £105 in the next period; the two values are equivalent.

1.3   PRESENT VALUES AND DISCOUNTING

The argument in section 1.2 suggests the following identity:

$$£100 = \frac{£105}{(1 + r)}.$$

Therefore

$$r = \frac{£105}{£100} - 1$$

$$= 5 \text{ per cent.}$$

With a pure interest rate of 5 per cent, £100 is the present value of £105 received in the next period. To translate period 1 wealth into current wealth it has to be discounted at the appropriate rate. In figure 1.1 the line linking the two amounts is a present value line. It has a slope equal to $-(1 + r)$, where in this case $r = 5$ per cent. It links amounts of consumption or wealth in the diagram of equal worth. The intersection with the horizontal axis shows present value (PV) and that with the vertical axis shows terminal value (TV). For by the same logic, £1 later must be worth more than £1 now. In general, if a constant rate of interest is assumed then the following relationship holds:

$$PV = \frac{A_n}{(1 + k)^n} \tag{1.1}$$

where PV is present value, A_n is a future amount of wealth (cash) received n periods ahead, and k is the appropriate discount rate (in this case assumed constant over the n periods).

Conversely, with a positive rate of interest, no one should be prepared to accept a future payment of less than its current cash value, compounded forward over the appropriate number of periods at the relevant interest rate. Thus terminal value is given by:

$$TV = A_0(1 + k)^n \tag{1.2}$$

where A_0 is the current value of the cash sum and all other symbols are as before.

So far discrete time has been considered; exactly the same principles hold in continuous time except that the mathematical technique employed would differ slightly and natural logarithms would be used.

Finally, the present value of a stream of cash flows is given by:

$$PV = \frac{A_1}{(1 + k)} + \frac{A_2}{(1 + k)^2} + \frac{A_3}{(1 + k)^3} + \cdots + \frac{A_n}{(1 + k)^n}$$

$$\therefore \quad PV = \sum_{t=1}^{n} \frac{A_t}{(1 + k)^t} \tag{1.3}$$

where A_t is the cash sum received in period t and k is the appropriate discount rate (assumed constant).

1.4　THE PRESENT VALUE OF AN ANNUITY

The practice of discounting and compounding, and the use of present and terminal values, are fundamental in both theoretical and practical finance. Consider the case of an annuity, a term referring to a series of equal payments made at equal intervals of time. These occur frequently in the form of interest payments on debentures or gilts, premiums on life assurance, depreciation funds, mortgage payments and so on. Suppose it is required to find the present value of the stream of payments A, the first of which is made at the end of the first period. Then:

$$PV_A = \frac{A}{(1 + k)} + \frac{A}{(1 + k)^2} + \frac{A}{(1 + k)^3} + \cdots + \frac{A}{(1 + k)^n}.$$

If V is $1/(1 + k)$, this expression becomes:

$$PV_A = AV + AV^2 + AV^3 + \cdots + AV^n. \tag{1.4}$$

Multiplying (1.4) by V yields:

$$VPV_A = AV^2 + AV^3 + AV^4 + \cdots + AV^{n+1}. \tag{1.5}$$

Subtracting (1.5) from (1.4) gives:

$$PV_A - VPV_A = AV - AV^{n+1}$$

$$\therefore \quad PV_A(1 - V) = AV(1 - V^n)$$

$$PV_A = \frac{AV(1 - V^n)}{(1 - V)}.$$

Substituting back $V = 1/(1 + k)$ gives:

$$PV_A = A\left(\frac{1}{1 + k}\right)\left\{\frac{1 - (1 + k)^{-n}}{1 - [1/(1 + k)]}\right\}$$

$$= A\left(\frac{1}{1 + k}\right)\left[\frac{1 - (1 + k)^{-n}}{(1 + k - 1)/(1 + k)}\right]$$

$$PV_A = A\left[\frac{1 - (1 + k)^{-n}}{k}\right]. \tag{1.6}$$

Tables for the calculation of the present value of an annuity are based on (1.6) assuming a payment of £1 per period. For greater values of A the result simply has to be multiplied by the value of A. For example, assume that there is a payment of £10 for five years and that the rate of interest (k) is 12 per cent. Calculation of the term in brackets in (1.6) (or recourse to the appropriate tables) yields a value of 3.6048. The multiplication of this value by £10 (A) gives the present value of the annuity, £36.048.

The use of (1.6) in this book will be more pragmatic; it is often mathematically convenient to assume that one is dealing with the present value of an infinite series of payments. Perusal of (1.6) shows that:

$$\lim_{n \to \infty} PV_A = \frac{A}{k}. \tag{1.7}$$

This follows since

$$\lim_{n \to \infty} \frac{1}{(1 + k)^n} = 0$$

(given that k is positive). This result will be used frequently in chapter 8 when we discuss capital structure.

1.5   THE VALUE OF A CAPITAL MARKET

For the moment the discussion returns to the two-period world of certainty. It can be assumed that, for each individual faced with the problem of how to allocate his consumption over the two periods, an indifference map can be constructed as shown in figure 1.2. This

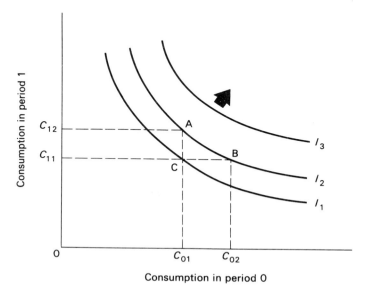

FIGURE 1.2   *An individual consumer's indifference map*

summarizes the individual's relative preferences for period 0 and period 1 consumption. All points along the same curve represent equivalent levels of utility or satisfaction.

Points A and B lie on the same indifference curve and yield equal utility. The fact that point A has less associated period 0 consumption $(C_{01} < C_{02})$ is compensated by the fact that it offers more period 1 consumption $(C_{12} > C_{11})$. Point C is inferior and is situated on a lower indifference curve, yielding less satisfaction. This is because it offers less consumption in the two periods taken together than either of the previous positions, and because more consumption is preferred to less, in terms of utility $(I_3 > I_2 > I_1)$, and the rational individual prefers to move in the direction of the arrow. Utility functions will be considered at greater length in chapter 3 (but for a full treatment see Fama and Miller).[16] The fact that the utility curves are convex to the origin suggests diminishing marginal utility of substitution of period 0 consumption for period 1 consumption and vice versa. This means that if, for example, an individual has a lot of period 0 consumption and little of period 1, he will require a lot of extra period 0 consumption to compensate him for any further reduction in his, already scarce, period 1 consumption.

Suppose now that an individual has an income (under the same conditions of a two-period world with certainty) which stems from a financial security that offers the combination of period 0 and period 1 consumption indicated by point D in figure 1.3.

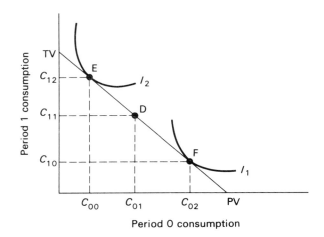

FIGURE 1.3 *The reallocation of consumption opportunities in the capital market*

In the absence of a capital market the individual would be stuck at point D in figure 1.3, with his consumption endowments of C_{01} in period 0 and C_{11} in period 1. Assume that a perfect capital market exists in the world of the hypothetical example. For a perfect market to exist the following assumptions have to hold:

(1) Each individual purchaser or seller of securities is so small, in relation to the total market in that security, that his actions can have no appreciable effect on either the total quantity traded in the market or the equilibrium price. He has to be a 'price-taker' and accept the market price as given.
(2) There are no restrictions on price movements or taxes.
(3) There are no dealing or transactions costs. The market is infinitely divisible and frictionless.
(4) There is complete freedom of entry and exit to the market, that is, no restrictions on access.
(5) There is perfect knowledge on the part of all participants in the market. They are all costlessly informed of market opportunities and prices.

These assumptions are unrealistic but they may be justified on the grounds that they lead to very powerful analytical results. Once the model has been built the assumptions can be relaxed.

For the purposes of the example the assumptions ensure that there will be one, general, equilibrium rate of interest at which all market participants will be able to trade. This is the situation depicted in figure 1.3 with the individual endowed as indicated by point D. Given the existence of the perfect capital market, a present value line with a slope equal to $-(1 + r)$ can be drawn through point D and will summarize all the various market opportunities (in this two-period world) now available to the individual. The present value of his endowment is indicated by the point of intersection of this line with the horizontal axis (marked *PV* in figure 1.3). This is the 'value' of his endowment; for a given interest rate, the value is immutable.

If a capital market exists, the individual is now free to reallocate his consumption over the two periods to any combination along this line. He can do this by borrowing or lending against his original endowment at the market rate of interest. If his preferences were as indicated by indifference curve I_2, its point of tangency E with the present value line would be his preferred position. He could move from D to E by lending $C_{01} - C_{00}$ current worth of consumption at the market rate of interest and in return receive $C_{12} - C_{11}$ in period 1. Alternatively, if his preferences were represented by curve I_1 and point F he could borrow $C_{02} - C_{01}$ units of current consumption in return for a repayment of $C_{11} - C_{10}$ worth of period 1 consumption. The individual's utility is increased by these actions. Given the nature of the utility map in figure 1.2, an optimal position is given by the point of tangency of the present value line and the highest attainable indifference curve. Clearly, in both cases point D is suboptimal and movement to either E or F will increase utility.

This means that the existence of the capital market increases everyone's utility, since if initial consumption endowment opportunities are not optimal they can be rearranged to suit individual preferences by appropriate combinations of borrowing or lending. Notice, however, that utility and not wealth has been increased by this. The present value of the endowment is unchanged. For this reason present value is a very useful *numéraire* or measure of value. If by some means the individual could increase the present value of his original endowment he would be even better off. This leads on naturally to a consideration of the goals or objectives usually adopted or assumed in the theory of finance.

1.6 THE MAXIMIZATION OF VALUE

The time value of money, the concept of present value, and the important related idea of discounting have been considered, all in the context of a world of certainty. It has also been demonstrated that the existence of a capital market increases investor utility. So far so good. However, what happens in the case of an investor who holds shares in a publicly quoted company? What policy would he prefer the company's management to pursue on his behalf? This is a central issue, since inevitably much of the theory of finance is concerned with the effects of corporate decisions, both real (where the concern is with the choice of productive and investment alternatives) and financial (where the choice is a matter of financial policy and financing instruments).

The investment decision

To analyse the investment decision, the assumption will be retained of the existence of a world of certainty in which there are consumption opportunities in two periods. Suppose that a firm, individually owned, is faced with the choice either of consuming its given stock of financial resources in financing the owner's current consumption,

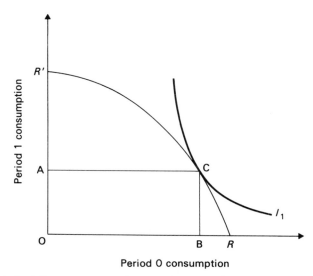

FIGURE 1.4   *The investment decision for an individually owned firm in the absence of a capital market*

equal to an amount OR in figure 1.4, or of investing some or all of it in a number of one-period investment projects. The rate of return achieved on these projects is equal to the income received from the project divided by the original investment outlay, and the resultant quotient is then reduced by the amount of the outlay to yield a rate of return as follows:

$$\text{rate of return} = \frac{\text{income} - \text{outlay}}{\text{outlay}},$$

$$\therefore \quad 1 + \text{rate of return} = \frac{\text{income}}{\text{outlay}}.$$

The one-period rates of return offered by these projects are ranked in descending order along the curve RR' in figure 1.4. For the sake of simplicity it is assumed that there are a large number of very small projects all offering slightly different rates of return; RR' is therefore continuous rather than 'stepped'. All the projects are independent, and can be taken up individually.

Given the production opportunity curve RR' in figure 1.4, and the owner's relative preferences for period 0 *vis-à-vis* period 1 consumption, as indicated by his indifference curves, his optimum strategy would be to move to point C, the point of tangency of the productive opportunity curve and his maximal attainable indifference curve. Given the normal assumptions about maximizing utility and the non-satiation of wants, higher levels of both period 0 and period 1 consumption give greater utility; the preferred position will therefore be as far to the top right-hand corner of figure 1.4 as possible. At point C the owner chooses to invest BR units of the equivalent of current consumption to obtain OA units of period 1 consumption. He consumes the remainder of the firm's endowment equal to OB units of current consumption.

Assume once again the existence of a perfect capital market. In such a market, period 0 consumption units can be traded for period 1 consumption units. The rate of exchange can be indicated by a series of present value lines of slope $-(1 + r)$. Given the existence of a capital market, the owner of the firm has a choice; he can either invest in the firm's available projects or lend his resources on the capital market at a rate of interest equal to r. The effect of these two alternatives is shown in figure 1.5.

The utility of the firm's owner(s) (it will shortly be seen that the argument can be generalized to the case of the firm owned by many shareholders) is clearly enhanced by the existence of a capital market, as can be seen from figure 1.5. Suppose that the owner's preferences were indicated by the 'family' of indifference curves represented by indifference curves I_{2a} and I_{2b}. In the absence of a capital market the point of tangency of the curves RR' and I_{2b} would mark his preferred position. Given the existence of a capital market, his dominant strategy is to take on investments up to point D on the curve RR'. A present value line EF with slope $-(1 + r)$ just comes into tangency with RR' at point D, and is therefore the maximum attainable present value line of the large number of lines, with a slope equal to the rate of interest, which could be drawn intersecting or coming into contact with RR'. Point D dominates all other positions on RR', since it has the highest attainable present value, in terms of current consumption units, as represented by E, its point of intersection with the horizontal axis. Present value can be used as a *numéraire* to measure the relative attractiveness of various combinations of consumption opportunities over various periods. Thus, given the production possibility curve, the optimum strategy is to choose that particular set of investments which yields the maximum present value, or movement to the right along the horizontal axis in figure 1.5. At point D the return offered by the last project taken on (the marginal project's return) is just equal to the market rate of interest.

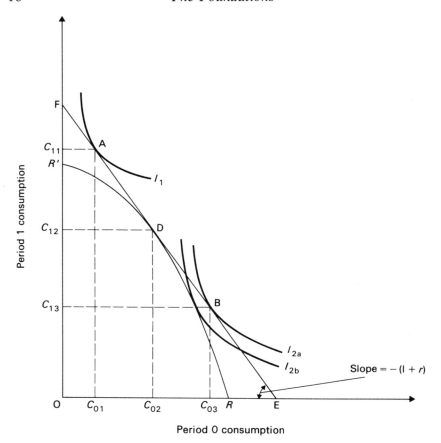

FIGURE 1.5   *The investment decision for a firm in the presence of a perfect capital market*

Procedure along RR' beyond point D would mean that the firm was taking on projects which offered a rate of return lower than the market rate of interest; this would be a suboptimal strategy. The firm would obviously be better served by lending out any remaining resources at the market rate of interest rather than taking on these inferior projects. In effect, at point D, the firm is equating yields at the margin. Furthermore, point D will be preferred irrespective of other preferences. The owner with preferences indicated by indifference curves I_{2a} and I_{2b} and one with preferences indicated by I_1 would both prefer movement to point D. The owner with a preference for current consumption, as represented by curve I_{2a}, would let the firm move to point D, which offers C_{02} units of current consumption and C_{12} units of period 1 consumption. Then he would 'borrow' or trade $C_{12} \rightarrow C_{13}$ units of period 1 consumption to obtain $C_{02} \rightarrow C_{03}$ units of current consumption, all that is required to move him to his preferred point B. He is clearly better off than he would have been in the absence of a capital market, in which circumstances he would have remained on a lower indifference curve I_{2b}. Likewise an owner with preferences indicated by curve I_1 could lend $C_{01} \rightarrow C_{02}$ units so as to move to point A. It can be perhaps be appreciated intuitively (for a more rigorous treatment see appendix 1.1) that if individual owners, irrespective of their preference, all prefer point D then many owners or shareholders, despite their preferences, will also prefer point D.

It follows that in a perfect market, characterized by the existence of a unique rate of interest, a separation theorem holds: the firm should maximize the present value of available investment opportunities, and by this means shareholder interests will be automatically maximized as well, irrespective of any individual differences in their time/consumption preferences. The firm's investment decision can be separated from any concern with shareholder preferences. The next question, which automatically follows, is how can this 'property' be turned into a decision criterion for evaluating investments?

The net present value and internal rate of return rules

Under the conditions assumed, two 'discounted cash flow' techniques will be considered that ensure that optimal investment decisions are taken: the net present value (NPV) rule and the internal rate of return (IRR) rule. The equation for NPV is as follows:

$$NPV = \frac{NCF_1}{(1+k)} + \frac{NCF_2}{(1+k)^2} + \cdots + \frac{NCF_n}{(1+k)^n} - I_0$$

$$\therefore \quad NPV = \sum_{i=1}^{n} \frac{NCF_i}{(1+k)^n} - I_0 \qquad (1.8)$$

where NCF_i is the net cash flow for the project in period i ($i = 1, \ldots, n$), I_0 is the original investment outlay in period 0 (for simplicity the assumption is made that only one outlay is involved), and k is the firm's marginal cost of capital.

The NPV rule suggests that the firm should discount all the net returns available from a project, for all periods of the project's life, at its marginal cost of capital (the cost of obtaining funds to finance the project). If, after undertaking this exercise, and deducting from the sum of discounted returns the original investment outlay, the net sum or *NPV* is positive, the project is profitable and should be undertaken. In figure 1.5 the marginal project at point D would have a zero *NPV*. It will be seen in later chapters that calculating a firm's marginal cost of capital, in practice, is a non-trivial problem. In the simplistic world assumed there is only one cost of capital, the pure interest rate r. In the two-period example in figure 1.5 the slope, or first derivative, of the curve RR' shows the yield on each project at each point on the curve. By definition, each project on the portion of the production possibility curve DR will have a positive *NPV*, since the gradient at all points on DR is greater than that of the market value line FE.

The internal rate of return calculation is as follows:

$$NPV = \frac{NCF_1}{(1 + R^*)} + \frac{NCF_2}{(1 + R^*)^2} + \cdots + \frac{NCF_n}{(1 + R^*)^n} - I_0 = 0$$

$$\therefore \quad NPV = \sum_{i=1}^{n} \frac{NCF_i}{(1 + R^*)^n} - I_0 = 0 \tag{1.9}$$

where R^* is that discount rate, the *IRR*, which when applied in (1.9) yields an *NPV* of zero, and all other symbols are as before.

The solution discount rate R^* is then compared with the firm's marginal cost of capital. All projects with an *IRR* greater than the marginal cost of capital are profitable and should be undertaken. In figure 1.5 the marginal project at point D has an *IRR* equal to the market rate of interest r, whereas all projects on DR have *IRR*s greater than r and are therefore profitable. Projects on R'D have *IRR*s less than r and are therefore unprofitable. In the simplified world of perfect capital markets and certainty, both the *NPV* and *IRR* rules lead to identical decisions concerning which projects should be undertaken.

The equivalence of the two approaches can be further appreciated from figure 1.6, which graphs at varying discount rates the *NPV* of the project shown in table 1.1. In the table the undiscounted cash flows are shown in the first row. As the discount rate is increased the *NPV* shown in the far right-hand column falls until finally, at 62 per cent discount rate, the solution rate for the *IRR* is achieved yielding an *NPV* of zero. The equivalence of the two rules can be seen in figure 1.6, in which the curve traces out the combinations of *NPV*s and discount rates from the example in table 1.1. It can be seen that

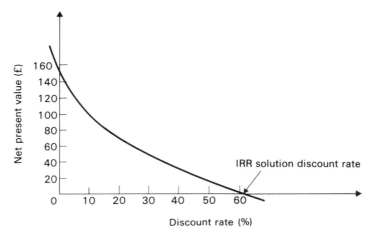

FIGURE 1.6   *The formal equivalence of the NPV and IRR investment criteria*

at all discount rates up to 62 per cent the project has a positive *NPV*, and is therefore profitable as long as the firm's marginal cost of capital is not in excess of 62 per cent. In the case of the *IRR* criterion, the *IRR* of 62 per cent will be greater than any marginal cost of capital up to 62 per cent, and the project is therefore profitable for any cost of capital less than 62 per cent. In this sense the two decision criteria yield identical results, and both are based on value maximization.

TABLE 1.1   *The discounted cash flows and NPV of a project at various discount rates*

Discount rate (%)	Period					NPV
	0	1	2	3	4	
0	− 100	100	50	50	50	150
10	− 100	90.9	41.3	37.6	34.2	104
20	− 100	83.3	34.72	28.94	24.1	70.96
30	− 100	76.92	29.59	22.76	17.51	46.78
40	− 100	71.43	25.5	18.22	13.0	28.15
50	− 100	66.66	22.22	14.82	9.88	13.58
62	− 100	61.73	19.05	11.76	7.26	approx 0

The inadequacy of the profit maximizing objective

Brief consideration reaffirms the primacy of value maximization as opposed to the economist's customary view that profit maximization is the relevant decision criterion. A major difficulty associated with the latter is the issue of defining profitability. There is a contrast between the economist's and the accountant's viewpoints.

The traditional accountant's view is to consider profitability as being an *ex post*, 'backward-looking' measure, concerned with the assessment of the surplus of business revenue over costs over an appropriate period, normally the accounting year. This immediately leads on to associated measurement problems – the consideration of how fixed costs and overheads ought to be allocated over the period. Underlying all this is the nature of the distinction between capital and income. These matters involve formidable practical and theoretical difficulties. For a start it is usually assumed that income cannot be paid from capital, and that capital values have to be maintained intact. Hicks suggested that, 'Income must be defined as the maximum amount of money which the individual can spend this week, and still expect to be able to spend the same amount in real terms in each ensuing week.'[17] However, this involves a change of perspective from the accountant's to the economist's point of view.[18]

The economist's view is an *ex ante* one, focused on the estimation of the discounted present value of the future benefits expected to accrue from the ownership of an asset, whether real or financial. As this view is 'forward looking' it necessarily involves choice and the estimation of the scale of future benefits and the appropriate discount rate. It is necessarily, therefore, a somewhat subjective viewpoint, which cannot be avoided in the determination of 'economic worth' or value.

Accountants, on the other hand, have tended to focus on the role of stewardship in the drawing up of accounts to represent an 'objective' picture of the manner in which a business has been run for the outside principals – the shareholders. Traditionally, accounts have been drawn up on a basis of historical costs with a view to the accepted canons of accounting wisdom – the principles of matching assets and liabilities, conservation (in all matters of valuation), and realization. The manifest inability of this approach to cope with the distortions introduced by high and persistent levels of inflation has led to a rethinking and a return to first principles. The adoption of a current cost accounting system has brought the accountant back to a consideration of economic value and suitable proxies for it.[19]

However, accounting profits remain a historical statement, and for that reason it is the economist's viewpoint that is fundamental to the analysis developed in this book. This is not to discount the crucial significance of accounting data, which obviously make important contributions to a number of the decision areas which will be considered in this book. As an informational input, such data may well contribute to estimations of economic worth; indeed, there is a growing literature concerned with analysing the impact of accounting data (particularly in the context of market 'efficiency' considered in chapter 4).[20]

Nevertheless, even if it is accepted that it is the economist's definition of value that is relevant to this book, it still cannot be taken that a straightforward definition of the maximization of economic profits is the appropriate decision criterion. This is not because of any deference to alternative 'managerial' or 'behavioural' theories of the firm, for despite the persuasiveness of these theories they have much less analytical and operational strength than the profit maximizing model.[21] It is because the profit maximizing model is one dimensional; it is suited to assumptions of certainty but not to the two parameters – expected returns and risk – which are the basis of the financial theories developed in this book.

A central feature of the theory of finance is the development of an analytical framework capable of handling both expected returns and risk. The essential foundations of this are developed in the course of the next two chapters. It will be seen that rational investors are assumed to dislike risk. Therefore a given level of expected returns subject to two different levels of risk will not be viewed or valued equally by investors. Much of chapter 4 will be devoted to the development of this idea, but some of the material in that chapter can be anticipated by consideration of figure 1.7.

It may well be the case that investors view all the points plotted along the line *RF–Z* in figure 1.7 as being equivalent. Higher expected returns or future profits, subject to high levels of risk, are regarded as equal to lower expected returns subject to a lower level of risk. Thus profit maximization, or the maximization of expected returns, is inadequate since it neglects any consideration of risk. There are various conceptual and definitional problems associated with profitability.[22] Henceforth these problems will be avoided by framing arguments in terms of expected returns subject to risk. The assessment of these factors will determine economic value.

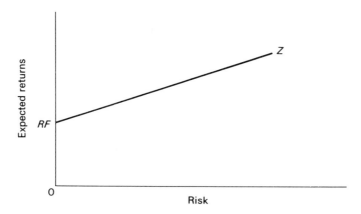

FIGURE 1.7   *Expected returns subject to different levels of risk*

Value maximization as the adopted decision criterion

Throughout this book it will be assumed that corporate decisions are taken with a view to value maximization. The maximization of the value of the corporation, and therefore the maximization of the value of the shareholder's interest, is assumed to be the optimum decision criterion. The reasons for this will be further developed in later chapters, but basic concepts sufficient to grasp its essential features have already been covered.

It was seen in the discussion of present value and the time value of money that future certain wealth can be expressed and measured in present value terms. By the same token, future uncertain or risky wealth can also be measured in present value terms. Admittedly certain further adjustments may be required to do this. Basically, estimations of the size of future increments of wealth will be adjusted downwards, or the discount rate employed to translate them into current value terms will be inflated (these matters will be considered in detail in chapters 4 and 6). Thus, in all the real and financial decisions considered, present value will be adopted as the appropriate *numéraire* and value maximization as the appropriate goal. This measure is chosen because it can take into account both the timing of increments of wealth and their relative riskiness.

1.7 EQUILIBRIUM, ARBITRAGE, AND THE VALUE ADDITIVITY PRINCIPLE

Many of the theories and proofs that will be considered will depend upon the assumption of 'equilibrium' conditions. When the market for any good or financial asset is in equilibrium, effective demand is equal to effective supply; their level of equilibration will determine value. Much of the theory assumes the existence of perfect markets and their concomitant, perfect knowledge, on the part of all market participants. If there are temporary deviations from equilibrium, forces will be set in motion which move the market back to equilibrium. In financial markets such a process is usually termed 'arbitrage'. If a financial asset is temporarily over- or underpriced, it is assumed that sharp-witted market operators (at least under perfect market conditions) will recognize this. Then they will either buy or sell as required by the circumstances and, by this process of arbitrage with a view to profit-taking, will force back the asset's value to its equilibrium level.

The value additivity principle is a natural corollary of the assumptions that markets are perfect and financial assets correctly priced. It follows on directly from the arguments considered in section 1.6 which showed that value maximization is the 'correct' decision criterion irrespective of individual investor time preferences. Similarly, financing considerations are also 'separate' given that there is one rate of interest in a perfect market, and this is used as the marginal cost of capital or 'hurdle rate' in an investment decision. Projects can therefore be independently evaluated according to their own merits on the basis of an appropriate decision criterion such as the *NPV* or *IRR* rules.

If projects can be valued independently, then the value of the firm can be determined by simplying summing the individual values of the 'bundle' of projects which collectively make up the activities of the firm. This is the value additivity rule, and can be formally stated as:

$$V = \sum_{i=1}^{n} P_i \qquad (1.10)$$

where V is the value of the company and P_i is the value of each individual project i. In practice this is not always likely to be the case, and some of the difficulties will be examined in later chapters.

24 *The Foundations*

1.8 MARKET IMPERFECTIONS AND RELATED DIFFICULTIES

Most of the models which will be developed are based on the assumption of perfect markets and in many of the following chapters considerable time will be spent examining how the models cope with the reintroduction of real-world imperfections and how they ultimately break down. The difficulties are formidable. To demonstrate the fundamental nature of the problem, the way in which the value maximization criterion copes with some relatively minor market imperfections is briefly examined.

Hirshleifer pointed out that if the market is assumed to have a borrowing rate greater than the lending rate (the 'normal' situation faced by a typical borrower) then the *NPV* rule becomes much more equivocal in its application.[23] The principle still holds, but problems arise in connection with the determination of the relevant marginal 'opportunity' cost of capital. This can be seen in figure 1.8.

In this figure, as previously, the firm's available investment projects are ranked along the curve RR' in descending order according to their yield. The market borrowing rate is equal to the slope of the line $R_B - R'_B$ and the market lending rate to the slope of the line

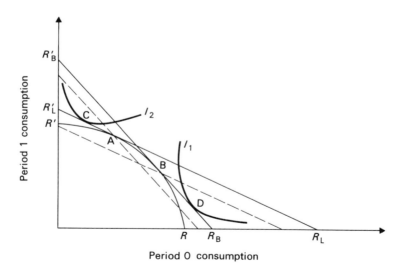

FIGURE 1.8 *The investment decision in a market with different borrowing and lending rates*

$R_L - R'_L$. The borrowing rate R_B is clearly greater than the lending rate R_L. Once again the firm maximizes its value by equating the yield on the marginal project with its marginal cost of capital. If it has limited internal funds and if reaching point B will involve some borrowing of funds, then it will not pay the firm to take on any projects beyond point B. This is because marginal projects along RR' beyond point B offer a yield less than the cost of borrowing (the slope of RR' beyond B is less than the slope of $R_B - R'_B$). However, if the firm did have sufficient internal funds, it would pay it to take on as many projects as it can afford along the section of RR' between points B and A, until it reaches point A. It will not be worth while progressing beyond A, since any further projects would offer a yield less than the market lending rate R_L. If the firm still has surplus funds it would be better lending them out at the market lending rate or distributing them to shareholders. Thus, in the presence of different borrowing and lending rates there is no longer a uniquely optimal strategy, and the firm should terminate its investment at either B or A or somewhere in between, according to its resources. It might be thought that a way out of this impasse, when faced with a lack of sufficient funds, would be to invite further subscriptions from shareholders and invest these funds so as to reach point A. This strategy would not necessarily suit all shareholders. If a shareholder had a preference for current consumption, as represented by indifference curve I_1, he would prefer the firm to take on projects up to point B. Then he would borrow against B to reach his preferred position D. Any other strategy would be suboptimal from his point of view. If the firm invested up to point A, he could borrow along the dotted line passing through point A, and this is clearly dominated by the parallel line through B. On the other hand, by similar logic, a shareholder with a preference for period 1 consumption would prefer the firm to take on projects up to point A. His preferences are represented by indifference curve I_2, and would lend against A to reach his desired point C. If the firm only invested up to point B, the shareholder's options would be determined by the parallel dotted lending line passing through B, and again positions along this line above B are clearly inferior. Thus, we have no unique interpretation of the investment decision rule. The optimal strategy will involve investing up to point A or point B or any of the intermediate positions, depending upon the relative preferences of shareholders. Our rule has broken down in the face of this relatively weak restriction on the raising of funds.

1.9   THE TERM STRUCTURE OF INTEREST RATES

A practical example of the application of discounting principles and of the problems posed by the existence of market imperfections is given by work on the term structure of interest rates. At any given moment in time there are likely to be a whole range or structure of interest rates available on the various debt instruments, whether they be company debentures or Government gilt-edged stock. Their respective rates will be influenced by factors such as their size of coupon payment, default of payment risk, marketability, tax treatment, eligibility as collateral, call provisions, transaction costs and the like, as well as period to maturity or 'term'. This section will concentrate on the last of these.

The yield to maturity on a financial asset is that yield or rate of return which, when employed as a discount rate and applied to the coupon payments and payment on redemption, gives a present value to these payments equal to the current market price of the asset. If a fixed interest security is assumed with n years until its redemption, annual year-end coupon payments of a constant amount C, and repayment at redemption of F, then the following relation holds between its market price B and its yield to redemption Y:

$$B = \frac{C}{(1 + Y)} + \frac{C}{(1 + Y)^2} + \cdots + \frac{C + F}{(1 + Y)^n}. \tag{1.11}$$

The existence of coupon payments on typical fixed interest securities causes further problems as the term of a security with coupon payments is not a completely unambiguous concept. Two fixed interest securities with the same issue and redemption dates but different coupon rates could be regarded as having different 'average terms'. For this reason the concept of 'duration' has been developed (see appendix 1.2).

Because of these difficulties, the following analysis will be confined to consideration of 'discount bonds', which are fixed interest securities issued at a discount, with no attached coupon payments, and redeemed at par n periods later. This permits concentration on the effects of term, at least in the theoretical analysis. In practice the empirical estimation of the shape of the yield curve is difficult. Ideally it would require the existence of a large number of discount bonds, all identical except in their term to maturity. This is not the reality, and perhaps only Treasury bills fall into this category. The

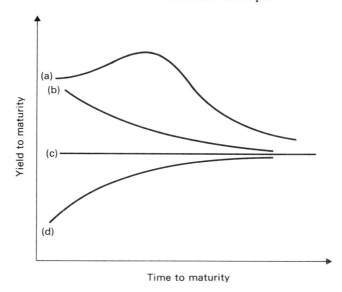

FIGURE 1.9   *Typical yield curves*

rest will have coupon payments and a sample will not be available over the full range of the maturity spectrum; the curve will have to be estimated or interpolated.[24] The result is likely to conform to one of the more frequently encountered shapes of the yield curve shown in figure 1.9.

In this diagram the yield to maturity, as defined in (1.11), is plotted up the vertical axis and the period to maturity along the horizontal axis. The overall level of interest rates will be a function of the supply and demand for loanable funds. In the following analysis this is assumed to be exogenous and the concern is with yields and term, which could exhibit the variety of forms shown in (1.9). Figure 1.9(a) depicts a humped term structure; in the short term yields will rise and in the longer term fall. Curve (b) shows a falling term structure, with high short rates succeeded by lower long rates. Curve (c) shows a flat term structure with no difference between short and long rates. Finally, curve (d) shows the most commonly encountered yield curve, with a rising term structure in which low short rates are followed by higher rates rising continuously with term.

In the analysis which follows, capital letters (R_t) stand for long-period rates at time t and lower case letters (f_t) for short or implied forward rates at time t. All operations are assumed to take place in a perfect market using discount bonds.

Suppose an investor is considering a fixed interest security for two periods and purchases one that matures after two periods. By so doing he will earn a return equal to the current 'long rate' appropriate for two periods, R_2. On the other hand the two-period security could be regarded as being equivalent to the purchase of two 'one-period' securities in succession, the first maturing at the end of the first period and then being replaced by the purchase of the second, maturing at the end of period two. The first security should give a return equal to the first-period forward rate (or 'spot rate' as it is usually termed), f_1, and the second a return equivalent to the second-period forward rate, f_2. The following identity is obtained:

$$(1 + R_2)^2 = (1 + f_1)(1 + f_2). \tag{1.12}$$

This means that, at any point in time, the existing term structure of interest rates contains an implicit set of forward rates. The long rate obtaining on the market over any period is equivalent to the geometric mean of the implied forward rates spanning the same period. Thus:

$$(1 + R_1) = (1 + f_1)$$
$$(1 + R_2) = \sqrt{[(1 + f_1)(1 + f_2)]}$$
$$\vdots \qquad \vdots$$
$$(1 + R_n) = \sqrt[n]{[(1 + f_1)(1 + f_2) \cdots (1 + f_n)]}. \tag{1.13}$$

The long rate or term yield is an average rate – an average of the forward rates over the same period – whereas the forward rate for any period is the marginal rate or yield which can be obtained by investing over that additional period. The yield at the margin is given by:

$$(1 + f_n) = \frac{(1 + R_n)^n}{(1 + R_{n-1})^{n-1}}. \tag{1.14}$$

There are three basic theories about the determination of these yields, which make up the term structure – the expectations theory, the liquidity or risk premium theory, and the market segmentation, hedging pressure, or institutional theory as it is variously called.

The strongest form of the expectations theory assumes that investors can forecast accurately what the future short-term rates will be, that they operate in a perfect market with no transactions costs, and that they have no preferred 'habitat'. This means that investors will hold financial instruments of any maturity if it suits them. These assumptions make (1.13) and (1.14) fully operational; implied forward rates have to be consistent with expected forward rates. If *ex ante* and *ex post* rates are not consistent, arbitrage will take place until they are. Given appropriate expectations, the theory can account for any of the shapes of the yield curve in figure 1.9, but it is difficult to test. Expectations cannot be observed, so some formulation about their nature and development has to be adopted.[25]

Hicks played a major part in developing the liquidity premium theory.[26] He posits the existence of a 'constitutional weakness' in the market on the long side. By this he means that the loans market is characterized by a surfeit of lenders wanting to lend short, such as the banks, and an excess of borrowers wanting to borrow long. All operators are risk averse, including the speculators who resolve the problem by borrowing short and lending long provided that they are paid a premium to compensate them for the risks involved. If there is an imbalance in the market of this type, and if investors are more concerned with principal rather than income risk (since a given change in interest rates will cause greater fluctuations in the value of longer-term than short-term fixed interest securities), then the above analysis will hold and long rates will, on average, be greater than short-term rates.

In this model the forward short-term rates implied by the term structure will be upward-biased estimates of the expected future spot rates, as a result of the existence of the liquidity premium. Thus the current long rate, spot rate, and expected forward rates have the following relation:

$$(1 + R_n) = [(1 + R_1)(1 + {}_{t+1}R_1 + LP_1)(1 + {}_{t+2}R_1 + LP_2)$$
$$\cdots (1 + {}_{t+n-1}R_1 + LP_{n-1})]^{1/n} \qquad (1.15)$$

where $(1 + R_n)$ is the current long rate for a loan of n periods, $(1 + {}_{t+1}R_1)$ is the current true expectation of the one-period spot rate (R_1) currently expected to hold in period $t + 1$, and LP_1 is the liquidity premium for period $t + 1$.

Expression (1.15) shows the true state of affairs, whereas the forward rates implied by the term structure are biased by the liquidity premiums as follows:

$$_{t+k}f_1 = {}_{t+k}R_1 + LP_k \quad \text{(for } k = 1 \cdots n - 1) \qquad (1.16)$$

where $_{t+k}f_1$ are the successive one-period forward rates implied in the term structure at period t. If the market does display the characteristics suggested, the liquidity premiums would be expected to be an increasing function of the maturity of the loan:

$$LP_1 < LP_2 < \cdots < LP_n.$$

This analysis can be contrasted with the expectations theory in terms of supply effects. In the 'pure' version of the expectations theory, the supply of securities has no effect when considered at the micro-level; as long as the security offers the appropriate yield, demand will be infinitely elastic. By contrast, in the liquidity premium theory expectations still play a major role but the introduction of risk, plus the assumption about the basic asymmetry of supply and demand in the market, introduce 'supply' effects. The problem is overcome by coaxing lenders to the long end of the market by paying them a liquidity premium.

In the 'hedging pressure' or 'market segmentation' theory, the influence of the supply of securities of different maturities becomes of paramount importance. Culbertson[27] is usually regarded as the primary architect of this theory, which runs as follows. It could be hypothesized that the banks and discount houses have only short-term liabilities and the pension funds and life assurance companies only long-term ones. If they are to avoid risk and achieve a fully hedged position, they must match their liabilities with assets of similar maturity. If they are not prepared to speculate and if their liabilities are singularly concentrated in a particular maturity, they will not be prepared to move outside their preferred habitat and purchase assets of a different maturity. In the strictest form, the theory suggests that expectations will play no part in determining the term structure, and the rates in any one section of the market will be determined solely by the real forces of supply and demand in that section. A further corollary is that the market is completely segmented, and if operators are not prepared to switch maturities then rates in different segments can have no effect on one another.

The extreme forms of the three theories have been outlined but they have also been combined in a number of hybrids. There seems to be fairly general agreement that both expectations and liquidity premiums are likely to play a part in determining nominal yields.[28] The problems arise from difficulties in the econometric testing and specification of the various hypotheses. The spectre of measurement error is ever present in the generation of the basic yield curve data. To test the expectations theory *ex ante* expectations have to be specified from *ex post* data. The models typically involve tests of joint hypotheses about both the influence of expectations and the manner in which they are formed. In the case of a rejected hypothesis it is difficult to be sure about which assumption is at fault. Given these difficulties it is very difficult to isolate the liquidity premiums.

The problems are compounded by the existence of inflation. Fisher suggested the following relationship between real and nominal interest rates.[29] If i is the nominal interest rate, r_i is the real rate of interest, and PI is the rate of change of prices according to an appropriate price index, then the real rate will be equal to the nominal rate deflated by the change in the relevant price index over the same period:

$$1 + r_i = \frac{1 + i}{1 + PI} \tag{1.17}$$

$$\therefore \quad (1 + r_i)(1 + PI) = 1 + i.$$

Simplifying and taking all terms except r_i to the right-hand side (RHS):

$$r_i = i - PI - r_i PI. \tag{1.18}$$

The normal convention is to assume that $r_i PI$ is very small and to use just the first two terms of the RHS of (1.18). Thus the 'Fisher effect' is obtained:

$$r_i \simeq i - PI. \tag{1.19}$$

This effect means that shifting inflationary expectations will also affect nominal interest rates. Indeed, Fama has used this fact to predict inflation from the behaviour of short-term rates.[30]

The conclusion is that the theoretical factors which are likely to influence the term structure of interest rates are fairly well understood but that the exact specification of the manner of their influence is elusive. It will be seen in later chapters that this pattern is repeated in much of the empirical work in finance.

Now that many of the basic concepts have been introduced the central concerns of the subject may be considered.

1.10 THE FUNDAMENTAL ISSUES IN CORPORATE FINANCE

The basic issues in corporate finance have been encapsulated in the following three main questions which, Solomon suggested, all financial managers have to address:

(1) What specific assets should an enterprise acquire?
(2) What total volume of funds should an enterprise acquire?
(3) How should the funds required be financed?'[31]

In facing these questions, the decision-takers must have a goal, or objective function, which will provide the criterion for assessing alternative courses of action. The appropriate criterion has already been introduced – the maximization of shareholder wealth, which is achieved by maximizing company value.

But to apply this rule as a practical decision tool requires an understanding of the factors which determine value. It has been mentioned that economic value is basically a function of expected returns and risk. Thus, chapters 2 and 3 are devoted to the development of a theoretical framework which can handle these two basic factors at the level of an individual decision-taker.

However, equilibrium valuation of both real and financial assets will be determined by the confluence of individual decisions in a market context. Therefore chapters 4 and 5 (in Part II) are devoted to theories of the determination of market value. Chapter 4 examines the implications of the assumption that rational investors hold diversified portfolios of financial assets; this leads directly on to a discussion of the capital asset pricing model and other equilibrium pricing models. Chapter 5 examines a model for use in the valuation of options and considers how it can be applied generally for valuing corporate liabilities. These two chapters should provide a basic grasp of the current understanding of the factors which determine market valuation.

This having been established, chapters 6, 7, and 8 (in Part III) are devoted to the central issues in corporate finance, as reflected in Solomon's three questions. Chapter 6 looks at the investment decision, and in the process seeks an answer to the first and second questions. Chapters 7 and 8 look more closely at the factors which determine company value, with particular attention to dividend policy, and the effects of capital structure or chosen financial 'mix' of debt and equity funding – in effect, the third of Solomon's questions. Throughout Part III frequent recourse is made to the models and insights provided by the material in Parts I and II. It is hoped that the 'unity' of the book's structure in part reflects the 'unity' of the current structure of thought.

However, many issues sit beckoning on the sidelines, and many of the central preoccupations of current thought are still unanswered.

There are also some potential drawbacks attached to the 'current orthodoxy' and inevitably certain issues and features of the financial landscape are not prominent from its chosen vantage point.

Chapter 9 (in Part IV) attempts to draw attention to this and to some of the more glaring and inevitable inadequacies in current knowledge.

TEST QUESTIONS

1. What is the relationship between the theory of finance and economics? How has this changed finance as a discipline?
2. Distinguish between value maximization and profit maximization.
3. What is the present value of an annuity of £20 for five years if the interest rate to be used for discounting is 10 per cent?
4. (a) Calculate the net present values of the following two streams of cash flows, given a discount rate of 15 per cent.

	Period 0	Period 1	Period 2
(1)	−£100	£110	£150
(2)	−£100	£150	£110

   (b) What are their internal rates of return?
5. The one-period (spot) interest rate stands at 5 per cent and the two-year rate stands at 7 per cent. What is the implied forward (spot) rate, one year hence, according to the expectations theory?
6. A £100 fixed interest security has a coupon rate of 10 per cent and is redeemable at par (£100) in four years. Assuming all payments are made annually at the year end, and the rate of interest is 12 per cent, what is its market value? Calculate the duration of the security (see appendix 1.2).
7. The nominal rate of interest is 15 per cent. The rate of inflation is 11 per cent. What is the real rate of interest?

APPENDIX 1.1   THE MAXIMIZATION OF VALUE AND SHAREHOLDER UTILITY

This demonstration that the individual shareholder's utility is maximized by maximizing the value of the corporation follows the proof given by Fama and Miller.[32]

In the case of the individually owned company, let C be the vector of an individual's consumption expenditure, $V(C)$ the present value of lifetime consumption, $V(E)$ the present value of lifetime earnings plus any original wealth, and $V(W)$ the present value of future withdrawals from the comapny (in effect the value of the company).

Individuals are assumed to want to maximize the utility of their lifetime consumption – that is, to seek

$$\max_{EW} U(C)$$

subject to

$$V(C) = V(E) + V(W)$$
$$T(W) = 0.$$

($T(W)$ could be regarded as the production constraint – in effect, all projects with positive NPVs are taken on.) This constrained maximization problem can be written as an unconstrained maximization problem in Lagrangian form:

$$\max_{EW} \{U(C) - \lambda_1[V(C) - V(E) - V(W)] - \lambda_2 T(W)\}$$

with the Lagrangian multipliers λ_1 and λ_2. By letting $\lambda_3 = \lambda_1/\lambda_2$, the problem can also be shown to be equivalent to finding two maxima – first

$$\max_{W} [V(W) - \lambda_3 T(W)] \qquad (1.20)$$

and then

$$\max_{E} \{U(C) - \lambda_1[V(C) - V(E) - V(W)]\}. \qquad (1.21)$$

The first stage of the maximization, (1.20), is equivalent to maximizing the value of the individual's ownership interest in the firm; the second stage, (1.21), is the maximization of the utility of his lifetime consumption, given the maximization of the valuation of his ownership of the company in (1.20). Thus, maximizing the value of the company is entirely consistent with maximizing his utility. Fama and Miller then generalize the argument to the case of the company owned by many shareholders by letting $V(W)$ be the proportionate interest of the individual shareholder's interest in the company, and $T(W)$ be his share of the company's production possibilities. The logic of the argument, therefore, remains identical for both the individual owner and the individual shareholder. In perfect capital markets their interests are best served by the maximization of company value.

Expression (1.11) showed that the total present value (or market price B) of a fixed interest security is made up of the sum of the present values of all its periodic coupon payments up to and including its redemption payment in period n. The concept of duration involves an analysis of the timing of the payments of these individual 'chunks' of present value which make up the total value of the security. The duration is calculated by taking a weighted average of the timing of this stream of payments and employing as weights the proportion of overall present value actually paid at each interval. If the time periods are $t = 1 \cdots n$, then the appropriate weights can be calculated from (1.11) by taking the present value of each individual payment divided by the total present value. Thus:

$$W_1 = \frac{C_1}{(1 + Y)} \frac{1}{B}, \ W_2 = \frac{C_2}{(1 + Y)^2} \frac{1}{B}, \ \ldots, \ W_n = \frac{C_n + F_n}{(1 + Y)^n} \frac{1}{B} \quad (1.22)$$

where W_t are the weights ($t = 1 \cdots n$), C_t are the coupon payments ($t = 1 \cdots n$), F_n is the redemption payment in period n, and B is the present value of the security.

The following summation calculates a security's duration:

$$D = \sum_{t=1}^{n} (tW_t) \quad (1.23)$$

where D is the duration, t is the timing of the payment ($t = 1 \cdots n$), and W_t are the weights (calculated as shown in (1.22)).

From these arguments it follows that two fixed interest securities with the same issue and redemption date but different coupon rates will have different durations, the one with the smaller coupon rate having the larger duration. The calculation of the duration of a 5 per cent security with three periods until redemption is as follows. The security of £100 nominal value is to be redeemed at par.

(1)	(2)	(3)	(4)	(5)
	Payments:			
	coupon	*Discount*	*Present value*	
Period	*redemption*	*factor*	*(2) × (3)*	*Duration*
(years)	*(£)*	*(10%)*	*(£)*	$\sum [(4)/B \times (1)]$
1	5	0.91	4.55	0.052
2	5	0.83	4.15	0.095
3	105	0.75	78.75	2.702
			$\sum = B = 87.45$	$D = 2.849$

The market price of the security is £87.45 and the yield is 10 per cent. The duration is calculated as 2.849 years.

Note should also be taken of the link between duration and price volatility. If $(1 + Y)$ is replaced by R, duration may be defined as:

$$D = \left(\frac{C}{R} + \frac{2C}{R^2} + \frac{3C}{R^3} + \frac{4C}{R^4} + \cdots + \frac{nC}{R^n} + \frac{nF_n}{R^n} \right) \bigg/ B. \tag{1.24}$$

However, it is known that:

$$B = \frac{C}{R} + \frac{C}{R^2} + \cdots + \frac{C}{R^n} + \frac{F_n}{R^n}. \tag{1.25}$$

If B is then differentiated with respect to R:

$$\frac{dB}{dR} = - \left(\frac{C}{R^2} + \frac{2C}{R^3} + \frac{3C}{R^4} + \cdots + \frac{nC}{R^{n+1}} + \frac{nF_n}{R^{n+1}} \right). \tag{1.26}$$

If both sides are multiplied by R:

$$R \times \frac{dB}{dR} = - \left(\frac{C}{R} + \frac{2C}{R^2} + \frac{3C}{R^3} + \cdots + \frac{nC}{R^n} + \frac{NF_n}{R^n} \right).$$

It can be seen that the term in brackets above is the same as the numerator in (1.24). This means that:

$$D = - \frac{dB}{dR} \frac{R}{B}$$

or:

$$D = \left(- \frac{dB}{B} \right) \bigg/ \left(\frac{dR}{R} \right). \tag{1.27}$$

It can be seen that (1.27) is the familiar price elasticity formula. Thus duration measures price elasticity as a function of the change in the required rate of return or yield.

NOTES AND REFERENCES

1. Williams, J. B. *The Theory of Investment Value* (1938), North-Holland, Amsterdam, 1964, p. 3.
2. Greene, T. L. *Corporation Finance*, Putnam, New York, 1897.
3. Meade, E. S. *Corporation Finance*, Appleton, New York, 1910.
   Dewing, A. S. *The Financial Policy of Corporations*, Ronald, Boston, 1938.
   Lyon, W. H. *Corporation and their Financing*, Heath, Boston, 1938.
4. Solomon, E. *Theory of Financial Management*, Columbia University Press, New York, 1963, p. 4.

5. Knight, F. H. *Risk, Uncertainty and Profit*, Houghton Mifflin, Boston and New York, 1921.

   Fisher, I. *Theory of Interest*, Macmillan, New York, 1930. See also: Fisher, I. *Rate of Interest*, Macmillan, New York, 1907.

   Williams, J. B. *The Theory of Investment Value* (1938), North-Holland, Amsterdam, 1964.

6. Hunt, P. and Williams, C. M. *Case Problems in Finance*, Irwin, Chicago, 1949.

   Also representative is: Howard, B. B. and Upton, M. *An Introduction to Business Finance*, McGraw-Hill, New York, 1953.

7. Lutz, F. and Lutz, V. *The Theory of Investment of the Firm*, Greenwood Press, Princeton, 1951.

   Dean, J. *Capital Budgeting*, Columbia University Press, New York, 1951.

8. Markowitz, H. M. 'Portfolio selection', *Journal of Finance* 7(1), March 1952, pp. 77–91.

   Markowitz, H. M. *Portfolio Selection: Efficient Diversification of Investments*, Wiley, New York, 1959.

9. See, for example; Sharpe, W. F. 'Capital asset prices: a theory of market equilibrium under conditions of risk'. *Journal of Finance* 29(3), September 1964, pp. 425–42.

10. Rubinstein, M. 'Mean variance synthesis of corporate financial theory', *Journal of Finance* 28(1), March 1973, pp. 167–81.

11. Cootner, P. H. (ed.) *The Random Character of Stock Market Prices*, M.I.T. Press, Cambridge, Mass., 1967.

12. Modigliani, F. and Miller, M. H. 'The cost of capital, corporation finance, and the theory of investment', *American Economic Review* 48(3), June 1958, pp. 261–97.

    Modigliani, F. and Miller, M. H. 'Corporate income taxes and the cost of capital: a correction', *American Economic Review* 55(3), June 1963, pp. 433–43.

    Miller, M. H. and Modigliani, F. 'Dividend policy, growth and the valuation of shares', *Journal of Business* 34(4), October 1961, pp. 411–43.

13. Black, F. and Scholes, M. 'The pricing of options and corporate liabilities', *Journal of Political Economy* 81(3), May/June 1973, pp. 637–54.

14. Fama, E. F. and Miller, M. H. *Thse Theory of Finance*, Holt, Rinehart and Winston, New York, 1972.

15. Hicks, J. R. *Causality in Economics*, Basil Blackwell, Oxford, 1979, p. 3.

16. Fama, E. F. and Miller, M. H. *The Theory of Finance*, Holt, Rinehart and Winston, New York, 1972, chapter 1, pp. 1–41.

17. Hicks, J. R. *Value and Capital* (2nd edn, 1946), Clarendon Press, Oxford, 1968, p. 174.

18. For a discussion of the two viewpoints see:

    Whittington, G. 'Accounting and economics', in Carsberg, B. and Hope, T. (eds) *Current Issues in Accounting*, Philip Allan, Oxford, 1977, pp. 192–212.

    Lee, T. A. *Income and Value Measurement*, Nelson, London, 1974.

19. See, for example:

    Inflation Accounting, Report of the Inflation Accounting Committee, HMSO, Cmnd 6225, September 1975.

    Standard Statement of Accounting Practice No. 16 (SSAP 16), March 1980.

20. See for example:

    Ball, R. and Brown, P. 'The empirical evaluation of accounting income numbers', *Journal of Accounting Research* VI, Autumn 1968, pp. 159–197.

Gonedes, N. J. 'Capital market equilibrium and annual accounting numbers', *Journal of Accounting Research* **XII**, Spring 1974, pp. 26–62.
See also the account given by: Ronen, J. 'The dual role of accounting: a financial economic perspective', in Bicksler, J. L. (ed.) *Handbook of Financial Economics*, North-Holland, Amsterdam, 1979, pp. 415–54.
21. See for example:
Baumol, W. J. *Business Behaviour, Value and Growth*, Macmillan, New York, 1959.
Cyert, R. M. and March, J. G. *A Behavioural Theory of the Firm*, Prentice-Hall, Englewood Cliffs, NJ, 1963.
Simon, H. A. *Administrative Behaviour* (2nd edn), Macmillan, New York, 1957.
22. For a discussion of the difficulties involved with the 'neo-classical' economist's definition of profits, see: Wood, A. *A Theory of Profits*, Cambridge University Press, Cambridge, 1975, chapter 1.
23. Hirshleifer, J. *Investment, Interest and Capital*, Prentice-Hall, Englewood Cliffs, NJ., 1970.
In developing his analysis Hirshleifer built upon the foundations provided by Fisher – see: Fisher, I. *The Theory of Interest*, Macmillan, New York, 1930.
24. For a discussion of some of the techniques see: Masera, R. S. *The Term Structure of Interest Rates*, Clarendon Press, Oxford, 1972, chapter 4.
25. The theory was fully developed by Lutz – see: Lutz, F. A. 'The structure of interest rates', *Quarterly Journal of Economics* November 1940, pp. 36–63.
Meiselman developed empirical tests based upon an 'adaptive expectations model': Meiselman, D. *The Term Structure of Interest Rates*, Prentice-Hall, Englewood Cliffs, NJ, 1962.
26. Sir J. Hicks *Value and Capital*, Clarendon Press, Oxford, 1939.
27. Culbertson, J. M. 'The term structure of interest rates', *Quarterly Journal Of Economics* November 1957, pp. 485–517.
28. For a good review of some of the models employed see: Dobson, S., Sutch, R. and Vanderfood, D. 'An evaluation of alternative empirical models of the term structure of interest rates', *Journal of Finance* **31**(4), September 1976, pp. 1035–65.
For a discussion of the general problems of fitting yields see: McCulloch, J. M. 'Measuring the term structure of interest rates', *Journal of Business* **44**(1), January 1971, pp. 19–31.
29. Fisher, I. *The Rate of Interest*, Macmillan, New York, 1907.
30. Fama, E. F. 'Short term interest rates as predictors of inflation', *American Economic Review* **65**, June 1975, pp. 269–82.
Fama, E. F. 'Inflation, uncertainty, and expected returns on treasury bills', *Journal of Political Economy* **84**(3), 1976, pp. 427–48.
See also: Nelson, C. R. and Schwert, G. W. 'Short term interest rates as predictors of inflation: on testing the hypothesis that the real rate of interest is constant', *American Economic Review* **67**(3), June 1977, pp. 478–86.
31. Solomon, E. *Theory of Financial Management*, Columbia University Press, New York, 1963, p. 8.
See also: Weston, J. F. *The Scope and Methodology of Finance*, Prentice-Hall, Englewood Cliffs, NJ, 1966.
32. Fama, E. F. and Miller, M. *The Theory of Finance*, Holt, Rinehart and Winston, New York, 1972, pp. 72–73.

CHAPTER 2

Risk and uncertainty

All knowledge resolves itself into probability, and becomes at last of the same nature with that evidence, which we employ in common life.[1]

This chapter will explore a very small portion of the ground in the shadow of Hume's controversial but incontrovertible eighteenth-century dictum. The treatment will be introductory, and of necessity will skate over many of the fundamental schisms of thought concerning probability and statistical theory.[2]

The treatment of risk in the theory of finance is largely based upon the use of subjective probability distributions, and is crucial in financial theory as financial decisions essentially involve two parameters – expected returns and risk. Subjective probability can be distinguished from objective probability as follows.

Objective probability views probability as the ratio of the number of 'positive' outcomes of an experiment to the total number of outcomes possible – in other words, as the 'relative frequency' of the positive outcomes. The experiment produces results which are objectively verifiable. The results can be used as the basis for a probability statement. Unfortunately this type of situation does not face the financial decision-taker very frequently. Consider the situation of a financial manager considering a particular investment project. It will be very unlikely that the project will be repeated frequently; it is much more likely to be a unique 'one-off' occurrence. The estimation of its probability of success cannot, therefore, be based upon the relative frequency of success of a number of identical projects in the past. This situation would require a subjective probability estimate of the likely outcome of the investment project.

Subjective probability involves the assignation of a number to represent the individual decision-taker's degree of belief concerning the likelihood of occurrence of some future event. The normal convention is to employ a 0 to 1 scale; complete certainty that a future event will occur is equated with a probability of 1, and less than complete certainty with a number between 0 and 1. One way of viewing subjective probabilities is to consider them in terms of betting odds. If you are prepared to give odds of 3 to 1 that the temperature will be above 25°C tomorrow, then you are assessing the probability as 3 chances out of 4, or 0.75, that the temperature will be 25°C plus. You may be basing your estimation on previous weather records, but you cannot be absolutely sure about the accuracy of your prediction. As the weather conditions are relatively settled you are fairly sure and you assign a reasonably high probability of 0.75 to your forecast.

2.1 PROBABILITY DISTRIBUTIONS AND RANDOM VARIABLES

A random variable is a variable whose value cannot be predicted with certainty. The normal convention is to place a tilde ($\sim$) over the variable concerned to indicate that it is random. Random variables are either discrete or continuous. Discrete random variables can only take on a limited number of possible values. The number of shares whose price rises on the London Stock Exchange tomorrow, or the number of firms that merge over the next year, are examples of discrete random variables. A continuous random variable can take any value within a range or continuum. For example, spot rates in the currency market might take any value down to fractions of a decimal point.

The random variables encountered in finance are not completely uncertain, but are normally assumed to be described by probability distributions. The function of a probability distribution is to associate probabilities with the various possible values of the random variable in accordance with the laws of probability previously discussed. Consider the following example. Suppose you are considering buying a house as a temporary investment prior to moving abroad in a year's time. The purchase price is £20,000, but your main concern is with $\tilde{X}$ – the sale price in a year's time. On the basis of a study of past trends in prices in the housing market, and projections concerning the state of the economy in the coming year, together with the likely flow of funds into the building societies, you construct a subjective probability distribution of estimations in the possible sale value of your house (table 2.1).

TABLE 2.1 *Subjective probability distribution of estimations of sale value of the house*

$\tilde{X}$ (price in £000s)	$P(\tilde{X})$ (probability distribution)
19	0.1
20	0.2
21	0.4
22	0.2
23	0.1
	1.0

On the basis of your study you have estimated that there is a small chance ($P = 0.1$) that the housing market will collapse in the coming year and that you will make a loss of £1,000 on your house. You are most confident in the estimation that you will make a gain of £1,000 ($P = 0.4$), and you consider there is a small chance ($P = 0.1$) that there will be a boom in house prices and you will make a gain of £3,000. The probability distribution sums to 1, which indicates that you feel you have included all possible sale values of the house. The information in table 2.1 could be represented in a histogram of the probability distribution, as shown in figure 2.1.

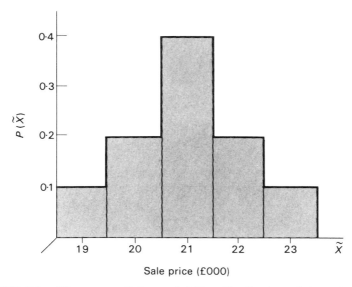

FIGURE 2.1 *Histogram of the probability distribution of the sale value of the house*

The example just considered is an illustration of a discrete probability distribution, and in the course of the analysis you have let the midpoint of a range of possible prices be representative of the whole range (you have let all prices in the range £18,500–£19,500 be represented by £19,000 and so forth for all sale prices considered).

The probability distribution you have derived can then be used to derive a measure of the expected value of your investment in the house and its riskiness (the variance or standard deviation of the probability distribution is used as a surrogate for risk). The expected value is found by multiplying each possible value of the discrete random variable by its probability and then summing the resulting products. In algebraic terms, the expected value or mean (μ) is given by:

$$\bar{X} = E(\tilde{X}) = \mu = \sum_{i=1}^{N} P(X_i)X_i. \tag{2.1}$$

The dispersion of the probability distribution is measured by the variance or standard deviation of the distribution. The variance of a random variable $\tilde{X}$ is:

$$\sigma^2(\tilde{X}) = \sum_{i=1}^{N} P(X_i)[X_i - E(\tilde{X})]^2 \tag{2.2}$$

and the standard deviation $\sigma(\tilde{X})$ is the square root of the variance.

In the example just considered of the investment in the purchase of a house, the expected value is a sale price of £21,000 and the standard deviation is £1,095.45. This can be calculated as shown in table 2.2. The expected value and the standard deviation of the

TABLE 2.2 *The calculation of the standard deviation of the investment in the house*

$\tilde{X}$ (price in £000s)	$P(\tilde{X})$	$P(\tilde{X})\tilde{X}$	$\tilde{X} - E(\tilde{X})$	$[\tilde{X} - E(\tilde{X})]^2$	$P(\tilde{X})[\tilde{X} - E(\tilde{X})]^2$
19	0.1	1.9	−2	4	0.4
20	0.2	4.0	−1	1	0.2
21	0.4	8.4	0	0	0
22	0.2	4.4	1	1	0.2
23	0.1	2.3	2	4	0.4
		$\sum = 21$ $E(\tilde{X}) = 21$			$\sum = 1.2$ $\sigma^2(\tilde{X}) = 1.2$ $\sigma(\tilde{X}) = \sqrt{1.2}$

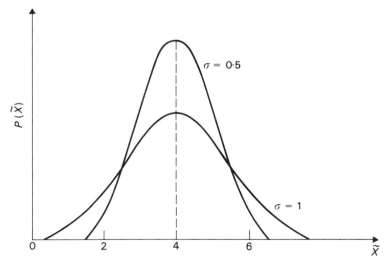

FIGURE 2.2   *The normal distribution*

expected return can then be employed for comparison with alternative investments. If you are merely interested in the house as an investment proposition, and not for its use value, you might find that investment in gilt-edged stock gave you a comparable return with a lower standard deviation, and on the basis of this you might choose to invest in gilt-edged stock.[3]

Up to this stage discrete distributions have been considered, but frequently in finance the analysis must be in terms of continuous distributions. More important, there are various theoretical distributions whose mathematical properties serve as useful approximations to the properties of continuous distributions.[4] One of the more commonly used is the normal distribution, the familiar bell-shaped curve shown in figure 2.2.

The normal distribution is a unimodal and symmetrical distribution. A particular normal distribution is distinguished by its mean (μ) and standard deviation (σ). [In figure 2.2 both curves have the same mean of 4 but different standard deviations of 0.5 and 1 respectively.] The normal curve has the important characteristics that 68 per cent of the total area under it must be within + or −1 standard deviation from the mean, and 95 per cent of the area under it within + or − two standard deviations from the mean. In the case of a probability distribution the total area under the curve will be equal to 1. A probability density function of random variable $\tilde{X}$ is normally distributed if it is described by the following expression.

$$P(\tilde{X}) = \frac{1}{\sigma\sqrt{(2\pi)}} \exp\left[-\frac{1}{2}\left(\frac{\tilde{X}-\mu}{\sigma}\right)^2 \right] \quad \text{for } -\infty \leq \tilde{X} \leq \infty \quad (2.3)$$

where σ is any real positive number and μ is any real number, positive or negative.

The assumption that distributions of returns ($\tilde{r}_X$) follow a normal curve is very common in finance because of the convenient properties of the normal curve. For example, investors, on the basis of this assumption, can be regarded as making their investment decisions purely on the basis of the mean and standard deviation of the probability distributions of returns on investments.

There are, however, a number of obvious drawbacks involved in the assumption of 'normality'. Two non-symmetric distributions could have the same mean and standard deviation yet be two quite distinct distributions as in figure 2.3. Indeed, in the case of the distributions illustrated in this figure, some commentators have suggested that investors should prefer distribution B because of the

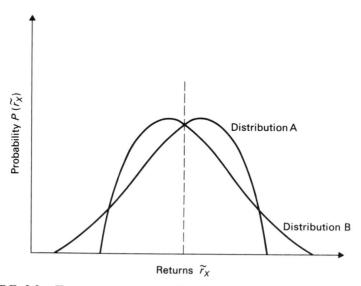

FIGURE 2.3   *Two non-symmetric distributions with the same mean and standard deviation*

small probability of much higher returns.[5] In these cases a measure of skewness is required.

In general, a distribution is described by statistical moments. These are now presented.

2.2 MOMENTS OF A PROBABILITY DISTRIBUTION

A probability distribution is defined by its moments.[6] The first moment about the mean is defined as:

$$M_1 = \sum P(\tilde{r}_X)[\tilde{r}_X - E(\tilde{r}_X)] = 0. \tag{2.4}$$

Naturally, the first moment is always equal to 0 (since $\sum P(\tilde{r}_X)\tilde{r}_X = E(\tilde{r}_X)$) and is of little interest to us. (The first moment about the origin is the mean: $\mu = E(\tilde{r}_X) = \sum P(\tilde{r}_X)(\tilde{r}_X)$.)

The second moment about the mean, the variance, we have already met:

$$M_2 = \sigma^2(\tilde{r}_X) = E[\tilde{r}_X - E(\tilde{r}_X)]^2 = \sum P(\tilde{r}_X)[\tilde{r}_X - E(\tilde{r}_X)]^2. \tag{2.5}$$

This moment measures the spread or the dispersion of the distribution.

The third moment of a distribution is defined as:

$$M_3 = E[\tilde{r}_X - E(\tilde{r}_X)]^3 = \sum P(\tilde{r}_X)[\tilde{r}_X - E(\tilde{r}_X)]^3. \tag{2.6}$$

This is the moment that measures the skewness of a distribution, as depicted in figure 2.3.

The fourth moment measures the 'peakedness' or 'kurtosis' of a distribution. The fourth moment is defined as:

$$M_4 = E[\tilde{r}_X - E(\tilde{r}_X)]^4 = \sum P(\tilde{r}_X)[\tilde{r}_X - E(\tilde{r}_X)]^4. \tag{2.7}$$

(For a further discussion of the properties of expectations and moments, see appendix 2.1.)

Although the four moments provide a comprehensive definition of statistical distribution, their use can prove mathematically cumbersome. For this reason, the bulk of financial literature concentrates on the use of the first two moments. This expediency causes a lot of disquiet, and in particular some concern has been expressed about the use of the second moment as a surrogate for risk. H. Markowitz was perhaps one of the first to review some of the alternative measures of risk, and a selection of these is featured in the next section.[7]

2.3 ALTERNATIVE SURROGATES FOR RISK

Semi-variance

Markowitz favoured the use of the semi-variance which would take into account only below-mean returns (BMR) on the grounds that an investor would be anxious to avoid these but would be favourably disposed towards above-mean returns. The semi-variance is defined as follows:

$$\text{semi-variance} = E[BMR - E(\tilde{r}_X)]^2$$
$$= \sum P(\tilde{r}_X)[BMR - E(\tilde{r}_X)]^2 \tag{2.8}$$

and the below-mean return is defined as those returns $(\tilde{r}_X)$ less than $E(\tilde{r}_X)$, i.e. satisfying $\tilde{r}_X < E(\tilde{r}_X)$. The semi-variance has a logical attractiveness, but has the disadvantage of being more mathematically cumbersome from the point of view of computer programming. Furthermore, if the distribution is symmetrical, it leads to exactly the same ranking of riskiness as the variance. One further point in its favour is that the utility function associated with it is more acceptable than that associated with the variance.[8]

Mean absolute deviation of returns (MADR)

The mean absolute deviation of returns $(MADR)$ is defined as:

$$MADR = \sum P(\tilde{r}_X)|\tilde{r}_X - E(\tilde{r}_X)| \tag{2.9}$$

where $|\tilde{r}_X - E(\tilde{r}_X)|$ is the absolute value of an individual return's deviation from the expected return.[9] It is very similar to the standard deviation except that the standard deviation and the variance both square deviations from the mean and therefore stress the larger deviations more than the smaller ones. This can be undesirable when one is trying to establish the parameters of random variables with large dispersions, such as share price movements. It has the disadvantage of being difficult to manipulate mathematically.

The coefficient of variation (CVR)

The coefficient of variation (CVR) is a 'normalized' standard deviation of returns which is found by dividing the standard deviation of

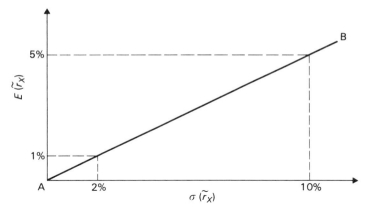

FIGURE 2.4   *All investments along the ray AB would have the same coeffi-cient of variation*

a probability distribution by its mean. It is defined as:

$$\text{coefficient of variation} = \frac{\sigma(\tilde{r}_X)}{E(\tilde{r}_X)}. \tag{2.10}$$

It provides a measure of the relative variability of returns. It could be argued that this is unnecessary as the standard deviation is a measure of riskiness which permits the comparison of probability distributions of different ranges of values to be compared. The *CVR* could further be regarded as misleading in a certain sense: as it is a measure of relative variability, any ray drawn through the origin of a diagram of risk/return space (see figure 2.4) will have the same *CVR*. Yet many investors would view an expected return of 2 per cent ($E(\tilde{r}_X)$) associated with risk ($\sigma(\tilde{r}_X)$) of 1 per cent as being less risky than an expected return of 10 per cent with a risk of 5 per cent. However, it has been employed in empirical studies[10] and the logic behind its use is very similar to the portfolio selection criterion suggested by Baumol.[11]

Thus, all the alternative measures of risk considered have their respective drawbacks and in terms of simplicity and convenience there are strong grounds for employing the variance or standard deviation as risk surrogates.

So far measures of risk have been considered that describe individual probability distributions of returns, but frequently financial decision-takers have to consider investment in a number of securities

or investment projects at the same time. This means that it is necessary to consider not only the individual probability distributions of
returns but also the interrelatedness of these probability distributions, so as to provide some measure of composite risk.

2.4 THE COVARIANCE OF RETURNS

Risk diversification or 'not putting all of one's eggs in one basket' is
a crucial element in many financial decisions. This can only be done
on a quantitative basis if we have a means of measurement of the
gains of diversification. One such measure is provided by estimations
of the covariance of returns. Suppose that you are considering investing in two securities, X and Y. The likely returns on these two
securities will be described by two random variables $\tilde{r}_X$ and $\tilde{r}_Y$ which
could be analysed in terms of a joint probability distribution.

Table 2.3 shows the joint probabilities of returns in the range 0–15
per cent for shares X and Y. The first entry in the top left-hand box
shows that there is an estimated 0.05 probability of the returns on
both X and Y being in the range 0–5 per cent. The adjacent box in
the row shows that there is a higher probability of 0.2 of having a
return in the range 5–10 per cent on X in association with a return
of 0–5 per cent on Y. The separate box at the end of the row shows
the sum of the probabilities in the row and indicates that there is an
overall probability of 0.35 of having a return on share Y in the range
0–5 per cent. The sums of the individual entries in the rows and
columns show the individual probability distributions for $\tilde{r}_X$ and $\tilde{r}_Y$,

TABLE 2.3 *Joint probability distribution of returns on shares X and Y*

$\tilde{r}_X$ (*return on share X*)

	0	5%	10%	15%	
5%		0.05	0.20	0.10		0.35
10%		0.10	0.30	0.03		0.43
15%		0.08	0.10	0.04		0.22
		0.23	0.60	0.17		$\sum = 1$

$\tilde{r}_Y$ (*return on share Y*)

whereas the individual entries in the main table show their joint probabilities. The entries in the main table, and the individual probability distributions given in the separate row and column, must sum to one if all possible outcomes have been considered.

The covariance of returns on shares X and Y is denoted $\sigma(\tilde{r}_X, \tilde{r}_Y)$ or $\text{cov}(\tilde{r}_X, \tilde{r}_Y)$, and it assesses the extent to which the two variables vary together. It is defined as:

$$\sigma(\tilde{r}_X, \tilde{r}_Y) = E\{[\tilde{r}_X - E(\tilde{r}_X)][\tilde{r}_Y - E(\tilde{r}_Y)]\}$$
$$= \sum P(\tilde{r}_X, \tilde{r}_Y)\{[\tilde{r}_X - E(\tilde{r}_X)][\tilde{r}_Y - E(\tilde{r}_Y)]\}. \quad (2.11)$$

The calculation of the mean, standard deviation, and covariance of returns of the values given in table 2.3 is shown in tables 2.4, 2.5, and 2.6.

The probabilities used in table 2.4 are taken from the bottom row of table 2.3 and show the overall assessed probabilities of the returns on share X being in the intervals 0–5, 5–10, and 10–15 per cent. In the calculation of the mean and standard deviation of the return on share X the midpoints of these ranges have been used in table 2.4. A similar exercise is conducted for share Y in table 2.5, with the probabilities of the returns being taken from the far right-hand column of table 2.3.

The respective means and standard deviations of returns on shares X and Y are calculated at 7.2 and 3.148 per cent for X and 6.41 and 3.089 per cent for Y. These values can then be utilized in the calculation of the covariance and correlation coefficient of $\tilde{r}_X$ and $\tilde{r}_Y$ as in table 2.6.

The nine possible combinations of outcomes of returns on share X with that of Y (low L, medium M, and high H) are shown in the two right-hand columns of table 2.6. The deviations of the returns on X and Y from their means are taken from column 4 of tables 2.4 and 2.5. The joint probabilities of the two returns being combined are taken from the central portions of table 2.3. The covariance of $\tilde{r}_X$ and $\tilde{r}_Y$ is calculated as -2.1769. The negative value reflects the tendency of one share to perform relatively well when the other is doing badly.

2.5   CORRELATION COEFFICIENT

Another measure closely related to the covariance is the correlation coefficient (ρ). From the joint probability distribution given in table 2.3 the expected value and the standard deviation of returns of X

TABLE 2.4   *The calculation of the mean and standard deviation of the returns on share X* (values taken from table 2.3)

(1) Probability of return	(2) Return (%)	(3) Prob. × Ret. (1) × (2)	(4) Ret. − $\bar{r}_X$ (2) − $\bar{r}_X$	(5) (Ret. − $\bar{r}_X$)² (4)²	(6) (Ret. − $\bar{r}_X$)² × Prob. (5) × (1)
0.23	2.5	0.575	−4.7	22.09	5.0807
0.60	7.5	4.5	0.3	0.09	0.054
0.17	12.5	2.125	5.3	28.09	4.7753
		$\sum = \bar{r}_X = 7.2\%$			$\sum = \sigma^2(\tilde{r}_X) = 9.91$
					$\therefore \sigma(\tilde{r}_X) = 3.148\%$

TABLE 2.5   *The calculation of the mean and the standard deviation of the returns on share Y* (values taken from table 2.3)

(1) Probability of return	(2) Return (%)	(3) Prob. × Ret. (1) × (2)	(4) Ret. − $\bar{r}_Y$ (2) − $\bar{r}_Y$	(5) (Ret. − $\bar{r}_Y$)² (4)²	(6) (Ret. − $\bar{r}_Y$)² × Prob. (5) × (1)
0.35	2.5	0.875	−3.91	15.2881	5.3508
0.43	7.5	3.225	1.09	1.1881	0.5109
0.22	10.5	2.31	4.09	16.7281	3.6802
		$\sum = \bar{r}_Y = 6.41\%$			$\sum = \sigma^2(\tilde{r}_Y) = 9.5419$
					$\therefore \sigma(\tilde{r}_Y) = 3.089\%$

TABLE 2.6   *The calculation of the covariance of X and Y*

Return on X	Return on Y	(1) $\tilde{r}_X - \bar{r}_X$	(2) $\tilde{r}_Y - \bar{r}_Y$	(3) Joint Probability	(4) Product (1) × (2) × (3)
L	L	(−4.7)	(−3.91)	(0.05)	0.9189
L	M	(−4.7)	(1.09)	(0.10)	−0.5123
L	H	(−4.7)	(4.09)	(0.08)	−1.5378
M	L	(0.3)	(−3.91)	(0.20)	−0.2346
M	M	(0.3)	(1.09)	(0.30)	0.0981
M	H	(0.3)	(4.09)	(0.10)	0.1227
H	L	(5.3)	(−3.91)	(0.10)	−2.0723
H	M	(5.3)	(1.09)	(0.03)	0.1733
H	H	(5.3)	(4.09)	(0.04)	0.8671
				$\sum = \text{cov}(\tilde{r}_X, \tilde{r}_Y) =$	−2.1769

and Y were calculated. The deviation of a security's return from its expected return can be expressed in 'normalized' units as follows:

$$d\tilde{x} = \frac{\tilde{r}_X - E(\tilde{r}_X)}{\sigma(\tilde{r}_X)}.$$

It is possible to consider these deviations in pairs for values of $\tilde{r}_X$ and $\tilde{r}_Y$:

$$d\tilde{X}\ d\tilde{Y} = \frac{\tilde{r}_X - E(\tilde{r}_X)}{\sigma(\tilde{r}_X)}\frac{\tilde{r}_Y - E(\tilde{r}_Y)}{\sigma(\tilde{r}_Y)}.$$

The correlation coefficient is derived by summing the product of all these paired deviations weighted by their probability:

$$\rho(\tilde{r}_X, \tilde{r}_Y) = \sum P(\tilde{r}_X, \tilde{r}_Y)\left\{\left[\frac{\tilde{r}_X - E(\tilde{r}_X)}{\sigma(\tilde{r}_X)}\right]\left[\frac{\tilde{r}_Y - E(\tilde{r}_Y)}{\sigma(\tilde{r}_Y)}\right]\right\}. \qquad (2.12)$$

The correlation coefficient can take any value in the range $+1$ to -1. If two variables are statistically independent they have a correlation coefficient of 0. Examples of perfect positive and perfect negative correlation are shown in figure 2.5.

The correlation coefficient $\rho(\tilde{r}_X, \tilde{r}_Y)$ could take any value between the two extreme values shown in figure 2.5. The weaker the level of association, the closer its value would be to 0.

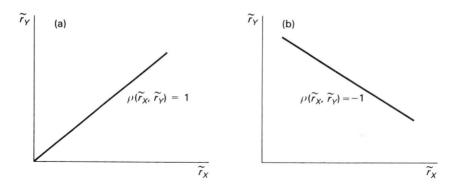

FIGURE 2.5   *(a) $\tilde{r}_X$ and $\tilde{r}_Y$ are perfectly positively correlated (b) $\tilde{r}_X$ and $\tilde{r}_Y$
are perfectly negatively correlated*

The only difference between the correlation coefficient and the
covariance is that the correlation coefficient is expressed in 'normalized' units. This means that:

$$\text{cov}(\tilde{r}_X, \tilde{r}_Y) = \rho(\tilde{r}_X, \tilde{r}_Y)\sigma(\tilde{r}_X)\sigma(\tilde{r}_Y). \tag{2.13}$$

The correlation coefficient of $\tilde{r}_X$ and $\tilde{r}_Y$, $\rho(\tilde{r}_X, \tilde{r}_Y)$, can be calculated
by simply dividing their covariance by their respective standard devi-
ations. In the example discussed in section 2.4 this yields a value of

$$\rho(\tilde{r}_X, \tilde{r}_Y) = \frac{-2.1769}{(3.148)(3.089)} = -0.2239.$$

The values of either of the two measures (as has been seen they are
very closely related) are crucial factors in determining the gains, in
terms of risk reduction, from the diversification of investments; they
are therefore important to both the individual investor considering
investment in a portfolio of shares, and the firm contemplating
investment in a number of different projects.

   The treatment of risk in finance has now been briefly introduced.
However, it would be impossible for a financial decision-taker to
come to a decision unless he had a predetermined attitude to the two
opposing parameters of expected return and risk. The determination
of such attitudes and their treatment in financial theory is the subject
of the next chapter.

1. Distinguish between 'subjective' and 'objective' probability.
2. Define 'risk'. In what ways can it be measured?
3. If a contemplated investment has an expected return of 20 per cent and a standard deviation of 10 per cent, is it possible to earn more than 30 per cent on the investment?
4. The subjective probability distribution of outcomes for an investment of £15,000 for a period of a year are as follows:

Probability	Outcome (£)
0.10	30,000
0.15	20,000
0.30	15,000
0.25	12,000
0.15	10,000
0.05	8,000

Calculate the expected return and the standard deviation of the rate of return.
5. Calculate the expected return, the standard deviation, the correlation coefficient, the covariance, and the coefficient of variation of the returns on the two securities X and Y, where the joint probability distribution is as follows:

		Return on X		
		2%	3%	4%
	0%	0.10	0.05	0.30
Return on Y	1%	0.05	0.30	0.05
	2%	0.05	0.05	0.05

6. Prove that the expected value of a random variable times a constant is equal to the constant times the expected value of the random variable; that is, prove that

$$E(\tilde{X}a) = aE(\tilde{X}).$$

Hint: see appendix 2.1.

APPENDIX 2.1   *Some properties of expectations and moments*

1. The expected value of a constant a plus a random variable $\tilde{X}$ is equal to the value of the constant plus the expected value of the random variable:

$$E(\tilde{X} + a) = E(\tilde{X}) + a. \tag{2.14}$$

Proof:

$$E(\tilde{X} + a) = \sum_{i=1}^{n} P_i(X_i + a) = \sum_{i=1}^{n} P_i X_i + \sum_{i=1}^{n} P_i a$$

$$= E(\tilde{X}) + a.$$

2. The expected value of a constant a times a random variable $\tilde{X}$ is equal to the constant times the expected value of the random variable:

$$E(\tilde{X}a) = aE(\tilde{X}). \tag{2.15}$$

The proof is along similar lines to the first proof.

3. The variance of a random variable plus a constant is equal to the variance of the random variable.

It is given that

variance $(\tilde{X})$ $\qquad = E\{[\tilde{X} - E(\tilde{X})]^2\}.$

$\therefore$ variance $(\tilde{X} + a) = E\{[(\tilde{X} + a) - E(\tilde{X} + a)]^2\}.$

But from the first proof:

$E(\tilde{X} + a)$ $\qquad = E(\tilde{X}) + a.$

$\therefore$ variance $(\tilde{X} + a) = E\{[(\tilde{X}) + a - E(\tilde{X}) - a]^2\}.$

The two as on the RHS cancel out, and hence:

variance $(\tilde{X} + a) = E\{[\tilde{X} - E(\tilde{X})]^2\} =$ variance $(\tilde{X})$.   (2.16)

4. The variance of a random variable $\tilde{X}$ multiplied by a constant a is equal to the square of the constant times the variance of the random variable.

$$\text{variance } (\tilde{X}a) = E\{[(\tilde{X}a) - E(\tilde{X}a)]^2\}$$

$$= E\{[(\tilde{X}a) - aE(\tilde{X})]^2\} \tag{2.15}$$

$$= E(\{a[(\tilde{X}) - E(\tilde{X})]\}^2)$$

$$= E\{a^2[\tilde{X} - E(\tilde{X})]^2\}.$$

$\therefore$ variance $(\tilde{X}a) = a^2 E\{[\tilde{X} - E(\tilde{X})]^2\}.$ (2.17)

NOTES AND REFERENCES

1. Hume, D. *Treatise of Human Nature*, Clarendon Press, Oxford, 1896, p. 181.
   Keynes attempted to extend Hume's observations and incorporate probability
   theory in a more general theory of knowledge. See: Keynes, J. M. *Treatise on
   Probability*, Macmillan, 1921.
   See also Ramsey's criticisms of Keynes on this matter: Ramsey, F. P. 'Truth and
   probability', reprinted in *Foundations*, Routledge and Kegan Paul, London,
   1978.
2. Raiffa distinguishes between various schools of thought in two branches of the
   employment of statistics. The first branch is the use of statistics for decision and
   practical action, which he divides into four groups comprising the followers of
   (a) R. A. Fisher, (b) Neyman and Pearson, (c) A. Wald, and (d) L. J. Savage. The
   second is the use of statistics for the purposes of inference and the development
   of scientific knowledge, where he broadly distinguishes between Bayesianists and
   non-Bayesian classicists. See: Raiffa, H. *Decision Analysis*, Addison-Wesley,
   Reading, Massachusetts, 1970, chapter 10.
3. This really leads on to portfolio theory, considered in chapter 4.
4. For discrete distributions the binomial distribution is employed. The normal,
   Poisson, and exponential distributions are amongst those used to represent
   continuous distributions. For a discussion of the above distributions see:
   Freund, J. E. and Williams, F. J. *Modern Business Statistics*, Pitman, London,
   1967, chapter 7.
5. See: Arditti, F. D. 'Risk and the required rate of return on equity', *Journal of
   Finance* 22(1), March 1967, pp. 19–36.
6. Apart from those probability distributions, such as the Cauchy distribution, that
   are not defined by moments.
7. Markowitz, H. M. *Portfolio Selection*, Wiley, New York, 1959. Markowitz
   devotes chapter IX to consideration of the semi-variance and in chapter XIII
   reviews various other possible measures of risk.
8. Markowitz, H. M. *Portfolio Selection*, Wiley, New York, 1959, pp. 290–1.
9. For a comprehensive review of this and the *CVR* see: Francis, J. C. and Archer,
   S. H., *Portfolio Analysis*, Prentice-Hall, Englewood Cliffs NJ, 1971, chapter XI,
   pp. 211–27.
10. Fisher, L. 'Determinants of risk premiums on corporate bonds', *Journal of Pol-
    itical Economy* 67(3), June 1959, pp. 217–37.
11. Baumol, W. J. 'An expected gain-confidence limit criterion for portfolio selec-
    tion', *Management Science* 10(1), January 1963, pp. 174–82.

CHAPTER 3

Utility theory

The multiplication of happiness is, according to the utilitarian ethics, the object of virtue.[1]

This chapter will be concerned with 'utility' in the narrower egotistical sense of its being the motive force behind consumption and investment decisions. For if valuation depends on estimations of future income, subject to varying levels of risk, a framework for evaluating individual decisions within this context is required. Decisions concerning future income and consumption possibilities are ultimately made with a view to the satisfaction or 'utility' attached by the individual decision-makers to those future possibilities. Any theory that seeks to explain the nature of decision-making requires a system of ranking which can be applied to order the various outcomes. The concept of expected utility is normally employed to do so. Utility theory has a long and chequered history in economic literature, although this can largely be ignored for present purposes.[2]

However, a landmark in the development of the concept was the eighteenth-century controversy concerning the famous St. Petersburg paradox. Prior to this, the prevalent idea had been that the individual, when confronted with a choice amongst various risky alternatives, should maximize the expected monetary value of the return. Nicholas Bernoulli demonstrated that this can lead to ludicrous results:

Peter tosses a coin and continues to do so until it should land 'heads' when it comes to the ground. He agrees to give Paul one ducat if he gets 'heads' on the very first throw, two ducats if he gets it on the second, four if on the third, eight if on the fourth, and so on, so that with each additional throw the number of ducats he must pay is doubled.[3]

The question is: what is the expected monetary value of this gamble? This could be regarded as the sum which Paul should be prepared to pay to participate in the game.

The straightforward expected monetary value of the bet can be calculated by weighting the value of the winnings by their probability of occurrence. Calculation reveals that Paul should be prepared to pay an infinite sum – but common sense rejects this as being absurd!

expected value in ducats

$$= (\tfrac{1}{2} \times 1) + (\tfrac{1}{4} \times 2) + (\tfrac{1}{8} \times 4) + (\tfrac{1}{16} \times 8) \cdots$$

$$= \tfrac{1}{2} + \tfrac{1}{2} + \tfrac{1}{2} + \tfrac{1}{2} \cdots$$

and this sum is infinite.

3.1 THE ROLE OF UTILITY

The solution proposed by Bernoulli was based on the idea that 'the determination of the value of an item must not be based upon its price, but rather on the utility it yields'.[4]

He suggested that utility should be regarded as being proportional to wealth.[5] This provides a solution with a finite utility to the original game, but if the amount awarded as a prize is increased much more rapidly after each toss of the coin, then a game can still be created for which the expected utility of participation is infinite.[6]

However, the principle adopted by Bernoulli was appropriate but the utility of wealth function chosen was not. If he had employed a utility function which was bounded from above, then none of the possible variations of the game could yield an infinite expected utility. In this case utility would never exceed a certain finite value irrespective of how large wealth became. Paul should calculate the expected utility he will enjoy, if he plays the game, by weighting the expected utility of the various levels of wealth he will enjoy, if he wins, by their probability of occurrence.

$$\text{expected utility } (EU) = \sum_{n=1}^{\infty} P_n U_n \tag{3.1}$$

where P_n is the probability that the gamble will give player wealth W_n, and U_n is the utility associated with wealth W_n along the player's utility of wealth curve.

If Paul's original wealth is w, he should calculate the expected utility he will enjoy if he plays the game in the following manner:

$$\text{expected utility } (EU) = \tfrac{1}{2}u(w + 1) + \tfrac{1}{4}u(w + 2) + \tfrac{1}{8}u(w + 4) + \cdots.$$

3.2 DEMONSTRATION OF THE BASIC PRINCIPLES VIA THE USE OF LOTTERIES

This famous problem serves as an introduction to most of the concepts required in a formal treatment of utility theory as applied to choices under risky conditions. Suppose you are sold a lottery ticket which offers two levels of prize. The first prize is a brand new car and each of the other prizes is a skateboard. A thousand tickets have been sold in the lottery; therefore the probability of winning (there is only one first prize) is 0.001, and the probability of losing and receiving a skateboard is 0.999. What is the value to you of participating in the lottery? We have already seen from the example of the St Petersburg paradox that this cannot be calculated merely from the expected monetary value of the prizes. The utility of the prizes has to be considered. If you value the car at 1,000 units of utility, or utils, and the skateboards at 1 util each, then weighting the utility of the two levels of prize by their probability of occurrence gives a means of assessing the expected utility of the lottery ticket:

$$(0.001 \times 1,000) + (0.999 \times 1) = 1.999 \text{ utils.}$$

In general, where a lottery ticket offers two prizes, X with probability P, and Y with probability $1 - P$, and if their respective utilities are given by $U(X)$ and $U(Y)$, then the utility of the lottery ticket L is given by:

$$U(L) = PU(X) + (1 - P)U(Y). \tag{3.2}$$

This simple case can be extended to cover any situation involving choice from a set of alternatives, or prospects, which the chooser can rank by means of preference ordering. Each prospect $(L, L_1, L_2, \ldots)$ is defined by a number of objects $(X, X_1, X_2, \ldots)$ which could be sums of money, or consumer durables, etc., which are to be had with certain associated probabilities $(P, P_1, P_2, \ldots)$.

The simplest case would be, as above, a prospect involving participation in a lottery with a possibility of receiving X or X_1, with associated probabilities of $P, 1 - P$; this could be written as:

$$L = (X, X_1; P, 1 - P). \tag{3.3}$$

It is also possible to make up more complex prospects which would give the opportunity of winning a lottery ticket, or the chance to participate in a lottery, rather than involving the straightforward choice of whether or not to purchase a lottery ticket. If you imagine the situation, this would be a lottery ticket which gives prizes that are, in turn, tickets in other lotteries! Formally this could be written

$$L_2 = (L, L_1; P, 1 - P)$$
$$= [(X, X_1; P, 1 - P),$$
$$\times (X_2, X_3; P_1, 1 - P_1); P_2, 1 - P_2]. \tag{3.4}$$

These prospects can be evaluated by means of the expected utility hypothesis. This suggests that for a prospect such as

$$L_2 = (L, L_1; P, 1 - P)$$

it is possible to associate with each of the component prospects L and L_1 a real number $f(L)$ and $f(L_1)$. By weighting these numbers by the probabilities associated with the prospect L and L_1, it is possible to calculate the expected utility of prospect L_2. This means that the expected utility of prospect L_2 is as follows:

$$L_2 = Pf(L) + (1 - P)f(L_1). \tag{3.5}$$

This is the method suggested in the solution to the St Petersburg paradox; the rule is that in a choice between two prospects, the one with the higher expected utility will be preferred.

As the prospects L and L_1 may involve the possibility of receiving objects X, X_1, and so on, this implies the existence of a utility function $U(X)$ defined on these objects.

Questions then arise concerning the type of utility function implied by the analysis, and also concerning the nature of the preference orderings required to ensure that the expected utility of the prospects can be taken to represent the preference orderings. Work on the latter question, in particular by Neumann and Morgenstern, and by Samuelson, has led to agreement about a set of postulates consistent with the expected utility hypothesis.[7]

3.3 THE FUNDAMENTAL AXIOMS

The assumptions are as follows:

(1) *Transitivity.* For the individual choosing there is a complete, transitive preference ordering of all possible alternative choices. This means that if X_1 is preferred to X_2, and X_2 is preferred to X_3, then X_1 is preferred to X_3.

(2) *Continuity of preference.* Suppose that, among three objects X_1, X_2, and X_3, X_3 is preferred to X_2 ($X_3 > X_2$) and X_2 is preferred to X_1 ($X_2 > X_1$). Then there is some probability value P for which receiving X_2, with certainty, is regarded as being equivalent to a prospect of X_3 with probability P and X_1 with probability $1 - P$. In effect there is some value P such that:

$$X_2 = (X_3, X_1; P, 1 - P).$$

(3) *Independence.* Suppose X_2 is preferred to X_1 ($X_2 > X_1$), and X_3 is any other prospect. Then the prospect $(X_2, X_3; P, 1 - P)$ is preferred to $(X_1, X_3; P, 1 - P)$. This also means that, in the particular case where $X_1 = X_2$, the prospect $(X_1, X_3; P, 1 - P) = (X_2, X_3; P, 1 - P)$.

(4) *High probability of success.* This assumption is fairly self-evident. It states that if two objects are regarded as being equivalent, that is $X_1 = X_2$, then the individual will choose the gamble or lottery ticket with the highest probability of success. For example, if

$$L_1 = (X_1, 0; P_1, 1 - P_1)$$

$$L_2 = (X_2, 0; P_2, 1 - P_2)$$

and if $P_1 > P_2$ and $X_1 = X_2$, then L_1 will be preferred to L_2.

(5) *Compound probabilities.* Suppose an individual is offered a lottery ticket, the prizes of which are, in turn, other lottery tickets. Then his attitude toward this compound lottery ticket would be equivalent to that suggested if he had worked out all the compound probabilities of winning and losing to find out what the compound ticket really offers him.

It is necessary to establish how reasonable these assumptions or axioms are, since they are the basic prerequisities of the construction of a Neumann–Morgenstern utility index. The first, I think you will agree, sounds reasonable enough.

The second, however, causes more difficulties. The following test example of it has been suggested. Suppose that you are faced with three prospects: X_1 is two candy bars, X_2 is one candy bar, and X_3 is being shot in the head. If the second axiom holds it should be possible to assign a probability P to X_3, and a probability $1 - P$ to X_1, such that the individual is indifferent between this uncertain prospect and the certain prospect of X_2 of receiving one candy bar. If the probability P of being shot in the head is infinitely small, it could be argued that the individual demands the second candy bar as compensation for the existence of this infinitely small but positive probability.[8]

The third axiom, called 'the strong independence assumption', could be illustrated as follows. If an individual is indifferent between receiving a new car or a luxury holiday cruise, then he will also be indifferent between two lottery tickets which offer the same probabilities of winning either prize. This can be taken a stage further and applied directly to lottery tickets as well.[9] Suppose the individual is indifferent between a second-hand car and a lottery ticket which offers him the chance of winning a luxury cruise. He should also be indifferent between a lottery ticket which offers him the chance of winning a second-hand car, and another which offers him the same probability of winning the first lottery ticket (the opportunity to participate in the first lottery with the chance of winning a luxury cruise).

The fourth assumption about the desire for a high probability of success seems straightforward enough, as long as no utility is attached to the act of gambling itself. For example, a person might prefer uncertainty about what will be served for dinner on Friday, so that he can enjoy the luxury of speculating during the journey home, to a 99 per cent certainty of being served fish.

The fifth postulate basically states that what should count, in an individual's evaluation of the prospect of receiving some objects, is the actual probability of receiving each object, and that the way in which the probability is determined, whether by drawing numbers from a hat, doubling up bets, or engaging in compound lotteries, is irrelevant.

The axioms are the prerequisites for drawing up a Neumann–Morgenstern utility index. The index is useful in situations where an individual is dealing with choices involving risky outcomes as it enables him to rank various prospects. The index has caused a lot of controversy as it is regarded as being a 'cardinal utility' index.[10]

3.4   METHODS OF RANKING

Associative measures merely associate items in different collections. Tags or brands on a farmer's cows might associate them with his farm but not distinguish between individual beasts.

Rankings or orderings allow the ordering of a set of items. For example, a force seven wind is not as strong as a force eight wind; the force number gives an indication of relative strength.

Cardinal measures are more restricted. For example, in the measurement of weights it is necessary to be able to measure the individual weights of two different bundles of goods, and then, on the basis of this, to be able to predict their combined weights. The Neumann–Morgenstern utility index is cardinal in the sense that it can be used for making predictions. It can be used to predict which of two lottery tickets a given individual will prefer from information about his ranking of alternative prizes and the probabilities of receiving those prizes in the lotteries concerned. In this sense it is cardinal, but note that no information is conveyed about the intensity of personal satisfaction involved.[11]

3.5   THE CONSTRUCTION OF AN INDIFFERENCE FUNCTION FOR MONEY OR WEALTH

The Neumann–Morgenstern assumptions about utility can be used in the construction of an indifference function for wealth. Suppose an individual is faced with a gamble in a lottery with two extreme outcomes: he either wins £100 or loses £25. These two extreme outcomes can be regarded as the boundaries of a whole class of basic reference lottery tickets (BRLT) with a lower reference prize $L = -£25$ and an upper reference prize $U = £100$. This is interpreted as meaning that a BRLT with probability P gives a P chance of winning £100 and a $1 - P$ chance of losing £25. The individual can then be asked what amount of certain wealth or certain money equivalent (CME) he would be prepared to accept instead of a particular gamble in the lottery.[12] A schedule can then be set up relating a number of different values of X or CMEs to P, the probability of winning in the lottery. The relation can be shown graphically as in figure 3.1.

The individual, for any value of X and P on the curve in figure 3.1,

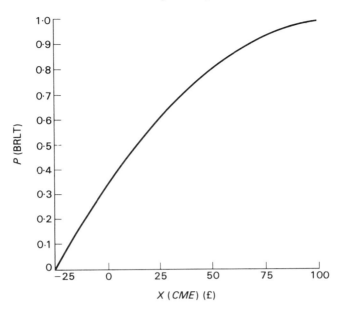

FIGURE 3.1 *The construction of an individual's wealth indifference curve*

is indifferent between receiving £X for certain and taking part in a lottery where he has a probability P of winning £100 and a probability $1 - P$ of losing £25. The curve is the individual's indifference curve for money or wealth. It can be seen that he regards certain wealth of £50 as being equivalent to a BRLT giving him a 0.8 chance (P) of winning £100, since the point (50, 0.8) lies on the curve. You will notice also that the curve increases at a diminishing rate, or in other words is concave towards the X axis. This leads to a very important consideration: the attitude of the individual towards risk.

3.6 RISK AVERSION

In most financial situations, individuals would be expected to display risk aversion. A risk averter will not accept a fair bet. This means that if he was faced with the situation shown below, he would regard the certain money equivalent of the bet as less than its expected monetary value.

$$\nearrow 0.5 \quad \text{win} \quad £X_1$$

○◁

$$\searrow 0.5 \quad \text{lose} \quad £X_2$$

For the risk averter facing this situation,

$$CME < \frac{X_1 + X_2}{2}. \tag{3.6}$$

Now suppose that he was offered the original fair bet, which involved equal probabilities of either winning or losing £100. If he rejects this bet this implies that he puts greater value on the loss in utility associated with losing £100 than on the gain in utility associated with winning £100. This suggests a utility of wealth curve of the type shown in figure 3.2.

The risk averter, if he is to reject a fair bet, must have a utility of wealth curve which increases at a diminishing rate or, in other words, one which displays diminishing marginal utility of wealth.

By similar reasoning, it can be shown that a risk-neutral individual would have a linear utility of wealth curve, as shown in figure 3.3. He would attach the same gain or loss of utility to an equal gain or loss of wealth. A risk preferrer, on the other hand, places greater utility on the gain of a given increment of wealth than on the loss of an equal amount of wealth. His utility curve rises at an increasing rate (figure 3.3), displaying increasing marginal utility of wealth.

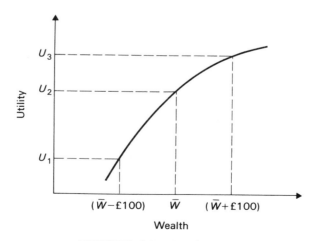

FIGURE 3.2 *A risk averter*

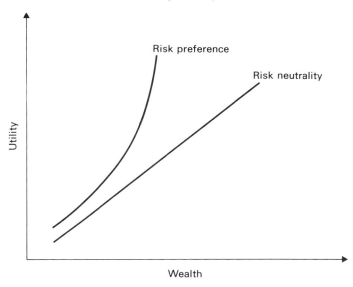

FIGURE 3.3 *Utility of wealth curves showing risk neutrality and risk preference*

3.7 GAMBLING AND INSURANCE

The utility of wealth functions so far considered are consistent either, in the case of risk aversion, with the purchase of insurance against loss and the avoidance of fair bets, or, in the case of risk preference, with the acceptance of fair bets and the refusal to insure against loss. Can this be reconciled with the fact that individuals frequently both insure against loss and participate in lotteries at the same time?[13]

In the individual case, the fact of purchase of insurance and participation in lotteries at one and the same time is consistent with the utility of wealth curve of the type shown in figure 3.4. In this figure the individual's current wealth is indicated by $\bar{W}$. He will accept fair bets which lead to an increase of wealth above $\bar{W}$ because on this section of the curve the marginal utility of wealth is increasing. He will also insure against losses leading to a reduction in wealth below $\bar{W}$ because on this section of the curve the marginal utility of wealth is decreasing.

This type of utility of wealth curve seems quite acceptable in the individual case; but however, can it be generalized to apply to all

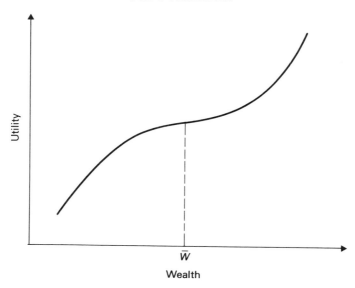

FIGURE 3.4   *A utility curve consistent with gambling and insurance*

individuals? This would suggest that only individuals with a current
level of wealth $\bar{W}$ will insure against loss and participate in lotteries.
Individuals with wealth below $\bar{W}$ will insure against loss and refuse
to accept fair bets, whereas individuals with a wealth greater than $\bar{W}$
will refuse to insure against loss yet accept fair bets. Thus the implication is that wealthy individuals would never purchase insurance
unless it led to a loss of wealth below $\bar{W}$. Yet this is clearly not the
case.

A utility curve which is consistent with both the purchase of insurance and the participation in lotteries at levels of wealth $\bar{W}_1$ (low
wealth) and $\bar{W}_2$ (high wealth) is shown in figure 3.5. The problem is
that this also leads to unacceptable results. For it implies that individuals with an intermediate level of wealth (between $\bar{W}_1$ and $\bar{W}_2$)
would refuse to insure against small losses but would gamble on fair
bets. This suggests that the number of people in this wealth bracket
would diminish over time, as either losses reduced their wealth to $\bar{W}_1$
or successful gambles moved them up to $\bar{W}_2$. Wealth would therefore be polarized around $\bar{W}_1$ and $\bar{W}_2$. This behaviour and type of
wealth distribution do not seem consistent with reality.

Perhaps the most sensible conclusion is to accept that in situations

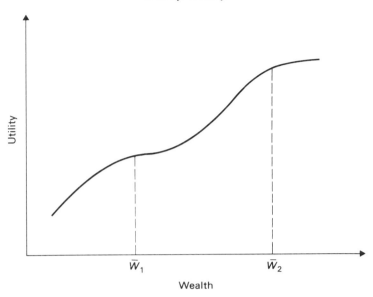

FIGURE 3.5 *A utility function consistent with gambling and insurance at two levels of wealth*

where significant amounts of personal wealth are at stake, and where an unfavourable outcome would involve impoverishment, individuals are likely to display risk aversion. However, where insignificant amounts of personal wealth are at stake, and where there is a separate utility attached to the act of gambling itself, then individuals are likely to display risk neutrality or even risk preference. This suggests that in the case of major financial decisions we can assume an attitude of risk aversion.

3.8 THE USE OF QUADRATIC UTILITY CURVES

Risk aversion implies a utility of wealth curve which increases at a diminishing rate. If the indifference curves are to have this property, and if the individual investor's choice among risky investment alternatives is to be based upon the mean and standard deviation of their expected returns, then a suitable class of utility curves with these characteristics is that of quadratic utility curves. These assume that utility is a quadratic function of wealth. This means that the utility of wealth function is of the form:

$$U(W) = a + bW - cW^2 \qquad (3.7)$$

where U is utility, W is wealth, and a, b, and c are constants (b and c are positive constants). It has already been noted that if an individual investor is risk averse his utility of wealth function must increase at a decreasing rate, or in other words he must display diminishing marginal utility of wealth. His marginal utility of wealth must be positive, though, as he may be expected to regard additions to his wealth as a 'good' thing even if they do not increase his overall satisfaction as much as previously when his total wealth was less. This suggests that if the utility of wealth function of (3.7) is considered, then the function will display the required characteristics only if:

$$W < \frac{b}{2c}, \quad b > 0, \quad c > 0.$$

This follows since:

$$\frac{dU}{dW} = b - 2cW. \qquad (3.8)$$

But small additions of wealth must yield positive utility, and therefore b must be positive; the whole expression must be positive only if $b - 2cW > 0$, or $W < b/2c$. Furthermore:

$$\frac{d^2U}{dW^2} = -2c. \qquad (3.9)$$

As $d^2U/dW^2 < 0$, $c > 0$, so that the function is at a maximum.[14] Thus, the quadratic utility function is only an approximation to the required function, over a limited range, as shown in figure 3.6.

It can be seen from the figure that the function displays positive but diminishing marginal utility of wealth over only a limited portion of its range. It is equivalent to the actual utility of wealth curve in the figure over its initial stages, and then the two become increasingly divergent (from the point where the 'dotted' utility of wealth curve continues above the quadratic utility curve). More important, the quadratic utility curve reaches a maximum where wealth $W = b/2c$. Beyond this point any further increases in wealth bring negative marginal utility and so serve to diminish total utility. This clearly does not make economic sense.

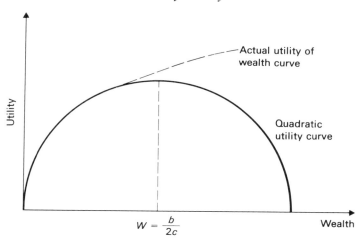

FIGURE 3.6 *The quadratic utility function is an approximation to the required function*

In most cases of financial decision-making the individual will be making decisions concerned with expected future returns, and he will be seeking to maximize the expected utility of those future returns. In this case, if expected returns are substituted for wealth the original utility function (3.7) as can be rewritten follows:

$$\text{expected } U = a + b \text{ (expected } R) - c \text{ [expected } (R^2)]. \quad (3.10)$$

The reason why much of financial theory employs quadratic utility curves is that this equation can be rewritten to make utility a function both of $E(R)$ (the mean of the probability distribution of expected returns) and of $\sigma(R)$ (the standard deviation of the probability distribution of expected returns). It can be shown that (3.10) can be rewritten as follows:[15]

$$\text{expected } U = a + b \text{ (expected } R)$$

$$- c(\text{expected } R)^2 - c\sigma^2(R). \quad (3.11)$$

This is one of the main points in favour of the use of quadratic utility functions. However, there is another technical difficulty associated with them in that they imply that risky assets are inferior goods. Suppose that at a certain level of wealth an individual chooses to hold a given amount of risky securities; the adoption of quadratic indifference curves suggests that if the wealth of this individual were to be increased he would hold less risky securities.[16] This suggests that risky securities are an 'inferior' good. In reality this would not be expected to happen, and risky securities are regarded as being 'normal' (in the sense that increases in wealth would lead to increases in demand for them). This leads on naturally to the consideration of attitudes to risk as a function of the individual decision-maker's level of wealth.

3.9 CONSTANT, DECREASING, OR INCREASING RELATIVE RISK AVERSION

It was seen previously that for an investor to display risk aversion it was necessary that his utility function display the characteristics dU/dW (or $U'(W)) > 0$ and d^2U/dW^2 (or $U''(W)) < 0$. The subsequent discussion of quadratic utility curves showed that these properties alone were not sufficient to ensure counter-intuitive behaviour of increasing risk aversion at higher levels of wealth.

The analysis of this problem was pioneered by Arrow and Pratt.[17] They suggested the following measure of absolute risk aversion:

$$A(W) = \frac{-U''(W)}{U'(W)}. \tag{3.12}$$

Inspection of (3.12) shows that $A(W)$ has the following properties: for a risk preferrer $A(W) < 0$; for a risk-neutral individual $A(W) = 0$; and for a risk-averse individual $A(W) > 0$. In addition, $A(W)$ will be unaltered in sign by an arbitrary linear transformation of the utility function.

As a measure of relative risk aversion Arrow and Pratt suggested;

$$R(W) = \frac{-U''(W)}{U'(W)} W = A(W)W. \tag{3.13}$$

Both of these measures are 'local' measures of risk aversion in that they are related to the level of W, though in the case of (3.13) the choice of units of W will not matter.

In the case of absolute risk aversion a utility function of the following type displays constant absolute risk aversion:[18]

$$U(W) = a - be^{-RW}. \tag{3.14}$$

(This follows where $b > 0$, since $[-U''(W)/U'(W)] = R$.)

In the case of constant relative risk aversion the following utility function has the appropriate properties:

$$U(W) = a - bW^{-R+1}. \tag{3.15}$$

(Again where $b > 0$, $[-U''(W)/U'(W)]W = R$, for all $W > 0$.)

For the above properties, and further related reasons, the logarithmic and power forms of utility functions have been receiving a lot of attention. Rubinstein has demonstrated that the generalized logarithmic utility model (GLUM) has a number of attractive properties, and has put forward persuasive arguments in favour of its adoption.[19] However, his arguments are beyond the scope of this text, and it is hoped that the brief survey just conducted will convey an idea of the type of requirements needed in the employment of utility functions in the theory of financial decision-making.

TEST QUESTIONS

1. Suppose someone has indicated the following set of preferences between three alternative objects of choice X_1, X_2, and X_3:

   $X_1 > X_2$

   $X_2 > X_3$

   $X_3 > X_1$.

   Does this conform with the axioms of rational choice? If not, how could the set of preferences be made to do so?
2. What is your implied attitude to risk if you are prepared to accept gambles on the basis of their expected monetary value?
3. Would a risk-averse individual accept the following bet?

   0.4   he gains £15

   0.6   he loses £10
4. Given the utility function $U(W) = 10 - 5e^{-2W}$:
   (a) Graph the function.
   (b) Is the marginal utility of wealth positive?
   (c) What is the implied attitude to risk?
   (d) Does it display increasing absolute risk aversion?

5. Draw a graph of a utility function which is consistent with an individual refusing to insure against loss yet refusing fair bets at the same time.

NOTES AND REFERENCES

1. Mill, J. S. 'Utilitarianism' (1861), reprinted in *Utilitarianism, On Liberty, and Considerations on Representative Government*, Dent, London, 1972, p. 17.
2. The debate goes all the way back to classical economics. Adam Smith was perhaps one of the first to point out the distinction between marginal and total utility in his famous treatment of the water/diamond paradox, and the difference between value in use and value in exchange. See: Smith, A. *The Wealth of Nations*, 1776, Book One, chapter 4.
3. Bernouili, D. 'Exposition of a new theory on the measurement of risk' (1738), translated by Sommer, L. *Econometrica* **22**(1), January 1954, pp. 23–36.
4. Ibid.
5. His solution was to suggest that utility should be equivalent to the logarithm of wealth.
6. See: Green, H. A. J. *Consumer Theory*, Macmillan, London, 1976, pp. 213–15.
7. Von Neumann, J. and Morgenstern, O. *Theory of Games and Economic Behaviour*, Wiley, New York, 1947.
   Samuelson, P. A. 'Probability, utility, and the independence axiom', *Econometrica* **20**(4), October 1952, pp. 670–8.
8. Alchian, A. A. 'The meaning of utility measurement', *American Economic Review* **43**(1), March 1953, pp. 26–50.
9. See; Baumol, W. J. *Economic Theory and Operations Analysis*, Prentice-Hall, Englewood Cliffs, NJ, 1965, chapter 22, pp. 512–29.
10. Ibid., p. 513.
11. See: Alchian, A. A. 'The meaning of utility measurement', *American Economic Review* **43**(1), March 1953, p. 28.
12. See: Raiffa, H. *Decision Analysis*, chapter 4, pp. 66–70.
13. Friedman, M. and Savage, L. J. 'The utility analysis of choices involving risk', *Journal of Political Economy* **56**(4), August 1948, pp. 279–304.
14. See: Green, H. A. J. *Consumer Theory*, Macmillan, London, 1976, p. 246.
15. If you have two random variables A and B with a joint probability distribution $P(A_i, B_j)$ for $i, j = 1, 2, 3, \ldots, n$, then the following theorems may be derived using the expected value operator.

Theorem 1 $\text{var}(A) = E(A^2) - [E(A)]^2$.

Proof $\text{var}(A) = E[A - E(A)]^2$ from the definition of variance

$$= E(A^2) - 2E(A)E(A) + [E(A)]^2$$

$$= E(A^2) - [E(A)]^2.$$

Theorem 2 $E(A^2) = \text{var}(A) + [E(A)]^2$.

Derivation $\text{var}(A) = E(A^2) - [E(A)]^2$ from theorem 1

$\therefore \quad \text{var}(A) + [E(A)]^2 = E(A^2)$.

See: Francis, J. C. and Archer, S. H. *Portfolio Analysis*, Prentice-Hall, Englewood Cliffs, NJ, 1971, appendix C, p. 235.
16. See: Sharpe, W. F. *Portfolio Theory and Capital Markets*, McGraw-Hill, New York, 1971, pp. 199–201.
17. Arrow, K. J. *Some Aspects of the Theory of Risk-Bearing*, Helsinki, 1965.
    Pratt, J. W., 'Risk aversion in the small and large', *Econometrica* **32**(1–2), January–April 1964, pp. 122–36.
18. See: Hey, J. D. *Uncertainty in Microeconomics*, Martin Robertson, Oxford, 1979, pp. 46–51.
19. Rubinstein, M. E. 'The strong case for the generalized logarithmic utility model as the premier model of financial markets', *The Journal of Finance* **31** (2), May 1976, pp. 551–571.

PART II

Theories of Market Valuation

CHAPTER 4

Portfolio theory and the analysis of capital markets

> It is of course true that as a rule a person will not enter on a
> risky business, unless, other things being equal, he expects to
> gain from it more than he would in other trades open to him,
> after his probable losses had been deducted from his prob-
> able gains on a fair actuarial estimate.[1]

This statement, written by Alfred Marshall at the turn of the century,
illustrates that the basic principles relevant to the analysis of individual risky ventures have been understood for a long time. They have
been put into practice, on an intuitive, 'rule of thumb' basis for many
years. The even older adage concerning the wisdom of 'not putting
all of one's eggs into one basket', particularly in the case where the
'eggs' are a number of financial instruments and the 'basket' is a
portfolio of investments or securities chosen by an investor, has also
been well taken. Thus, the idea of risk diversification is certainly far
from new. What is relatively new is the provision of a formal theoretical framework in which both the analysis of the benefits of risk
diversification, and the choice of a particular portfolio (a group of
investments or securities suited to the requirements of an individual
investor), can be made on a 'scientific' basis. This development
stemmed largely from the work of Harry Markowitz.[2]

In developing his analysis Markowitz made a number of crucial
assumptions with respect to both the behaviour of investors and the
nature of their analysis of the potential returns available on portfolios of securities. (Most of the concepts employed have already
been encountered in chapters 2 and 3.) The assumptions are:

(1) Investors are assumed to be concerned with maximizing the
    expected utility of their portfolio of securities over the single
    period under consideration.

(2) Investors are assumed to have beliefs about the potential returns available on individual securities in the form of subjective probability distributions of expected returns. The mean of the distribution is taken as a measure of expected return and the variance as an indication of its risk. It is also assumed that investors have an estimate of the covariability of the expected returns on the securities available.

(3) It follows that, when combinations of securities are chosen to form various portfolios, these portfolios can be completely described, from the investor's point of view, by the mean and variance of their expected returns. (For a treatment of alternative portfolio selection criteria see appendix 4.1.)

(4) Investors have utility functions of a type which enables them to choose portfolios solely on the basis of their estimated risk and expected return, and that in this choice the investors display risk aversion. (The utility functions are of the quadratic type considered in chapter 3.) From this it follows that, at a given level of risk, investors prefer more returns to less, and that at a given level of return they prefer; less risk to more.

Further assumptions normally made to facilitate the analysis are that investors can effect transactions in the market without incurring any dealing costs or tax liabilities, and that they can put any proportion of their portfolio into any security. The last assumption implies that securities are infinitely divisible.

The above approach suggests that portfolio selection is a three-stage process consisting of: security analysis, portfolio analysis, and portfolio selection. Each of the three stages will now be considered in turn.

4.1 SECURITY ANALYSIS

The first stage of the process requires the investor to generate subjective probability distributions to represent his estimation of the returns he expects to be forthcoming over the single period for which he intends to hold the portfolio, on all available securities. The mean and the standard deviation of each security's distribution will summarize his expectations of the returns available on that security. He is also required to make an estimation (in the manner considered in the previous chapter) of the covariability of all the securities considered systematically, in their various combinations, in pairs.

There are a number of ways in which the investor can tackle this problem. A careful study of historical data related to the securities, taken together with an assessment of likely trends in the economy and in the relevant market sectors, plus a careful evaluation of the current information relevant to the companies concerned, could yield a series of predictions about the likely returns promised by the securities over the planned holding period. An estimate of the covariability of the securities could be obtained, likewise, by careful study of previous data, plus projections of any factors likely to alter their relatedness of returns over the planned investment period. This obviously involves a considerable workload in the generation and assessment of a large quantity of data. To meet this problem, some short-cut methods have been suggested, based upon econometric forecasting techniques, which utilize the relationship between the return on all securities and the return on a market index, or number of indices, to produce the required information. These single- and multi-index methods will be considered in section 4.14.

4.2   ARE THE RETURNS ON SECURITIES NORMALLY DISTRIBUTED?

The single-period return on a share, if tax considerations are ignored, could be defined as follows:

$$_{t-1}r_t = \frac{d_t + (s_t - s_{t-1})}{s_{t-1}} \tag{4.1}$$

where $_{t-1}r_t$ is the one-period return, d_t are any dividends paid over the period, s_{t-1} is the share price at the beginning of the holding period, and s_t is the share price at the end of the holding period.

The assumption that the returns on securities, as defined above, are normally distributed is obviously of fundamental importance to portfolio theory. Does this assumption seriously violate reality?

There have been a number of studies of the distributions of both daily and monthly returns on individual securities and on market indices of securities, the earliest being Bachelier's long-neglected study of the distribution of returns of the Paris Bourse at the beginning of this century.[3] Interest was renewed in the fifties by the work of Osborne who, like Bachelier, employed arguments founded on the central limit theorem to support the conclusion that the distribution of returns is approximately normal.[4] Later studies by Fama and Mandelbrot drew attention to the fact that the distribution of returns is more peaked about the mean and fatter in the tails than the normal distribution. This led to the suggestion that the distribution of returns conforms to the non-normal stable class of Paretian distributions, of which the normal is but a special case.[5] An alternative and equally uncomfortable explanation would be that the distribution is non-stationary, experiencing movements in its mean and dispersion over time. A study of British data by Brealey found similar slight departures from normality, and further evidence that the distribution of monthly returns is skewed to the right.[6] However, taking the natural logarithm of returns:

$$\ln\left(\frac{d_t + s_t}{s_{t-1}}\right),$$

which would be consistent with using continuously compounded rather than simple returns, would have the effect of reducing the right skewness of monthly returns. Nevertheless, if the distribution of security returns is stable and normal it should be invariant under addition, and there should be no difference between the distribution of daily and that of monthly returns. Thus there are some important doubts, but the crucial question is: can the assumption of normally distributed returns be employed as a working hypothesis? Most authorities would seem to accept that it can.

4.3 THE COMBINING OF SECURITIES TO FORM PORTFOLIOS

A portfolio is simply a collection or group of securities considered in total as a single investment unit. A portfolio could be defined very broadly and be taken to include property, antiques, works of art, bullion, and commodities, as well as financial securities. However, this discussion will be limited to the consideration of a portfolio of shares, though the principles which will be developed would still apply for the evaluation of any type of portfolio. When any particular portfolio is assessed, the concern will be with its overall characteristics – its expected return and its risk. This follows directly from the previously cited assumptions, though obviously there are circumstances when other criteria will be of direct concern too. In times of political and economic 'crisis', gold bullion is placed at a considerable premium, perhaps because of its acceptability, liquidity, and up to a point, its portability. But in normal circumstances it can be assumed that all potential investments can be fitted into the risk/expected return framework.

The careful assessment of securities which must be undertaken before their combination into portfolios can take place has already been considered. Security analysis provides the foundation for subsequent portfolio analysis, but it is the contribution of each security to portfolio performance, rather than its individual performance, which is the paramount concern. In terms of the total portfolio, the value of the initial holding in each security can be expressed as a proportion of the value of the total portfolio. In this manner a 'weight' can be assigned to each security held in the portfolio. If the weight for security i is denoted x_i, then at the beginning of the holding period:

$$x_i = \frac{\text{value of funds invested in security } i}{\text{total value of funds invested in the portfolio}}.$$

As the total value of the portfolio is determined, at the start of the holding period, by the amount of funds invested in each security, it follows that:

$$\sum_{i=1}^{N} x_i = 1. \tag{4.2}$$

4.4 THE RETURN ON A PORTFOLIO

The return on a portfolio is obviously going to be determined by the return on the securities included in it; it will be a weighted average of the returns on the component securities:

$$R_\text{p} = \sum_{i=1}^{N} x_i r_i \tag{4.3}$$

where R_p is the return on the portfolio, x_i is the 'weight' for security i (the proportion of the portfolio invested in security i), and r_i is the rate of return on security i.

An illustration of how the return on a three-security portfolio, chosen from a 'universe' of five securities, could be determined, is shown in table 4.1. In this table you will see that security 4 and security 5 are not included in the portfolio, and therefore $x_4 = 0$ and $x_5 = 0$. In the original portfolio selection model developed by Markowitz the x_i values were constrained by $1 \geq x_i > 0$. This means that the choice was simply one of whether or not to include a security in a portfolio. If a security was left out it had an x_i value of 0. At the other extreme, if all the funds were put into one security, the chosen

TABLE 4.1   *The calculation of a return on a portfolio*

Security (i)	% rate of return (r_i)	Proportion of the portfolio invested in security i (x_i)	(x_i)(r_i)
1	5.0	0.2	1.0
2	10.0	0.4	4.0
3	12.0	0.4	4.8
4	18.0	0.0	0.0
5	14.0	0.0	0.0
		$\sum = 1$	$\sum = 9.8\%$ = portfolio return

security would have an x_i value of 1 and the others would have weights of 0. This was restrictive and unrepresentative of actual investor behaviour in that the model excluded both borrowing and lending and 'short sales'. ('Short-selling' is a form of speculation which relies on the fact that a seller of securities may not have to 'deliver' them to the purchaser immediately. Thus, a speculator can sell securities which he does not possess in the hope that, when the time comes for delivery, he will be able to purchase them on the market at a price below that of his original sale.) In the normal case we would expect the x_i values to be positive fractions.

It is evident from table 4.1 that a very large number of portfolios could be constructed from a mere five securities, and that a range of portfolio returns from 5 to 18 per cent could be obtained, merely by varying the security weights x_i. If the maximization of portfolio return was the sole investment criterion, then this could be achieved by putting the entire portfolio funds in security 4 and thereby obtaining a return of 18 per cent. This strategy ignores the other portfolio investment dimension – risk – and it could well be that the investor would find it unacceptably risky. This brings us to the consideration of portfolio risk and the possible benefits available from diversification.

4.5   THE RISK OF A PORTFOLIO

The calculation of portfolio risk is a slightly more difficult matter than the calculation of portfolio return. It will not be sufficient merely to take a weighted average of the individual component securities' risk, as this will not fully indicate the benefits of diversification. Both the individual riskiness of securities and the extent of their covariability of returns will have to be considered in order to measure portfolio risk. The total risk of a portfolio can be measured by calculating its variance by means of the following formula:

$$V_p = \sum_{i=1}^{N} x_i^2 \sigma_i^2 + \sum_{i=1}^{N} \sum_{\substack{j=1 \\ j \neq i}}^{N} x_i x_j \rho_{ij} \sigma_i \sigma_j \tag{4.4a}$$

where x_i and x_j are security weights, σ_i^2 is the variance of each security's return, ρ_{ij} is the correlation coefficient of the return on security i and j, and σ_i and σ_j are the standard deviations of the returns on securites i and j.

Expression (4.4a) is the sum of two terms. The first sums the products of the variance σ_i^2 of each security and the square of its portfolio weight x_i^2. The second sums the products of the covariability ρ_{ij} of each security i considered pairwise with every other security j in the portfolio, weighted by the respective portfolio weights (x_i, x_j) and the respective standard deviations (σ_i, σ_j), for all pairs $i = 1, \ldots, N$ and $j = 1, \ldots, N$ with the exceptions of $j = i$.

This expression could be simplified by noting that if security i is paired with itself $(j = 1)$ then $\rho_{ij} = 1$, and it follows that the expression $x_i x_j \rho_{ij} \sigma_i \sigma_j$ becomes equivalent to $x_i^2 \sigma_i^2$. Thus the first term in (4.4a) could be regarded as the diagonal factors in the full covariance matrix shown in tables 4.2 and 4.3. It follows that (4.4a) can be simplified to:

$$V_p = \sum_{i=1}^{N} \sum_{j=1}^{N} x_i x_j \rho_{ij} \sigma_i \sigma_j. \tag{4.4b}$$

Furthermore, from (2.13):

$$\text{cov}_{ij} = \rho_{ij} \sigma_i \sigma_j.$$

This means that expression (4.4b) could be written as:

$$V_p = \sum_{i=1}^{N} \sum_{j=1}^{N} x_i x_j \, \text{cov}_{ij}. \tag{4.4c}$$

At first sight, the calculation of the risk or variance of a portfolio's returns may seem rather complicated, but the example shown in tables 4.2 and 4.3, in which the risk of a three-security portfolio has been calculated, should help clarify the process. In table 4.2 the characteristics of the three securities and their portfolio weights are shown.

TABLE 4.2 *Security characteristics and portfolio weights*

Security 1	Security 2	Security 3
$\sigma_1 = 8\%$	$\sigma_2 = 12\%$	$\sigma_3 = 15\%$
$\rho_{12} = 0.3$	$\rho_{21} = 0.3$	$\rho_{31} = 0.5$
$\rho_{13} = 0.5$	$\rho_{23} = 0.4$	$\rho_{32} = 0.4$
$x_1 = 0.2$	$x_2 = 0.4$	$x_3 = 0.4$

The calculation of the risk of a portfolio of three securities with the above characteristics and portfolio weights is shown in steps in table 4.3. This table is drawn up in pairs with algebraic values on the LHS and their corresponding numerical values on the RHS.

In table 4.3(a) the correlation coefficient for each of the three securities in the portfolio is considered pairwise with every other security. At the outside of the table in both a vertical and a horizontal direction is the standard deviation of each of the securities. The numerical

TABLE 4.3 *Calculating portfolio risk*

(a)

	σ_1	σ_2	σ_3
σ_1	ρ_{11}	ρ_{12}	ρ_{13}
σ_2	ρ_{21}	ρ_{22}	ρ_{23}
σ_3	ρ_{31}	ρ_{32}	ρ_{33}

(d)

	8	12	15
8	1	0.3	0.5
12	0.3	1	0.4
15	0.5	0.4	1

(b)

	x_1	x_2	x_3
x_1	$\rho_{11}\sigma_1\sigma_1$	$\rho_{12}\sigma_1\sigma_2$	$\rho_{13}\sigma_1\sigma_3$
x_2	$\rho_{21}\sigma_2\sigma_1$	$\rho_{22}\sigma_2\sigma_2$	$\rho_{23}\sigma_2\sigma_3$
x_3	$\rho_{31}\sigma_3\sigma_1$	$\rho_{32}\sigma_3\sigma_2$	$\rho_{33}\sigma_3\sigma_3$

(e)

	0.2	0.4	0.4
0.2	64	28.8	60
0.4	28.8	144	72
0.4	60	72	225

(c)

	$x_1 x_1 c_{11}$	$x_1 x_{12} c_{12}$	$x_1 x_3 c_{13}$
	$x_2 x_1 c_{21}$	$x_2 x_2 c_{22}$	$x_2 x_3 c_{23}$
	$x_3 x_1 c_{31}$	$x_3 x_2 c_{32}$	$x_3 x_3 c_{33}$

(f)

	2.56	2.304	4.8
	2.304	23.04	11.52
	4.8	11.52	36.0

$$V_{\text{p}} = \sum_{i=1}^{3} \sum_{j=1}^{3} x_i x_j c_{ij}$$

$$\sigma_{\text{p}} = \sqrt{V_{\text{p}}}$$

$$V_{\text{p}} = 98.848$$

$$\sigma_{\text{p}} = 9.94\%$$

values corresponding to the symbols in table 4.3(a) appear in table 4.3(d). Notice that every numerical value in the table apart from those on the diagonal appears twice, as by definition $\rho_{12} = \rho_{21}$. In table 4.3(b) are given the correlation coefficients weighted by the standard deviations of the two securities in each pair. Table 4.3(e) gives their respective numerical values. Note that the figures in table 4.3(e) are obtained by taking each numerical entry from table 4.3(d) and multiplying it by the value at the head of its respective row and column; that is, by the standard deviations of the two securities.

In table 4.3(c) the covariance of each pair of securities (note that $c_{ij} = \rho_{ij}\sigma_i\sigma_j$) is weighted by their respective portfolio weights. Once again the values in table 4.3(f) are obtained by taking the elements within each box in table 4.3(e) and multiplying them by their respective row and column heads, in this case their respective portfolio weights. Finally, the variance of the portfolio is calculated by summing all the entries within table 4.3(f); in the example the sum of all the entries is 98.848. The portfolio standard deviation is found by taking the square root of the variance; in this case the standard deviation is 9.94 per cent.

It can be seen from this small example that, even though the basic computational steps are straightforward, there are an enormous number of computations involved in calculating the risk of a portfolio comprising a large number of securities. A computer will readily accomplish the task but computer time is expensive, and therefore a number of 'short-cut' methods have been developed which will be considered in section 4.14.

The measures of risk and of returns that were required have now been obtained. In the example these are actual values; a portfolio selection problem would deal with expected values, but the mathematics and methods of calculation would be identical. In the example the portfolio chosen seems to be rather risky. Its return is 9.8 per cent but its risk is 9.94 per cent. If the calculations were *ex ante* or 'before the event', as would normally be the case, then the prospect of an expected portfolio return of 9.8 per cent and an associated expected level of risk of 9.94 per cent might not be an attractive proposition. The assumption has been the distributions of security returns and therefore of portfolio returns are normal. From the properties of the normal distribution it is known that 95 per cent of the outcomes will be within two standard deviations of the mean. This means that there is a 0.95 probability that the actual portfolio return will be in the range $E(R_p) - 2\sigma_p < E(R_p) < E(R_p) + 2\sigma_p$. In the example, the return will be in the range $-10.08\% < 9.8\% <$

29.68%. An outcome in the top half of the range would be acceptable but the possibility of a large negative return might be viewed with disquiet. Could the portfolio be rearranged to reduce its risk?

4.6   THE BENEFITS OF DIVERSIFICATION

The gains in risk reduction from portfolio diversification depend inversely upon the extent to which the returns on securities in a portfolio are positively correlated. Ideally the securities should display negative correlation. This implies that if a pair of securities has a negative correlation of returns, then in circumstances where one of the securities is performing badly the other is likely to be doing well, and vice versa in reverse circumstances. Therefore the 'average' return on holding the two securities is likely to be much 'safer' than investing in one of them alone. It can be seen in the example portfolio considered in section 4.4 that none of the securities displayed negative correlation.

In normal circumstances, as evidenced by the securities in the example portfolio, most securities will display a degree of positive correlation, as all are likely to be similarly influenced by external trends in the economy. Nevertheless, there will still be some gains from risk diversification as long as the securities are not perfectly positively correlated. This can be most readily demonstrated by the consideration of a two-security portfolio's riskiness, as follows.

Risk in a two-security portfolio

If (4.4b) is expanded, an equation is obtained which shows how the variance of a two-security portfolio would be calculated:

$$\sigma_p^2 = x_1^2 \sigma_1^2 + x_2^2 \sigma_2^2 + (2x_1 x_2 \rho_{12} \sigma_1 \sigma_2). \tag{4.5}$$

Inspection of (4.5) shows that x_1 and x_2 are going to be positive fractions as, by assumption, $x_1 + x_2 = 1$. If security 1 and security 2 are risky it follows, by definition, that σ_1 and σ_2 are positive. It follows that any gains from risk diversification depend upon the bracketed third term, and within this the crucial factor is ρ_{12}. If $\rho_{12} = +1$, indicating perfect positive correlation, then there will be no gains from risk diversification. If ρ_{12} is a positive fraction there will be some gains from diversification, as the value of the third term will be reduced. If $\rho_{12} = 0$, the third term will disappear and there will be considerable gains from diversification. If ρ_{12} is negative, the

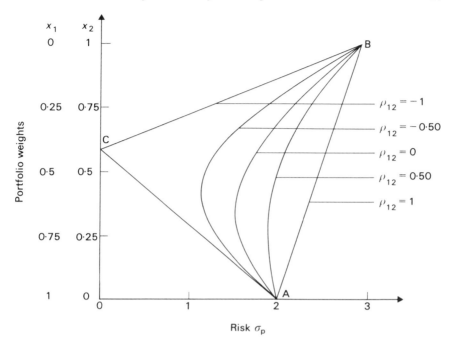

FIGURE 4.1 *The variation of risk in a two-security portfolio*
(note: $x_2 = 1 - x_1$)

third term will be negative and there will be even greater gains as overall riskiness will be further reduced. In the limit maximum gains come where $\rho_{12} = -1$. Figure 4.1 shows the various possibilities.

In this figure are shown the portfolio risks of all possible two-security portfolios that can be formed by combining a security 1 with a risk of $\sigma_1 = 2$ and a security 2 with a risk of $\sigma_2 = 3$, at five different degrees of correlation of their returns. The gains are entirely dependent on the degree of correlation and with a negative correlation of -1 it is possible to entirely diversify away risk. (If $\sigma_1 < \sigma_2$, this would be achieved in a two-security portfolio by setting the x_1 weight to $x_1 = \sigma_2/(\sigma_1 + \sigma_2)$.) At point A all the investor's funds are invested in security 1 and they are all in security 2 at point B. With perfect positive correlation of returns, combining the two securities to form portfolios results in a linear change in composite riskiness, plotted along line AB. Lower degrees of correlation enable risk diversification, and the relation of portfolio risk levels available between A and B becomes curvilinear. At the limit, with perfect negative correlation, they become linear again, and at point C it is possible to diversify away all risk.

4.7   THE 'EFFICIENT' SELECTION OF PORTFOLIOS

In the enumeration of Markowitz's assumptions at the beginning of this chapter it was mentioned that investors are assumed to choose portfolios on the basis of the mean and variance of their expected returns, and furthermore that they are rational and display risk aversion. Together these assumptions imply that investors will only consider investing in what Markowitz termed 'efficient' portfolios – portfolios which promise the greatest expected return for estimated levels of risk. This is shown in figure 4.2.

Suppose an investor is faced with the choice of which portfolio to choose from portfolios A, B, C, and D in figure 4.2. Portfolios C and D both offer the same level of expected return $E(R_1)$, but portfolio D is more risky than C and therefore a risk-averse investor would chose portfolio C. By similar logic, at a level of returns $E(R_2)$ he would prefer A to B. Thus A and C dominate B and D, but what about the choice between A and C? At a given level of risk σ_1, A offers the greater level of expected returns; therefore A is preferred to

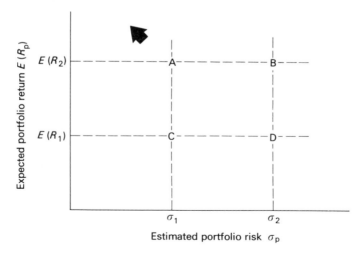

FIGURE 4.2   *Portfolio choice and efficiency*

the other three available portfolios and is termed the 'efficient' portfolio in this set of four portfolios. In general, risk aversion implies
that the rational investor will want to take on as much expected
return as possible and minimize the amount of risk in his portfolio.
He will therefore try to move in the general direction of the arrow in
figure 4.2.

It was seen in figure 4.1 that it is possible to combine two securities to form a number of portfolios offering various levels of risk and,
by implication, various levels of expected return. The same principle
holds for portfolios, and as any two existing portfolios could be
combined to form a number of other portfolios, the continuing
assumptions of infinite security and portfolio divisibility suggest that
a dominating 'efficient set' of portfolios could be generated. This is
shown in figure 4.3.

In this figure the curve marked 'efficient frontier' traces the locus
of the combinations of risk/return on all available efficient portfolios.
Portfolios on the curve obviously dominate the risk/return combinations available on portfolios and securities to the right of it. Portfolios offering risk/return further to the left of the efficient frontier
would be preferred, if available, but the investor's estimations of the
risk/return characteristics of currently available portfolios suggests

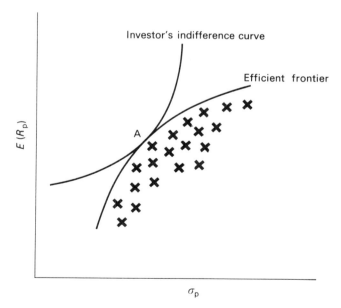

FIGURE 4.3   *The efficient frontier and portfolio selection*

that these are currently unattainable. The efficient frontier marks the optimal set of portfolios available to the investor. His optimal port-folio, indicated by the point at which he chooses to locate himself on the efficient frontier, will depend upon his relative aversion to risk. The investor depicted in figure 4.3 chooses a portfolio at point A, which is the point of tangency between his highest available indiffer-ence curve in risk/return space and the efficient frontier. The nature of investor indifference curves was first introduced in chapter 3 and will be further developed in section 4.8.

4.8   INVESTOR INDIFFERENCE CURVES

It was seen in chapter 3 that quadratic utility curves are particularly suited to this type of analysis, as they allow expected utility to be determined solely by the mean and variance of expected returns. It was also noted that risk aversion implies diminishing marginal util-ity of wealth. An individual investor's utility curves in a simple one-period investment model can be expected to vary according to the size of his initial wealth endowment and the proportion of his wealth that he decides to invest in a portfolio for the period concerned.[7] Given these factors it is possible to depict for each investor a whole family of utility curves, with each curve representing a constant level of expected utility, as shown in figure 4.4.

The indifference curves have a positive slope, which indicates that expected utility increases with higher levels of expected wealth, as would be expected. The point at which each curve cuts the vertical axis indicates a certain level of return which the investor regards as being equivalent to all the risk/return combinations along the indif-ference curve. In figure 4.4 the investor is indifferent between R_1 and all the risk/return combinations along I_1. The first derivative, or the slope, of the indifference curve gives an indication of the rate at which the investor is prepared to trade higher expected returns for having to take on higher levels of risk. At low levels of expected returns/risk on I_1 the investor is prepared to take on d units of risk to obtain c extra units of expected returns, but at higher levels of expected returns/risk he will only take on b units of risk if compen-sated by a units of expected returns.

The ratio a/b is greater than the ratio c/d and thus the slope of the indifference curve is increasing. This is exactly what would be expected given risk aversion and attendant diminishing marginal utility of wealth. It means that on a given indifference curve at

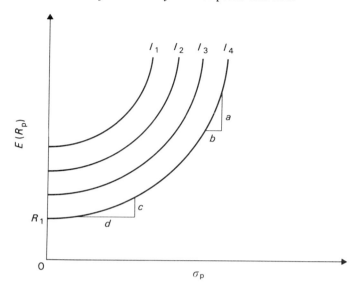

FIGURE 4.4   *A set of investor's indifference curves*

relatively high levels of risk, large additions to expected returns will only be accepted if they involve taking on relatively small increases in risk. It also follows, as noted in figure 4.3, that investors will want to move in the direction of the top left-hand side of figures 4.3 and 4.4. In terms of expected utility, in figure 4.4, $I_4 > I_3 > I_2 > I_1$.

4.9   THE NATURE OF THE EFFICIENT FRONTIER

In section 4.4 it was shown that the expected return on a portfolio is simply a weighted average of the expected returns of its component securities. As portfolios are merely groups of securities, a large number of new portfolios could be formed simply by combining existing portfolios in different proportions. The return available on a third portfolio P_3 formed from two existing portfolios P_1 and P_2 could be calculated as follows:

$$E(R_{P_3}) = x_1 E(R_{P_1}) + (1 - x_1)E(R_{P_2}) \tag{4.6}$$

where $E(R_{P_i})$ is the expected return on the portfolio considered, and x_1 is the portfolio weight (in the two-security or portfolio case $x_1 + x_2 = 1$, and therefore $x_2 = 1 - x_1$).

Theories of Market Valuation

The expected return on the portfolio formed from two existing portfolios will just be a weighted average of their individual expected returns, and therefore the expected return of the third portfolio will vary linearly with the chosen weights. The risk of the composite portfolio P_3 can be calculated in an identical manner to the risk on a portfolio combining two securities, as follows:

$$\sigma_{P_3}^2 = x_1^2 \sigma_{P_1}^2 + (1 - x_1)^2 \sigma_{P_2}^2 + x_1(1 - x_1)\rho_{P_1 P_2} \sigma_{P_1} \sigma_{P_2} \qquad (4.7)$$

where $\sigma_{P_i}^2$ is the variance of the portfolio considered, and $\rho_{P_1 P_2}$ is the correlation coefficient of expected returns on portfolios P_1 and P_2.

This is an identical equation to the one illustrated in figure 4.1, which related the risk of a two-security portfolio to variations in portfolio weights, given different degrees of correlation of returns. Once again the key factor is the degree of correlation, in this case of the two portfolios' expected returns. The standard deviation of the third portfolio would vary linearly with the chosen weights in cases where the two original portfolios' expected returns were either perfectly negatively or perfectly positively correlated, and curvilinearly for all cases of correlation between these two extremes. The implications of this in expected return/risk space are shown in figure 4.5.

If two portfolios are combined to make further portfolios, the locus of expected return/risk combinations available must be convex towards the expected return axis, apart from the extreme case of perfect correlation, though some points of minimum variance on the

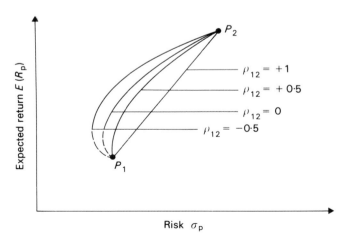

FIGURE 4.5   *The combining of two portfolios to make further portfolios*

efficient frontier will be inefficient as indicated by the dotted line in figure 4.5. This means there can be only one unique point of tangency with investor indifference curves. This can be utilized in the quadratic programming technique which can be employed to generate efficient portfolios.

4.10 EFFICIENT SET COMPUTATION AND PORTFOLIO SELECTION

The equation for the calculation of portfolio risk was expressed in terms of portfolio variance. To keep the generation of the efficient set relatively simple, the efficient set will be derived in terms of expected returns and variance, as shown in figure 4.6.

At the point of tangency between the investor's indifference curve and the efficient frontier in figure 4.6, a line could be extended through the point of tangency, with a slope equal to the slope of the two curves at the point of tangency, down to point Z_1 where it cuts the horizontal axis. A number of parallel lines could also be drawn, distinguished from the original line by the fact that they cut the horizontal axis at a different point of intercept – Z_2 and Z_3 in the

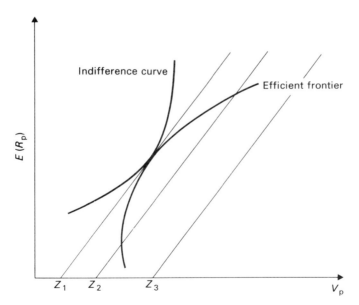

FIGURE 4.6 *Derivation of the efficient set*

case of the two lines drawn in figure 4.6. The general equation of a straight line could be employed to define these lines in terms of expected return/variance space:

$$V_p = Z + \lambda E(R_p) \tag{4.8}$$

where V_p is the portfolio variance, $E(R_p)$ is the portfolio expected return, Z is the intercept with the horizontal axis, and λ is the gradient of the line (equal to the risk/expected return trade-off at the point of tangency on the investor indifference curve).

The investor wants to maximize his expected utility; this is equivalent to reaching the highest attainable indifference curve or, in figure 4.6, to minimizing the value of Z. Furthermore, this will hold for any investor, no matter what the exact shape of his indifference curve. All will have a preferred position at the point of tangency of their respective indifference curves with the efficient frontier; the only difference will be that the slope of the line through the point of tangency will vary. Indeed, if the slope of the line was varied through all values from 0 to ∞, whilst minimizing the value of Z, all points on the efficient frontier would be traced out. This is exactly the method employed in the quadratic programming solution to portfolio selection, outlined as follows. By rearrangement of (4.8):

$$Z = -\lambda E(R_p) + V_p. \tag{4.9}$$

If (4.3) and (4.4c) are used to substitute for $E(R_p)$ and V_p, the objective becomes:

$$\text{minimize} \quad Z = -\lambda \sum_{i=1}^{N} x_i er_i + \sum_{i=1}^{N} \sum_{j=1}^{N} x_i x_j c_{ij} \tag{4.10}$$

for all λ, $0 \le \lambda \le \infty$

Subject to

$$\sum_{i=1}^{N} x_i = 1$$

and $x_i > 0$ for all $i = 1, \ldots, N$.

er_i is the expected return on security i.

Expression (4.10) is the essence of the quadratic programming solution to the original portfolio selection problem, as proposed by Markowitz, but it could also be determined, as he originally demonstrated, by geometric analysis, or by calculus[8] (see appendix 4.2).

It was mentioned at the beginning of this chapter that portfolio analysis is conceptually a three-stage process, but use of the programming algorithm turns it, in practice, into a two-stage one as the efficient set and the chosen portfolio are derived at the same time. The original Markowitz formulation ruled out short-selling and made no provision for either borrowing or lending, yet capital markets are characterized by these activities. A further problem lay in the 'unwieldiness' of the model in terms of the considerable computational workload involved.[9] For a start there are N expected returns and N variances required for each security considered, and then the covariance matrix (as shown in table 4.3(b)) requires $N(N - 1)/2$ calculations. This means that in total a 100-security portfolio would require a data input of 5150 coefficients before a computer program could be run.

Markowitz's achievement was initially normative rather than positive. He provided a theoretical framework, previously lacking, in which the advantages of risk diversification could be rationally analysed. The empirical positive applications of his work were developed by Tobin, Treynor, Lintner, Sharpe, Mossin, and Fama.[10] Before some of these advances are discussed, the next logical step in the development of the theory will be considered – the introduction of borrowing and lending.

4.11 BORROWING AND LENDING

The treatment of the holding of a riskless asset – cash – was developed by Tobin. His analysis was then modified and extended, to incorporate borrowing and lending, by Sharpe and Lintner.[11] Suppose it is assumed that security 1 is riskless. What would be its characteristics? The return on the security would be equal to the pure interest rate, or the risk-free rate, which will be denoted RF. The risk of the security, σ_1, is by definition 0. Furthermore, the covariance of this security with any other security i is given by

$$C_{1i} = \rho_{1i}\sigma_1\sigma_i = 0 \quad (\text{as } \sigma_1 = 0).$$

This means that any two-security portfolio which includes a riskless security will have the following expected return:

$$E(R_\text{p}) = x_1\,RF + x_2\,e_2 \tag{4.11}$$

where x_1 and x_2 are the weights in the two-security portfolio, RF is the risk-free or pure interest rate, and e_2 is the expected return on security 2. This is the familiar expected return; it is a weighted average and will vary linearly with the chosen portfolio weights.

The riskiness of a two-security portfolio including a riskless asset is more interesting and is as follows:

$$\sigma_p^2 = x_1 \sigma_1^2 + x_2 \sigma_2^2 + 2x_1 x_2 \rho_{12} \sigma_1 \sigma_2. \tag{4.12}$$

As $\sigma_1 = 0$, this becomes

$$\sigma_p^2 = x_2^2 \sigma_2^2$$

$$\therefore \quad \sigma_p = x_2 \sigma_2. \tag{4.13}$$

Expression (4.13) shows that the risk of a two-security portfolio including a riskless security is entirely dependent on the risk of the risky security and the proportion of the portfolio put into that security, and this is a linear relation too. The implications of this are shown in figure 4.7.

If the constraint $0 \leq x_i \leq 1$ is relaxed to allow $x_i \leq 0$, then both borrowing and lending, and short-selling, can be introduced. Whether the investor borrows or lends is determined by his attitude to the riskless security. In terms of figure 4.7, if he positions himself at point A he is choosing to put all of his funds in the risk-free security. He earns a certain return equal to the risk-free rate *RF*.

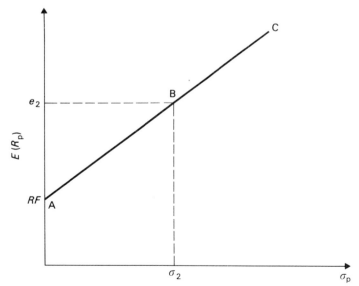

FIGURE 4.7 *Borrowing and lending in a two-security portfolio*

This could be thought of as being equivalent to putting all his money in a riskless deposit account with a bank (ignoring inflation and default risk).[12] It is equivalent to lending, as the investor is loaning his funds to the bank in this example. If the investor lends, the weight attached to security 1 will be positive in the region $0 \leq x_1 \leq 1$. If the weight x_1 is a positive fraction, the investor is both lending and putting some of his money in risky security 2, since the constraint that $\sum_{i=1}^{N} x_1 = 1$ still holds. If this is the case he is positioning himself somewhere along the line AB in figure 4.7. If he puts all his funds into the risky security and does not lend at all, he is at point B in the diagram. If it is further assumed that the lender can borrow at the same risk-free rate at which he can lend, then an $x_1 \leq 0$ indicates that the investor is borrowing funds and reinvesting them in the risky security as well as committing all his original funds to security 2. As this process is not immediately intuitively obvious, the example will be considered of an investor borrowing an amount equal to half his original funds. This means $x_1 = -0.5$. What happens to the expected return and risk of his portfolio?

$$E(R_\mathrm{p}) = -0.5RF + 1.5e_2 \quad (x_1 + x_2 = 1).$$

It can be seen that he can considerably 'gear up' his return by this policy. He is committed to repaying the risk-free rate on funds equal to half the value of his portfolio, but he was reinvested borrowed funds in security 2 with higher expected returns of e_2. Thus his prospective return is much greater. Unfortunately few things are 'free' in this world, and examination of the risk attached to this particular strategy shows that this is the case in financial markets. It is known that risk in a two-security portfolio comprising a riskless security is given by:

$$\sigma_\mathrm{p} = x_2 \sigma_2 = 1.5\sigma_2.$$

Therefore the risk is much greater, and as would be expected there is a trade-off between higher prospective returns and higher risk in this strategy. If the investor chose this policy he would be located at point C in figure 4.7.

An identical form of analysis could be undertaken to obtain the expected return/risk characteristics of any portfolio consisting of a riskless asset and one other risky security or portfolio, and the results would be identical. The implications of this are shown in figure 4.8.

Given the opportunity to invest in a riskless asset, the investor could combine any portfolio on the efficient frontier with the riskless

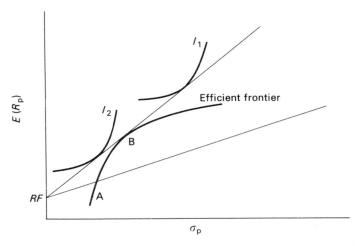

FIGURE 4.8   *The inclusion of a riskless asset and the separation theorem*

asset and obtain a linear combination of expected returns/risk, as indicated by the line *RF*–A in figure 4.8. However, no rational investor would choose portfolio A when choice of portfolio B, yielding expected returns/risk combinations along the line extended through *RF*–B, is obviously dominant. The choice of the optimum portfolio B is completely independent, or separate, from the investor's relative attitude to risk, as indicated by his indifference curves. It would not matter whether his preferences were indicated by indifference curve I_1 or I_2. He would always choose portfolio B as the portfolio to combine with either borrowing or lending. This particular separation theorem was first developed by Tobin, though subsequently Sharpe and Lintner modified and generalized it further.[13]

It should also be noted that the introduction of borrowing and lending has greatly simplified the efficient frontier which is now linear. All previous points of efficiency on the old frontier passing through AB are now dominated by the line extended from *RF* through B. So only point B of the original efficient frontier remains efficient. It will be seen in a later section of this chapter that the linearity of the efficient frontier is of crucial importance in empirical testing of the theoretical extensions of Markowitz's original portfolio selection model.

The introduction of borrowing is analogous to the treatment of short-selling, which could be viewed as the investor issuing a security. Suppose he sells on the market a promise to deliver a security with a particular level of expected return and risk. (Perhaps he sells a claim on a security that he does not currently possess, in the belief that when the time comes for delivery he can purchase and deliver it.) If the market has confidence in his ability to deliver it will pay him the market value of the claim he sells. The investor could treat the short-selling of any of the securities in his portfolio by assigning it an appropriate negative x_i value. In effect short-selling is a more 'risky' form of borrowing than borrowing at the riskless rate, but offers the prospect of a greater amount of funds rased for a given level of uncertain liability. If things go wrong it could be a very expensive form of borrowing; if the price of the security he has sold short rises very markedly after he has sold it short, then when the time comes for delivery he may have to pay a great deal for the purchase of it so that he can deliver it.[14]

The insights developed so far – from consideration of portfolio theory, to its extension to include borrowing and lending, and the subsequent development of the separation theorem – are of crucial importance in the next sections, which will consider the implications of these insights for the pricing of risky assets, in equilibrium, in the capital market.

4.12 THE CAPITAL MARKET LINE

The generalization of the analysis obtained from portfolio theory to a general equilibrium pricing model for risky assets was achieved almost contemporaneously by Sharpe, Lintner, and Treynor.[15] Initially, there was some confusion concerning the alleged inconsistency of the Sharpe and Lintner formulations, but Fama subsequently resolved this by proving that both derivations were essentially part of the same model.[16]

The model was broadened to encompass the entire capital market by making the sweeping assumptions indicated below. Their realism could be doubted, but Sharpe's paraphrasal of Friedman's assertion should be noted – that 'the proper test of a theory is not the realism of its assumptions but the acceptability of its implications'.[17]

To derive equilibrium conditions in the capital market the following assumptions must be made:

(1) All transactions take place within a perfect capital market in which all relevant information is freely available to all operators.

(2) There are no transactions costs or taxes.
(3) There is one unique risk-free rate and all investors can both borrow or lend an unlimited amount at this rate, without affecting the rate, and there is no prospect of bankruptcy.
(4) All investors have the same time horizon or, in other words, are investing for a single period of identical duration.
(5) All investors are rational and risk averse, and they make their investments decisions on the basis of the mean–variance rule.
(6) It is a world of 'idealized uncertainty' in which all investors have identical or homogeneous expectations with respect to the probability distributions of expected returns on all securities. This means that they all agree in their estimation of the risk and expected return offered by each security.

In a capital market which reflected these assumptions all investors would face the same efficient frontier, as they have identical expectations. The separation theorem suggests that there would be only one unique optimum portfolio, which will be termed the market portfolio and which is indicated by point M in figure 4.9. Apart from those investors who were lending all their funds by investing in the riskless asset, every investor would combine either borrowing or lending with investment in this portfolio, unless they chose neither to borrow nor to lend but to put all their funds in portfolio M. These alternative strategies are indicated in figure 4.9.

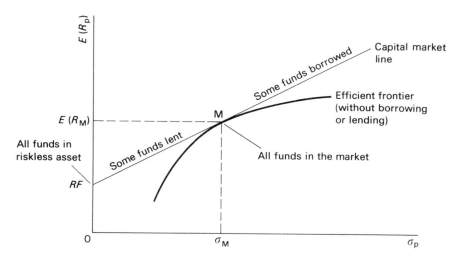

FIGURE 4.9   *The capital market line*

The optimum portfolio M is termed the market portfolio for good reasons. Only securities included in that portfolio will be demanded in the capital market. If a security has a price it must be in the market portfolio, and therefore all securities must be included. If the market is in equilibrium there should be no tendency for the prices of securities to alter. This means that the weighting of each security included in the market portfolio should be as follows:

$$x_{iM} = \frac{s_i Q_i}{\sum_{i=2}^{N} s_i Q_i} \qquad (4.14)$$

where x_{iM} is the weighting of security i in the market portfolio, s_i is the equilibrium price of security i, and Q_i is the total number of units of security i outstanding. (NB: Security 1, the riskless security, is excluded by definition.)

In other words the weighting of each security in the market portfolio must be equivalent to the ratio of its total market value to the total market value of all other risky securities outstanding in the market.

The line in figure 4.9 extended from RF through point M and beyond is termed the capital market line. It summarizes the equilibrium expected return/risk trade-off available to all investors in the capital market. In equilibrium all efficient portfolios will plot along this line. In a sense the separation theorem considered previously has now been generalized even further and now applies with respect to the same market portfolio for all investors in the market. Thus the choice is not of which optimum risky portfolio to hold; the only suitable portfolio is the market portfolio. Individual investors merely have to choose where to position themselves along the capital market line. In effect the choice consists of how much borrowing or lending they should practise, in conjunction with investment in the market portfolio.

The slope of the capital market line is sometimes termed the 'price of risk', as it indicates how much extra risk has to be borne in order to obtain an extra unit of expected return. An expression to show this can easily be derived by utilizing (4.6) and (4.7) to obtain an indication of the expected return and risk of a portfolio made up of a risk-free asset and the market portfolio. Its expected return would be given by:

$$E(R_p) = x_1 RF + (1 - x_1)E(R_M). \qquad (4.15)$$

Its risk would be indicated by:

$$\sigma_p = (1 - x_1)\sigma_M,$$

and manipulation of this expression shows that:

$$(1 - x_1) = \frac{\sigma_p}{\sigma_M} \quad \text{and} \quad x_1 = 1 - \frac{\sigma_p}{\sigma_M}.$$

Substitution of these values back into (4.15) yields:

$$E(R_p) = RF + [E(R_M) - RF]\frac{\sigma_p}{\sigma_M} \qquad (4.16)$$

where $E(R_p)$ is the expected return on any efficient portfolio, RF is the risk-free rate, σ_p is the risk of the efficient portfolio, σ_M is the risk of the market portfolio, and $E(R_M)$ is the expected return on the market portfolio.

Expression (4.16) is the equation of the capital market line and it indicates the expected return available on any efficient portfolio, of a given level of risk, assuming the initial assumptions hold. It does not apply to either inefficient portfolios or individual securities, but its very existence has important implications for their pricing which are covered by the capital asset pricing model considered in the next section.

4.13   THE CAPITAL ASSET PRICING MODEL

It has already been seen that in equilibrium all securities must be held in the market portfolio. The fact that all securities are held as part of an efficient portfolio has a crucial effect on the way in which their equilibrium prices are determined. The appropriate equation for the valuation of securities under these conditions is the following; it gives the equation of the security market line, or the capital asset pricing model (CAPM) as it is more commonly termed:

$$E(r_i) = RF + \frac{[E(R_M) - RF)]\text{cov } r_i R_M}{\sigma_M^2} \qquad (4.17)$$

where $E(r_i)$ is the expected return on security i, $\text{cov } r_i R_M$ is the covariability of returns on security i with returns of the market portfolio, σ_M^2 is the variance of returns on the market portfolio, and all other notation is as previously defined. (The proof of this important relationship is given in appendix 4.3.)

It is immediately apparent that the only difference between the equation of the capital market line and that of the capital asset pricing model is in the measure of risk adopted. A moment's thought suggests why this might be the case. The reason why investors hold securities in portfolios is to reap the benefits of risk diversification. It follows that part of the total risk of any security *i*, measured by σ_i, can be diversified away in an efficient portfolio; therefore the market, in equilibrium, should only reward investors for bearing that portion of a security's risk which cannot be removed by diversification in an efficient portfolio. Undiversifiable risk is usually termed 'systematic risk' and it is determined by the covariability of returns on an individual security with those of the market portfolio. This measure, $\mathrm{cov}\ r_i\,R_M/\sigma_M^2$, is usually termed the 'beta' (β) coefficient, and thus the capital asset pricing model is frequently written as follows:

$$E(r_i) = RF + [E(R_M) - RF]\beta_i \tag{4.18}$$

where $\beta_i = \mathrm{cov}\ r_i\,R_M/\sigma_M^2$.

In equilibrium all securities should plot along the security market line shown in figure 4.10. In this figure, point A represents the market portfolio. As the returns on the market portfolio provide the performance benchmark, by definition, they, have a beta coefficient of 1; using (2.13) in the expression for β_i,

$$\beta_i = \rho(R_M,\,R_M)\sigma_M\,\sigma_M/\sigma_M^2 = 1.$$

Any security with a beta of 1 would earn a premium above the risk-free rate identical to the premium available on the market portfolio: $E(R_M) - RF$. It follows that less risky securities with a lower

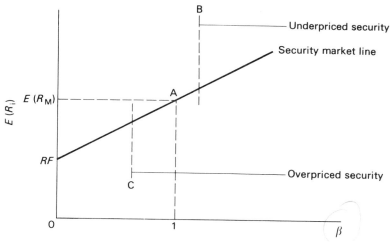

FIGURE 4.10   *The security market line*

why $\beta \gtrless 0$ only?

beta will earn a lower return, and vice versa in the case of securities with a higher beta. It is important to remember that the measure of risk is an individual security's covariability of its returns with returns of the market portfolio. An individual security may be very risky indeed in terms of its unique and overall risk as measured by the standard deviation of its returns. But if it has a 'perverse' relationship with the market portfolio – it performs well when the market portfolio is performing poorly, and badly when the market portfolio performs well – then it has the valuable attribute of reducing market portfolio risk when included in that portfolio. For this reason it would be much sought after, and would command a high price. This means that its return would be relatively low. The security at point C in figure 4.10 is overpriced; its return is not commensurate with its systematic risk. The security at B is underpriced, with too high a return. Investors would perceive this, and the resultant selling and buying pressure in the two respective cases would push the prices of the two securities back to a point where they both plotted on the security market line.

The sceptical reader might, at this point, comment that this is all very well but, apart from those investors who invest via a unit trust or investment trust company, or those who have exceedingly large funds, how can an individual investor afford to invest in the market portfolio? In practice, must not the transaction costs be prodigious? Fortunately this is not the case. The investor need invest in only a few well-chosen securities in order to eliminate most of the unsystematic risk from his portfolio, as will be shown in the next section.

Various empirical studies have given support to both the measures and views of risk implicit to the portfolio selection model that has been considered. Ibbotson and Sinquefield have investigated the actual rates of return available on American common stocks, corporate bonds, Government bonds, and Treasury bills over the period 1926–76.[18] The risk-related returns over the period were exactly as portfolio theory would predict, with common stocks displaying the highest average annual real rate of return.

The concept of systematic risk is also intuitively appealing in that one would expect certain economic forces and general factors to influence the whole economy, and certain other more specific factors to influence particular industrial sectors. This means that some influences on security risk will be so general that it will be impossible to avoid them via portfolio diversification. An early study by King found evidence in support of this view, and Officer found evidence of a link between the variability of the market factor of New York

Stock Exchange prices and general business fluctuations, as represented by changes in industrial production.[19]

The relationship between market and industry factors and movements in security prices are utilized in some of the 'short-cut' methods which can be employed in the generation of the data requirements for portfolio selection models. The use of these index models is considered in the next section.

4.14 THE USE OF INDEX MODELS

The tremendous data input required to utilize the Markowitz model has already been considered. Sharpe added to the scope for its practical application by developing his single-index or 'diagonal' model. The model relies on the hypothesis that the returns on all securities are very significantly correlated with movements in the market as a whole. He applied least-squares regression analysis to produce a line of best fit relating movements in an individual stock's rate of return to movements in an overall market index, typically an ordinary share index. This produced the following relation:

$$r_i = \alpha_i + B_i I + U_i \qquad (4.19)$$

where r_i is the rate of return on security i, α_i is a constant (in this form $\alpha_i = RF(1 - \beta_i)$ and $B_i = \beta_i$ to be consistent with CAPM; see section 4.15), B_i is the slope of the regression line, indicating the relation between returns on security i and movements in the market index, I is the return on the market index, and U_i is an error term with an expected value of zero and a variance of σ_{U_i}. The estimation of this relationship is depicted in figure 4.11.

Treynor referred to this linear relationship as the 'characteristic line' of a security.[20] Once this relationship has been established for all the stocks under consideration, by empirical investigation of historical data, then it can be used for making predictions of future security returns – given the assumption that security betas are reasonably stable over time. Blume, in a series of empirical studies, has provided evidence that they are reasonably stable over time, though there is a tendency for securities with either high or low betas to gradually regress towards the overall market beta of 1.[21]

A few further assumptions are required to make the model applicable for predictive purposes. There is assumed to be no dependency between the size of the prediction error U_i and the level of the index. The rates of return on individual securities are assumed to be linked

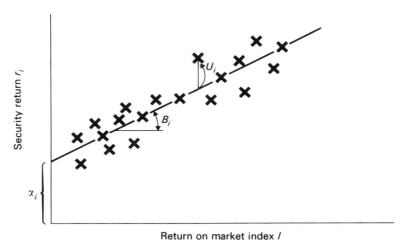

FIGURE 4.11 *Estimating the 'characteristic line' of a security*

solely via their relationship with the market index. There is assumed to be a complete lack of independent correlation of the returns of individual pairs of securities. In effect this assumes that all the 'off-diagonal' U_i are zero; hence the reference to this model as the 'diagonal model'. Given these assumptions, and knowledge of the appropriate regression equations, all that is required to predict individual security returns is a prediction of the level of the market index. On the basis of this one prediction both portfolio expected return and variance can be estimated. An individual security's expected return is estimated as follows:

$$er_i = \alpha_i + B_i\,EI \qquad (4.20)$$

where er_i is the expected return on security i, and EI is the predicted level of the market index.

Given the predictions of individual security returns it is a simple matter to aggregate them to get a prediction of portfolio expected return:

$$E(R_p) = \sum_{i=1}^{N} x_i(\alpha_i + B_i\,EI). \qquad (4.21)$$

Before the estimation of portfolio variance is considered it should be noted that in this model there are only two potential sources of risk:

(1) Prediction error in the forecast of the future level of the index EI; strictly speaking this is the mean of a subjective probability distribution of standard deviation σ_{EI}.

(2) Prediction error in the forecast of each individual security's return, of standard deviation σ_{U_i}.

It follows that the risk of an individual security's expected returns can be written as:

$$\sigma_{er_i}^2 = B_i^2 \sigma_{EI}^2 + \sigma_{U_i}^2, \tag{4.22}$$

that is

total risk = systematic risk + unsystematic risk.

It follows that total portfolio risk will be given by:

$$\sigma_p^2 = \sum_{i=1}^{N} \sum_{j=1}^{N} x_i x_j B_i B_j \sigma_{EI}^2 + \sum_{i=1}^{N} x_i^2 \sigma_{U_i}^2. \tag{4.23a}$$

Expression (4.23a) supports the previous claim that a small portfolio consisting of relatively few stocks can be effectively diversified. Suppose there is an equally weighted portfolio of 20 securities; then each $x_i = 0.05$. If it is assumed that the distribution of the error term in (4.23a) is normal and stable, then it can be appreciated that the weighted sum of this term will rapidly approach zero as the number of securities in the equally weighted portfolio is increased. This means that even in the case of an equally weighted portfolio of 20 securities, most of the risk will by systematic. The relationship between the number of securities in a portfolio and its level of unsystematic or diversifiable risk is shown in figure 4.12.[22]

This means that (4.23a) can be rewritten as

$$\sigma_p^2 \simeq \sum_{i=1}^{N} \sum_{j=1}^{N} x_i x_j B_i B_j \sigma_{EI}^2 \tag{4.23b}$$

Once the composition of the portfolio has been determined, the $x_i B_i$ values will be known and only $N + 1$ risky terms remain; given a knowledge of all the securities' characteristic lines, only $N + 2$ computations are required rather than the $N(N + 3)/2$ required in the full Markowitz model. If the responsiveness of the portfolio to movements in the market index is designated Res(p), then to the original model has been added one decision variable Res(p) and one constraint Res(p) $= \sum_{i=1}^{N} x_i B_i$.

This approach can provide a very convenient and practical means of assessing a portfolio, especially if recourse is made to a risk

$\downarrow B_{(P)}$

TABLE 4.4　Portfolio assessment on the basis of risk measurement service data

Sedol number	Company name	Industry	Market capit'n	Market ability	Beta	Vari-ability	Specific risk	Std error	Qly ab return	Ann ab return	Actual return	Gross yield	P/E ratio	Price 28:9:79
1241	A. A. H. Limited	Transport	17	3T	0.77	26	18	0.10	5	3	19	8.9	7.6	117
2084	Aaronson Bros Ltd	Timber	22	2T	1.26	43	30	0.15	11	6	27	6.7	6.8	82
2040	Abbey Ltd	Ind. Hold	8	5	0.91	33	28	0.27	−1	−10	1	14.9	2.9	35
2169	Abbey Panels Ltd	Mtr. Comp	1	5	1.06	35	39	0.21	12	37	48	5.6	6.6	72
1100	A. B. Electronic Compnts	Lgt. Elec	8	3	0.74	39	34	0.16	−1	58	73	5.4	7.0	194
2761	Aberdeen Construction	Constrct	11	2T	0.97	40	33	0.16	17	0	17	7.9	6.2	97
2987	Aberdeen Invs	Inv. Trst	1	4	0.29	22	21	0.10	−5	17	29	6.1	22.6	70
3009	Aberdeen Trust Ltd	Inv. Trst	31	2T	1.02	29	16	0.09	2	−10	4	6.4	23.8	94
3504	Aberthaw Cement	Cement	5	3	0.86	37	31	0.15	−5	−26	−13	9.2	4.7	122
5306	Abwood Machine Tools	Mch. Tool	1	5	0.57	52	51	0.27	20	39	53	7.0	10.9	18
1207	A C Cars Ltd	Mtr. Vhcl	1	5	0.48	36	35	0.24		1	12	2.0	6.4	36
1304	A. C. E. Machinery	Ind. Plnt	2	5	0.48	20	16	0.15		−13	5	4.3	13.9	132A
6268	Acorn Securities Cap	Inv. Trst	4	4	0.98	30	21	0.12	−12	−19	−5			97
6246	Acorn Securities Inc	Inv. Trst	1	4	0.55	28	24	0.12	4	−8	2	26.1	6.4	60
6321	Acrow Ltd 'A' N.V.	Mch. Hand	33	3T	1.12	41	30	0.15	−20	−55	−40	8.3	3.5	54
6309	Acrow Ltd	Mch. Hand	2	4T								4.1	7.1	108
7045	Adams & Gibbon Ltd	Mtr. Dist	1	3	0.84	46	41	0.18	22	9	25	8.6	5.8	80
8004	Advance Laundries	Laundry	9	3T	0.89	31	23	0.13	11	18	31	9.6	7.8	32
8101	Adwest Group Ltd	Misc. Eng	37	2T	0.69	31	25	0.12	3	14	29	5.3	7.5	382
8606	Aero & Gen. Instrument	Instrmnt	2	4	0.72	54	49	0.21	−3	14	28	2.7	9.8	155

Source: Reproduced with the permission of the London Business School, Risk Measurement Service, October 1979.

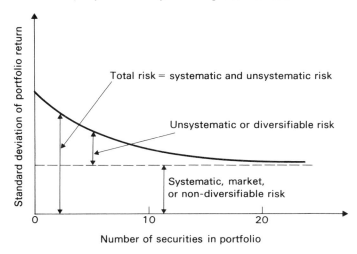

FIGURE 4.12 *Risk diversification and the number of securities in a portfolio*

measurement service such as that provided by the London Business School, an extract from which is shown in table 4.4. The following example shows how the risk and return of a three-security portfolio could be estimated on the basis of information given in table 4.4.

Suppose you have invested 50 per cent of your funds in A. B. Electronic Components, 25 per cent in Aberthaw Cement, and 25 per cent in Adams and Gibbon Ltd. The beta or responsiveness of your portfolio could be calculated as shown in table 4.5.

The beta of the portfolio is 0.795, and is just a weighted average of the beta values taken from table 4.4. Recourse to the capital asset pricing model gives a prediction of the expected return on this portfolio. Suppose that the risk-free Treasury bill rate is 12 per cent and

TABLE 4.5 *Calculating the portfolio beta*

Company	Beta (B_i)	Portfolio weight (x_i)	$(x_i)(B_i)$
A. B. Electronic Compnts	0.74	0.50	0.37
Aberthaw Cement	0.86	0.25	0.215
Adams & Gibbon Ltd	0.84	0.25	0.21
			$\sum = 0.795$

that, on average over the last sixty years, the annual return on shares has been 9 per cent more than the Treasury bill rate. This suggests an expected return on the market of 21 per cent. CAPM suggests that:

$$E(R_p) = RF + B_p[E(R_M) - RF].$$

substituting the values from table 4.5:

$$E(R_p) = 12 + (0.795)\ (9)$$

$$E(R_p) = 19.155\%.$$

The risk on the portfolio can be divided into its systematic and non-systematic components. Suppose that the variability or standard deviation of returns on the market index is 24 per cent. The market risk of the chosen portfolio is given by:

$$\text{market risk} = \text{beta} \times \text{market variability}$$
$$= 0.795 \times 24$$
$$= 19.08\%.$$

The square of this value would be equivalent to (4.23b). It would be synonymous with total portfolio risk only in a perfectly diversified portfolio, since it measures systematic risk. As there are only three securities in this portfolio there is bound to be a considerable amount of unsystematic risk, which can be calculated as shown in table 4.6 using the information about each security's specific risk from table 4.4. To perform the calculation we utilize the final term in (4.23a).

TABLE 4.6   *The calculation of portfolio unsystematic risk*

	Portfolio weight (x_i)	Specific risk (σ_{U_i})	$(x_i)(\sigma_{U_i})$	$(x_i)^2(\sigma_{U_i})^2$
A. B. Electronic Compnts	0.50	34	17.0	289
Aberthaw Cement	0.25	31	7.75	60.06
Adams & Gibbon Ltd	0.25	41	10.25	105.06
			$\sum =$	454.12

Portfolio specific risk $= \sqrt{454.12} = 21.31\%$

The total portfolio risk is made up of systematic and unsystematic risk:

$$(\text{portfolio variability})^2 = (\text{systematic risk})^2$$
$$+ (\text{unsystematic risk})^2$$
$$= (19.08)^2 + (21.31)^2$$
$$= 364.05 + 454.12$$
$$= 818.17.$$
$$\text{portfolio variability} = \sqrt{818.17} = 28.6\%.$$

The extent to which you have diversified risk successfully can be assessed by examining the proportion of total portfolio risk which is unsystematic:

$$\text{efficiency of diversification} = \frac{\text{unsystematic risk}}{\text{total risk}}$$
$$= \frac{454.12}{818.17} = 55.5\%.$$

As would be expected, a three-security portfolio is not particularly well diversified, and in this case 55.5 per cent of its total risk is diversible unsystematic risk.

The single-index model as used above on the one hand, and the full Markowitz covariance model on the other, could be regarded as the two polar extremes of approaches to the portfolio selection problem. There are also a number of 'gradations' in between these two extremes provided by the use of multi-index models. The essence of their approach is the linkage of the returns on securities in particular sectors of the market with a particular index which more closely reflects conditions in their sector. This approach is necessarily more computationally cumbersome, depending upon the number of indices employed, but it still falls far short of the workload of the full Markowitz approach.

Cohen and Pogue tested the Markowitz model and found evidence that the portfolios it selected, even on the shaky basis of using average historical returns as a predictor of expected returns, still matched, and in some cases outperformed, actual portfolios chosen by Mutual Funds. They also tested the relative effectiveness of single-index and multi-index models, and found that the single-index usually performed better than the multi-index model.[23] This may have been influenced by the restriction of their study to common stocks. Wallingford found contrary evidence that a two-index model usually dominated a single-index model, but there are some doubts about the effects of the relatively small sample he employed.[24] However, Elton and Gruber have provided further confirmation of the usefulness of various forms of multi-index models.[25]

4.15 EMPIRICAL TESTS OF THE CAPITAL ASSET PRICING MODEL

One of the great attractions of the CAPM was that its simple linear form apparently lent itself to relatively straightforward empirical testing. More recently there have been serious doubts expressed about this, which have considerably undermined the earlier work on CAPM testing. Before these doubts are considered, a brief review is given of some of the findings of a selection of the major studies.[26] Jensen pinpoints an acute distinction between tests of the market model, defined in (4.19), which simply postulates a linear relationship between security returns and returns on a market index, and tests of the CAPM, which is similar but has much more rigorous specifications.[27] The derivation of the CAPM was considered in sections 4.12 and 4.13, and (4.17) indicated that the return on any security is equal to the risk-free rate plus a premium given by

$$\frac{[E(R_M) - RF]\text{cov } r_i R_M}{\sigma_M^2}.$$

Jensen shows the relationship between the two models in the following manner.[28] It is possible to rearrange (4.18), defining the CAPM as:

$$E(r_i) = RF(1 - \beta_i) + \beta_i E(R_M). \tag{4.24}$$

On the other hand the market model, which was considered as the single-index model, suggests that the expected return on security i (from (4.19)) is given by:

$$E(r_i) = \alpha_i + B_i E(R_M) + E(U_i)$$
$$= \alpha_i + B_i E(R_M). \tag{4.25}$$

(By definition the expected value of the error term is zero.)

(NB: In tests of both models a market index is used, as a proxy for the market portfolio in the case of the CAPM.)

Furthermore, as the definition of β_i and B_i in the two models is identical, both models are identical if $\alpha_i = RF(1 - \beta_i)$ (given the assumptions that the market index is a good proxy for the market portfolio, that B_i is stable over time, and that the estimation techniques are 'efficient').

Some of the research done on the market model by King and by Blume has already been encountered.[29] Some of King's findings weakened the market model in that they gave evidence that the error terms in the regression equations are not independent because of industry effects, and this implied the potential utility of multi-index models. Further work, paralleling Blume's study of the stability of security betas, has been done on the stability of the betas of managed portfolios, such as those of the mutual funds in the USA. Jensen produced evidence that the betas of these funds are relatively stable over time, indicating fairly constant attitudes towards risk on the part of their management.[30]

Indeed, one of the valuable spin-offs from the development of modern portfolio theory is that it has facilitated the development of models suited to the testing of managed fund performance. Two studies were made by Sharpe and Treynor employing similar methodologies, though different measures of risk.[31] Sharpe employed a reward to variability ratio:

$$\text{reward to variability ratio} = \frac{\text{Av}(R_{P_i}) - RF}{\sigma_{P_i}} \qquad (4.26)$$

where $\text{Av}(R_{P_i})$ is the average historical rate of return on the chosen portfolio, RF is the risk-free rate, and σ_{P_i} is the standard deviation of historical returns of the chosen portfolio.

Treynor took a slightly different approach using a reward to volatility ratio:

$$\text{reward to volatility ratio} = \frac{\text{Av}(R_{P_i}) - RF}{B_{RP_i}} \qquad (4.27)$$

where B_{RP_i} is the covariability of historical returns on portfolio i with returns on a market index, divided by the variance of index's returns, and the other variables are as before.

Casual inspection of the two measures reveals that Sharpe is employing total risk as a risk measure, whereas Treynor is only employing systematic risk. In a well-diversified portfolio unsystematic risk should have been reduced to insignificant levels and therefore, if the funds being ranked have well-diversified portfolios, the

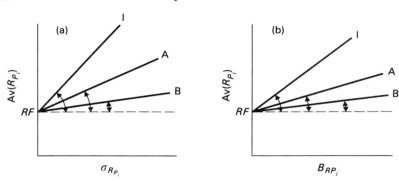

FIGURE 4.13   *The (a) Sharpe and (b) Treynor methods of ranking port-*
folio performance

two measures should provide similar rankings. An illustration of the
two methods of portfolio performance ranking is given in figure 4.13,
and in both diagrams portfolio *A* is preferred to *B*, as *A* has a higher
reward to variability and reward to volatility ratio. The points
marked *I* indicate the return on a stock market index *I*. Neither
portfolio *A* nor portfolio *B*, in either case, give a return as good as a
naïve policy of investing in a randomly diversified portfolio, which
gives a return equal to the return on the index. Both studies used the
return on the index as a benchmark. In figure 4.13 the slope of the
line linking the risk-free rate and the portfolio ranks the fund; the
greater the slope the higher the rank. Sharpe found that only 11 of
the 34 mutual funds he studied performed better than the market
index, and this was before adjustment for management expenses.

However, both of these performance measures suffer from being
based upon the market model. The return on a market index is only
an imperfect proxy for the return on the Markowitz efficient market
portfolio required by the CAPM, and as will be seen shortly these
methods suffer from built-in bias, particularly in their evaluation of
the performance of high-risk portfolios. Firth employed an approach
similar to that of Sharpe, and found similar results, in a recent study
of 300 UK unit trusts (the equivalent of USA mutual funds).[32]

Direct tests of the CAPM are a little more tricky. Many of the
tests have been cross-sectional, and have involved regressing the
average return on a cross-sectional sample of securities against the
covariability of each security's return with the return on a market
index, over some time period. (To avoid specification error the beta

coefficients are normally estimated in a different time period from the one at which the model is tested.) The regression would typically be of the form:

$$\tilde{r}_{it} = \tilde{\gamma}_{1t} + \tilde{\gamma}_{2t} B_i R_M + \eta_{it} \tag{4.28}$$

where $\tilde{r}_{it}$ is the return on security i at time t, $\tilde{\gamma}_{1t}$ is a constant, $\tilde{\gamma}_{2t}$ is a constant and η_{it} is a random error term with zero expected value.

Black, Jensen, and Scholes applied this approach, but found that typically the intercept was greater than the risk-free rate and the slope of the line less than the CAPM would predict.[33] This suggests that low beta stocks earn a greater than predicted return and high beta stocks less. This is illustrated in figure 4.14. (Roll's criticisms of the empirical methodology, considered later in this section, would account for this.)

The actual methodology employed by Black, Jensen, and Scholes, and in a subsequent study by Fama and Macbeth,[34] involved regressing the returns of portfolios of different levels of beta, as measured by the betas of their component securities, against their displayed levels of systematic risk. Fama and Macbeth found support for three of the four hypotheses they tested:

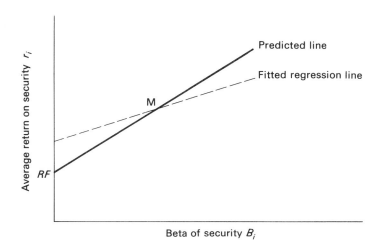

FIGURE 4.14 *Typical results of cross-sectional regressions of security returns on security betas*

(1) There is a linear relationship between the expected return of a security and its risk in an efficient portfolio.
(2) The beta coefficient is a complete measure of risk in an efficient portfolio.
(3) Higher risk is associated with higher return in a market characterized by risk-averse investors.
(4) They found no support for the fourth hypothesis that the Sharpe–Lintner form of the CAPM holds, because of the existence of the relationship depicted in figure 4.14.

The lack of support for the fourth hypothesis is perhaps a little worrying, but it is certainly not particularly surprising if note is taken of some of the implications of relaxing the assumptions underlying the CAPM. In practice investors will have different tax positions, different time horizons, and different expectations, and the borrowing rate will normally be higher than the lending rate and will vary according to the credit standing of the investor. The implications of some of these factors are shown in figure 4.15.

The mere introduction of different borrowing and lending rates, shown in figure 4.15, means that there will no longer be a linear efficient frontier. This change means that the efficient frontier will plot along the line extended through R_L, the lending rate, to M_2, the

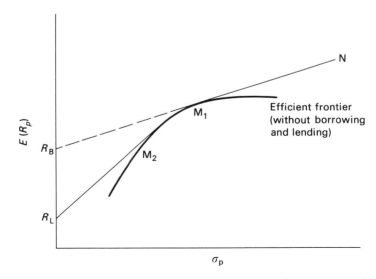

FIGURE 4.15   *The efficient frontier with different borrowing and lending rates*

point of tangency with the efficient frontier in the absence of borrowing and lending. Then the curvilinear portion $M_1 M_2$ will be efficient. Finally a line extended through the borrowing rate R_B to the point of tangency with the efficient frontier M_1 becomes part of the efficient frontier along the section M_1 to N. This one change undermines the strict foundations of the CAPM, and the relaxation of the other assumptions implies that there will be a number of different frontiers, of the type illustrated above, facing various investors, depending upon their expectations, tax positions, and so on.

Is the damage irreparable, or is the CAPM sufficiently robust to still give a good general guide to equilibrium risk/expected return relationships? Black made an attempt to get round these problems by suggesting a number of alterations to and restrictions on the basic portfolio model.[35] He developed a model which included a zero beta portfolio (whose returns are uncorrelated with those of the market portfolio), and demonstrated that equilibrium expected return/risk relationships could be expressed as a linear function of combinations of the zero beta and market portfolio. He also developed a variant of the model in which riskless lending was permitted but borrowing proscribed, and in certain circumstances this could be consistent with the production of the type of results implied by tests of the CAPM illustrated in figure 4.14. Brennan has also generalized the existence of different borrowing and lending rates to conditions consistent with market equilibrium.[36] The problems considered so far, in the specification and testing of the model, were vexatious but not fundamentally damaging.

Much more fundamental doubts have been raised by the work of Roll and Ross, who have amplified and extended earlier doubts expressed by Fama.[37] Roll provided strong theoretical arguments in support of Fama's conclusion that the literature had not produced a meaningful test of the Sharpe–Lintner CAPM. He suggested that the ability to test the validity of the CAPM hinges ultimately on whether or not it is possible to correctly identify the composition of the mean–variance efficient market portfolio; and that all the other implications of the model, such as the linearity of expected return in relation to beta, follow on from the market portfolio's efficiency and are not independently verifiable. The true market portfolio would involve investment in every individual existing asset in positive proportions (as all must have a price). In practice, all the empirical tests have employed proxies for the market portfolio, perhaps an equally weighted market index containing a sample of stocks. These proxies are not necessarily mean–variance efficient, and therefore testing them tells us nothing about the characteristics of the true market portfolio. Thus it is possible to theoretically envisage an appropriate test, but in practice no truly robust empirical test has yet been applied.

Further limitations are implied by the required movement from *ex ante* beliefs to tests of *ex post* observations. If the *ex post* observations are to be interpreted as being representative of *ex ante* beliefs, then the stochastic process generating security returns must be stationary. In contrast, Ross claims that most of these difficulties can be avoided by the use of an arbitrage pricing model (APT), which has recently received a good deal of theoretical and empirical attention.[38]

4.16   THE ARBITRAGE PRICING MODEL

Ross argues convincingly in favour of the advantages of APT on the grounds that CAPM is weighed down by a great deal of excess baggage. The separation principle which leads to all investors holding the market portfolio and gearing their position to their desired risk level relies on a string of assumptions mentioned previously, including homogeneous *ex ante* expectations which are realized *ex post*, and the existence of a mean–variance efficient market portfolio. This has to include all assets and is not properly proxied by the return on some market index.

The arbitrage pricing model, on the other hand, assumes as a first principle a linear return-generating process. Suppose that returns are generated by a two-factor model:

$$\tilde{r}_j = A_j + B_{j1}\tilde{R}_{P_1} + B_{j2}\tilde{R}_{P_2} + \tilde{U}_j. \qquad (4.29)$$

Expression (4.29) shows that the return $\tilde{r}_j$ on any asset j is some constant A_j, plus a function of the stochastic returns on R_{P_1} and $\tilde{R}_{P_2}$, plus a random error or 'noise' term $\tilde{U}_j$, which is assumed to be completely independent of the returns on the two factors. For example, it could be assumed that the first factor $\tilde{R}_{P_1}$ is some general index of stock market prices, and the second $\tilde{R}_{P_2}$ a specific industry index. This would be consistent with King's findings mentioned previously, but the approach is very general and any number of factors could be specified.[39] Indeed, Sharpe's 'diagonal' model could be viewed as an example of a single-factor generating model, the major difference being that the APT is more flexible, allowing for any number of factors. The only equilibrium requirement is that there should be no opportunity for arbitrage profits; therefore any equilibrium should be characterized by a linear relationship between each asset's expected returns and the loadings B_{ij} on each common return generating factor.

In equilibrium, in a well-diversified portfolio, unsystematic risk will be diversified away and so $\tilde{U}_j$ will disappear, leaving the systematic risk attached to holding $\tilde{R}_{P_1}$ and $\tilde{R}_{P_2}$. This means that the return on some composite portfolio would be given by:

$$\tilde{R}_{P_c} \simeq A_c + B_{c1} \tilde{R}_{P_1} + B_{c2} \tilde{R}_{P_2}. \tag{4.30}$$

Furthermore, to prevent the existence of arbitrage profits, A_c, B_{c1}, and B_{c2} must be linearly related for all values of R_{P_c}. If RF is the return on a riskless asset, it follows that:

$$A_c - RF \simeq [E(R_{P_1}) - RF]B_{c1} + [E(R_{P_2}) - RF]B_{c2}. \tag{4.31}$$

Ross claims that this arbitrage relationship has a number of important advantages over CAPM. It can be seen that the market portfolio does not feature in it all, and therefore tests can be done on small subsets of data with no requirement that the market portfolio be mean–variance efficient. It is a 'minimalist' model in the sense that, apart from requiring investors to be risk averse and non-satiated with respect to wealth, and requiring that there be no arbitrage opportunities in equilibrium, there is a minimum of assumptions. It can also be readily generalized to intertemporal models, and is consistent with option pricing theory.

The model is very attractive and work on it is still in its infancy. The major difficulty is that the factor analysis usually employed to analyse return distributions will isolate the influence of a number of factors but provides no means of identifying them.[40] A leap is still required to identify factors additional to the market one and there is a temptation to arbitrarily specify factors and test for their effects.

4.17 MULTIPERIOD PORTFOLIO THEORY

The models of portfolio decision-making and asset pricing that have been considered so far have all been single-period models in which decision-makers are concerned with maximizing the expected utility of terminal wealth. There have been numerous extensions of the model into a multi-period context, but despite their ingenuity I think that most authorities would agree that they have not been entirely satisfactory.[41] The problem stems from the fact that either a number of restrictive, unrealistic assumptions have to be made to make the models tractable and determinate, or the more general, realistic models are mathematically complete but applying them and solving them in practice is infeasible. Elton and Gruber suggest a division of multiperiod models into two classes according to the nature of the postulated objective function – those models which maximize the utility of terminal wealth, and those which maximize the utility of multiperiod consumption.[42] The account which follows will consist of a brief thumb-nail sketch, as the mathematics required is complex and beyond the scope of this text. To avoid unnecessary complications perfect markets and an absence of taxation and transaction costs are the normal assumptions.

The multiperiod models based on the maximization of terminal wealth assume an objective function of the following type:

$$\max \ EU(TW_T) \tag{4.32}$$

where EU is the expected utility, determined by $f(U)$, the assumed utility of wealth function, and TW_T is the terminal wealth at horizon period T. It is assumed that the investor has in mind a future terminal point in time – the horizon period – at which he plans to consume his terminal wealth, and whose expected utility he intends to maximize. Interposed between the present and this horizon are a number of discrete time periods, and at the beginning of each he will choose a portfolio of assets to hold over the period concerned. His wealth at the end of the planning period, dependent on the return achieved on the portfolio held over the period, will be reallocated to a new portfolio to be held over the next period, and so the process will be repeated up to the horizon. Mossin points out that there is no excuse for the fact that this approach completely ignores any opportunities for intermediate consumption during the holding period; it is unrealistic but it simplifies the analysis.[43] Brief reflection suggests that at any point in the decision process of choosing sequences of portfolios, the optimum policy will depend both on the success of investments made in previous periods and on the current information available about future probability distributions of returns. However, in the last planning period before the horizon the decision is of the one-period form already encountered. If the previous notation is retained and it is assumed that there are n assets, the first of which is riskless, then the portfolio choice at the beginning of the last period will determine terminal wealth:

$$TW_T = \sum_{i=2}^{n} x_{i, T-1} \tilde{r}_{i, T-1} + x_{1, T-1} RF_{T-1} \tag{4.33}$$

where $x_{i,\,T-1}$ are the proportions of the portfolio invested in risky securities $i = 2, 3, \ldots, n$ at $T - 1$, $\tilde{r}_{i,\,T-1}$ is the expected return on the risky securities at $T - 1$, $x_{1,\,T-1}$ is the proportion invested of the portfolio in the riskless asset in period $T - 1$, and RF_{T-1} is the return on the riskless asset during $T - 1$.

The total wealth available at the beginning of any period must be split between the amount invested in risky assets and the amount put into the riskless asset, since consumption has been ruled out. This is shown in the following identity:

$$TW_{T-1} = \sum_{i=2}^{n} x_{i,\,T-1} + x_{1,\,T-1}$$

$$\therefore \quad x_{1,\,T-1} = TW_{T-1} - \sum_{i=2}^{n} x_{i,\,T-1}. \tag{4.34}$$

Substituting (4.34) into (4.33):

$$TW_T = \sum_{i=2}^{n} x_{i,\,T-1}\tilde{r}_{i,\,T-1} + \left(TW_{T-1} - \sum_{i=2}^{n} x_{i,\,T-1} \right) RF_{T-1}$$

$$\therefore \quad TW_T = \sum_{i=2}^{n} (\tilde{r}_{i,\,T-1} - RF_{T-1}) x_{i,\,T-1} + RF_{T-1} TW_{T-1}$$

$$\tag{4.35}$$

Expression (4.35) shows that the last-period decision problem is to choose that set of investments which, given the value of wealth at the beginning of the last period TW_{T-1}, maximizes the expected utility of terminal wealth TW_T. The expression also shows the nature of the link between wealth at the beginning and the end of any period. It is 'recursive'; therefore a procedure of beginning by solving for the last period, and then by solving for the last but one period, means it is possible to work backwards using the 'backward recursive' process until eventually an optimum first-period decision is achieved.

More generally, the optimum decision at the beginning of any period is to maximize the expected utility of wealth at the end of the period, given the value of wealth at the beginning of the period, by making the choice on the basis of an appropriate utility of wealth function at the beginning of the period, which can be employed for choosing an appropriate portfolio on the basis of the expected distribution of returns on the assets available. This is reflected in the following expression:

$$\max_{x_{i,t-1}} EU(TW_t) = f(U)_{t-1}(TW_{t-1}) \tag{4.36}$$

where

$$\max_{x_{i,t-1}} EU(TW_t)$$

is the maximization of terminal wealth on the basis of the composition of the portfolio chosen at $t-1$, $f(U)_{t-1}$ is the appropriate utility of wealth function applicable at $t-1$ for selecting the optimum portfolio at $t-1$ on the basis of the probability distributions of expected returns, and (TW_{t-1}) is the wealth available at $t-1$ for investment.

To solve this problem a dynamic programming algorithm would be employed, and TW_t would be defined as in (4.35), which gives the explicit form for the last period but equally applies to any period. Thus, the problem is now completely specified mathematically, and essentially involves a long chain of consistent 'one-period' decisions. In practice it could still be extremely cumbersome to handle and involve an inordinate number of computations since a change in any one decision could affect all the others. Potential difficulties arise because the nature of the utility of wealth function $f(U)_t$, on the basis of which portfolio decisions are made in any given time period, has not been specified. The utility function may be 'state dependent' on the lines discussed in section 4.18. In effect this could mean that the utility function would be affected by both the level of an investor's wealth at the beginning of any period, and by his expectations concerning the level of his wealth in future periods. To avoid these possible complications further assumptions are usually made about his utility functions, concerning various issues already met in chapter 3 and this chapter.

It is normally assumed that investors are risk averse and that their utility of wealth function is concave, monotonically increasing – that is, of the type previously employed in the discussion of one-period portfolio models. Utility functions of the logarithmic or power form conform to these specifications, and Rubenstein has put forward persuasive arguments for their employment, in particular the logarithmic form.[44] These also have the attractive feature that the ranking they provide, of the relative merits of risky assets as portfolio components, is independent of the actual amount invested. This means that the rankings are constant under a linear transformation. The implication of this is that, in any particular decision period, one unique portfolio will be optimum for an individual investor regardless of the size of his wealth at the beginning of the period. Without this property he might have a different optimum portfolio for every conceivable level of initial wealth. Furthermore, these functions enable the investor to behave myopically. This means that he can treat each individual decision period as if it were his last one. This follows from the fact that the amount of wealth invested does not affect the rankings, and therefore expectations concerning the level of future wealth are irrelevant. This last characteristic means that the multiperiod problem and the single-period portfolio problem are equivalent, and that the multiperiod problem is merely a chain of single-period problems without the problem of consistency. Thus, the multiperiod portfolio problem has been greatly simplified, but at considerable cost in terms of restrictive assumptions.

The other main approach, based on the maximization of the utility of multiperiod consumption, has the attraction of being ostensibly more realistic. It considers intermediate consumption, and it initially involves fewer restrictions on the objective function.[45] The individual is assumed to maximize the utility of his consumption over each period in his lifetime up to his death, when his final wealth could be treated as a bequest. Given the utility function the problem can be formulated on lines similar to those employed in the previous model and the solution involves a recursive relationship solved by dynamic programming. To make the model tractable further assumptions are then required and these essentially make the model equivalent to the one-period model. Fama suggests that at the beginning of each period the investor acts as if:

(1) Consumption opportunities and their prices are known.
(2) The distribution of one-period wealth relatives or returns on all assets are known at the onset of the previous period.
(3) Utility is independent of the information set or state of the world.[46]

The further standard assumptions about risk aversion and concave monotonically increasing utility of wealth functions are also required. To make the model even more tractable 'separable utility' functions can be assumed; these postulate that the utility of consumption in any given period is unrelated to past or future consumption.[47]

The challenge in multiperiod portfolio theory therefore remains one of the development of manageable general models without the dead weight of the restrictive assumptions.

4.18   STATE PREFERENCE THEORY

The most elegant, generalized, formal analytical model of investment decisions under uncertainty is provided by state preference theory. This was initially developed by Arrow and Debreu and then greatly extended by Hirshliefer, who essentially regarded his contribution as an extension and generalization of Fisher's theory of riskless choice over time to encompass an explicit treatment of risky choice.[48] He develops a model in which the objects of choice are commodities real and financial, and the choosers making the decisions are economic agents. They make their choices on the basis of a preference or utility function, and each individual agent is constrained in his chosen allocation by his wealth. The model also includes balance equations to ensure that individual choices in aggregate are consistent and productive of equilibrium.

'States' of the world, the foundation of the model, can be either broadly or narrowly defined, but they have to be mutually exclusive and exhaustive. This means that the total probability of any given number of states expected to occur at a given point in time must be equal to one. Two very broad states might be defined as peace or war at time t. A very narrow definition might be 'ICI shares will stand at 350p and I win a £100 on "spot the ball"'. The state terminating a series of discrete time periods from $t = 1$ to $t = T$, by producing event E at time T, has to be defined so as to include all the contingent events during $t = 1$ to $t = T$ which lead inexorably to the final event E_T, and so states may have to be very precisely defined.

This precision of definition means that commodities demanded can be very clearly defined as well. A 'pure' financial claim or asset would pay £x in the appropriate state, should it occur, and nothing in any other. The traditional mean–variance portfolio approach is much less precise, and its securities are bundles of pure commodities which promise varying returns across a large number of states. The state preference approach therefore affords more direct access to the exact specification of the consumption opportunity which underlies the demand for financial assets.

Choices between consumption opportunities at any given point in time are determined by utility functions, but utilities are state specific. This means that they can vary according to the state of the world. If in one state you are married with a child, and in another a bachelor, then in the two states the utility of money to you could well be different. This flexibility is absent in mean–variance analysis, in which utilities at a given time are assumed constant across all states.

The actual value of wealth available for consumption at a given time will depend on which state occurs. States can be so defined that a given investor receives a particular return on one asset or group of assets. If the state occurs the return is guaranteed by assumption. The uncertainty arises from the probability of occurrence of any given state.

The simplified version of the theory which follows draws heavily upon Hirshliefer's pioneering treatment.[49] This brief version concentrates on financial claims and ignores the determination of productive opportunities, which can be readily accommodated within the model. The model will be reduced to the consideration of two time periods, $t = 0$ and $t = 1$. Thus the choice faced by an individual is between how much of his original endowment of wealth over the two periods to allocate to certain consumption in the present, CS_0, and the time plus risk choice of uncertain consumption in $t = 1$ in the two alternative states S_a and S_b. In order to demonstrate certain properties of the assumed preference function, employed for determining time state consumption preference, consider the choice between consumption in the two alternative period 1 states, CS_a and CS_b as shown in figure 4.16.

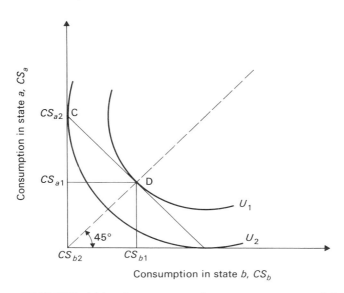

FIGURE 4.16 *Consumption choice in two-state model*

In this figure the dotted line passing through the origin at 45° is the certainty line. If we assume that $CS_{a1} = CS_{b1} = £500$, then whatever state occurs the individual is guaranteed £500 worth of consumption. The utility curves illustrated are consistent with an individual attaching equal subjective probability estimates to the occurrence of the two states; this points to another novel feature of the theory, that probabilities are implicit in the preference curves. In this case $Pr(S_a) = Pr(S_b) = 1/2$. Convex indifference curves of the type shown are consistent with risk aversion. Consider the points marked C and D in figure 4.16. At point C it will be assumed that CS_{a2} has a value of £1,000 if state a occurs, and nothing if state b occurs, and that the probabilities of occurrence of both states are 0.5. Very few people are likely to be so imprudent as to prefer a prospect of $Pr(CS_{a2}) = 0.5(£1,000)$ plus $Pr(CS_{b2}) = 0.5(0)$ to a prospect of $Pr(CS_{a1}) = 0.5(£500)$ plus $Pr(CS_{b1}) = 0.5(£500)$, especially if receiving nothing in state b does not mean a trivial loss of wealth but absolute impoverishment. If this is so, then point C will be on a utility curve representing a lower level of utility than point D, and this is consistent with utility curves of the type shown which are convex towards the origin. If all the utility curves are of this shape, then this implies risk aversion.

In this simple example three 'pure' time–state claims could be considered. There are three prospects of consumption: CS_0, CS_a and CS_b. If a pure commodity of security is regarded as one offering one 'unit' of consumption in one state alone then in this example three pure commodities can be thought of as offering the following prospects of the distribution of units of consumption:

$(CS_0, 0, 0,)$

$(0, CS_a, 0,)$

$(0, 0, CS_b).$

Suppose the individual has an initial endowment of wealth W, representing levels of potential consumption across the three states; for the ith individual these levels will be denoted W_0^i, W_a^i, W_b^i. Given the prices of pure commodities it will be possible to reallocate this wealth across states, should he so desire. The total value of his wealth will be equal to the amount of his consumption endowment in each state multiplied by the price at which it will sell, as shown in the following expression:

$$W^i = \pi_0 W_0^i + \pi_{1a} W_a^i + \pi_{1b} W_b^i \tag{4.37a}$$

where π_0, π_{1a}, π_{1b} are the prices of units of wealth in the appropriate states and time periods.

Alternatively this relation could be expressed in terms of the original endowment of consumption across states and time periods, valued in terms of units of consumption, as follows:

$$W^i = \pi_0 C_0^i + \pi_{1a} C_a^i + \pi_{1b} C_b^i. \tag{4.37b}$$

Hirshleifer suggests that certain consumption in the present can be considered equivalent to cash and therefore could be employed as a *numéraire*, and thus $\pi_0 = 1$.[50]

The fact that units of consumption, or wealth, can be priced in different times and states suggests that there must be an appropriate discount rate for trading units between states across time periods. This discount rate will reflect the nature of the investor's utility function, which itself incorporates an assessment of the subjective probability of future states. It will also be influenced by the investor's 'time bias', if evident, in the trading of marginal utility in one time period against that in another. However, it is assumed that marginal utilities are independent in the sense that they are not influenced by potential outcomes in other states. It follows that (4.37a) can be reformulated in terms of the present value of future wealth or consumption, discounted at the appropriate rate for trading between the current period and the future state a or b:

$$W^i = W_0^i + \frac{W_{1a}^i}{1 + R_{1a}} + \frac{W_{1b}^i}{1 + R_{1b}} = C_0^i + \frac{C_{1a}^i}{1 + R_{1a}} + \frac{C_{1b}^i}{1 + R_{1b}}$$

$$\tag{4.38}$$

where $1 + R_{1a}$ is the appropriate discount rate for trading units between the current period and state a, and $1 + R_{1b}$ is the discount rate for trades between the present and state b.

Now that a set of discount rates has been obtained for trading units of wealth or consumption across states, the risk-free interest rate can be defined. It must equal the price that is required to be paid to guarantee a unit of wealth or consumption, whatever state occurs. Therefore, in the simple model

$$\frac{1}{1 + RF} = \frac{1}{1 + R_{1a}} + \frac{1}{1 + R_{1b}}. \tag{4.39}$$

Everything that is required to complete this simple model of time–state pure exchange has now been obtained. Each individual would have a preference function, as shown for individual i in the following:

$$EU^i = F(C_0^i, C_{1a}^i, C_{1b}^i, \text{Pr}_{1a}^i, \text{Pr}_{1b}^i) \tag{4.40}$$

where EU^i is the expected utility of individual i. The RHS of (4.40) is the individual's time–state preference function; note that consumption opportunities in states and the probabilities of states are integral to it.

Each individual will want to maximize his expected utility and each will be subject to a wealth constraint of the type shown in expression (4.38), for in the absence of productive opportunities he will not be able to increase the present value of his wealth endowment W^i.

This means that every individual will face conservation equations as shown below:

$$\sum C_0^i = \sum W_0^i$$
$$\sum C_{1a}^i = \sum W_{1a}^i$$
$$\sum C_{1b}^i = \sum W_{1b}^i. \tag{4.41}$$

It also follows that, for the system to be in equilibrium and for the maximization of individual i's utility, the trade-off in utilities of consumption across time–state claims must be equal to the time–state discount rates for wealth/consumption:

$$\left.\frac{\partial C_{1a}^i}{\partial C_0^i}\right|_{EU^i} = -(1 + R_{1a})$$

$$\left.\frac{\partial C_{1b}^i}{\partial C_0^i}\right|_{EU^i} = -(1 + R_{1b})$$

$$\left.\frac{\partial C_{1a}^i}{\partial C_{1b}^i}\right|_{EU^i} = \frac{1 + R_{1a}}{1 + R_{1b}}. \tag{4.42}$$

This system of equations can be viewed in terms of the original 'Fisherian' analysis of two-period consumption allocation under certainty, considered in chapter 1. In the previous analysis of the present value rule, in figure 1.3, it was shown that any given amount of wealth could be reallocated into various bundles of two-period consumption according to the terms given by the prevailing market rate of interest and the constraint that the present value of the wealth or consumption could not be altered. The individual's preferred combination of consumption opportunities was indicated by the point of tangency of his highest attainable indifference curve and the present value line. At that point the slope of the present value line, given by the market rate of interest, equalled the slope of his indifference curve. A similar relationship across two periods, but holding for two different states and therefore under uncertainty, is shown in the first two equations in (4.42).

The third equation in (4.42) shows that the ratio of the marginal utility of consumption in state *a* to that in state *b* is, in turn, equal to the ratio of the time–state discount rates for consumption in states *a* and *b*. This is a standard microeconomic theory result which follows inexorably from the geometry of the analysis.

4.19   THE IMPLICATIONS OF PARAMETER PREFERENCE THEORY

The system of analysis can be readily extended and generalized in a number of ways. It could incorporate production decisions by firms by including a production function; then the optimum decisions and value of the firm can be determined. It is perhaps not surprising that under the formal analysis the 'separation' of the investment and financing decisions holds once again. Individuals can delegate the taking of investment decisions to the firm's managers who can serve their interests by maximizing the value of the firm. The individual shareholders can then reallocate their consumption opportunities according to their own preferences. Financing decisions can be included in the analysis, and in appropriate conditions the Modigliani–Miller theorem (which will be introduced in chapter 8, and shows that the 'package' of financial claims issued by a company has no effect on its overall value) can also be reproven in a state preference framework. However, there are a number of important provisos.

For the system to work and be determined as outlined above there must be 'complete' markets. This means that there must be at least as many securities issued as there are 'pure securities' or individual time–state claims. As there are conceivably a tremendous number of states there are likely to be 'incomplete' markets with considerably less financial securities (shares in firms and so on) than pure securities (equivalent to the pure commodities defined in section 4.18). Financial securities can be considered as bundles of pure securities, but with incomplete financial markets all possible combinations of pure securities will not be available. This means that some individuals will have non-marketable time–state claims. The present value of wealth constraint (4.38) will no longer hold, and therefore there will be implications for the equilibrium pricing process. The separation theorem will break down, the problem of interdependence between the investment and the financing decision will return.

Security valuation in a state preference context has been further developed by Myers, who analysed the effects of the introduction of borrowing, restrictions on short-selling, and non-homogeneous investor expectations.[51] Hirshleifer suggested that the standard Markowitz portfolio theory can be interpreted as being a special restricted case of state preference theory. The requirements are that the utility function employed is constant, irrespective of the state of the world, and furthermore that it is quadratic, or else that all available returns are normally distributed.[52] These arguments have been extended and generalized.[53] The development of CAPM and the concept of a market price of risk are dependent on the principle of portfolio separation: the optimal investment policy combines borrowing or lending with investment in the market portfolio. All investors find this optimal irrespective of their risk preferences. Cass and Stiglitz showed that, in addition to quadratic functions, logarithmic, power, and exponential utility functions would yield similar results, and Ross has extended the classes of distributions of returns for which portfolio separability hold. Work by Rubinstein, and by Klaus and Litzenberger, has further examined the extent of the complementarity of the valuation approaches embodied in the employment of logarithmic utility, mean–variance and the state preference models.

Indeed all equilibrium pricing models require 'separability' of some form. The option pricing model considered in the next chapter provides a means of valuing a contingent claim over a succession of trading periods. To accomplish this, the diffusion process which governs the price behaviour of the security against which the option is written has to be assumed given. It can then be demonstrated that a hedged position can be created involving a long position in the option and a short position in the stock, or vice versa, which will completely eliminate risk (if continuously adjusted). To avoid arbitrage opportunities this should earn the risk-free rate of return. This application of the rule that assets of identical characteristics should earn the same rate of return provides a means of valuing contingent claims.

State preference theory could be viewed as providing an 'umbrella' or overall theoretical framework within which the various other

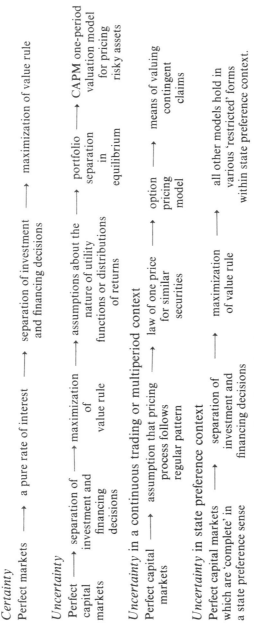

FIGURE 4.17 *The relationship between the various approaches to valuation*

approaches to security valuation could be placed. A schematic representation of this linkage is shown in figure 4.17.

It is reassuring that the models are consistent in the manner intimated, but it will also be noted that they share a foundation built on the assumption of perfect capital markets. This is the difficulty, and as soon as realistic market imperfections are admitted the models begin to crumble and the attractive properties, such as separation principles in various forms and the primacy of the maximization of value rule, tend to disappear. This is a difficulty that will be encountered frequently but will just have to be tolerated.

These developments have important implications in many areas and they will be met repeatedly in later chapters.[54]

In section 4.20 will be considered another important, and closely related, activity of the capital markets – the processing of information into the pricing of securities. In the consideration of attempts to measure the 'effectiveness' with which this is carried out, some of the models developed earlier in the chapter will be encountered.

4.20 EFFICIENT CAPITAL MARKETS: IMPLICATIONS AND TESTS

In the previous consideration of portfolio theory it was seen that a crucial input into portfolio choice was the investor's subjective probability estimation of the likely one-period returns available on securities. These estimations would be based upon all relevant, available information, both historical and current, ranging from the most general economy-wide information to company-specific, as long as it was considered relevant to the pricing of the company's securities. This pricing or valuation process will be considered more extensively in chapter 7. Essentially attempts to 'price' a company's securities can be viewed as estimations of the security's 'fundamental' or 'intrinsic' value. This could be viewed as the discounted present value of all future benefits or returns likely to accrue from ownership of the security. If the estimation of this value successfully incorporates all available information pertaining to the security, then the market is said to be 'efficient' (not to be confused with efficiency in portfolio theory). Strictly speaking there are three forms of 'efficiency' frequently encountered in the literature:

(1) Weak form: security prices fully reflect all historical relevant information.

(2) Semi-strong form: security prices fully reflect all publically available relevant information.
(3) Strong form: security prices reflect all that is knowable and relevant to the pricing of the securities.

The theory has been continually refined and made more robust, largely through the efforts of Fama, but it has had a long gestation period.[55]

The original work by Bachelier, encountered in section 4.2, was later paralleled by the studies of Cowles and Kendall.[56] Osborne's work was also supported by the empirical findings of Fama, and Granger and Morgernstern, amongst others.[57] The finding that security prices appeared to move randomly was unusual in that it predated an explanatory theory of price behaviour, though this was subsequently provided by Samuelson.[58] The concept of efficiency is extremely important in that it implies that capital markets are working effectively and correctly forming prices on the basis of available information. Thus, returns are appropriate for given levels of risk and the capital market allocatory system is working properly. This suggests that investors can expect a 'fair' return and firms a realistic cost of capital. There are various ways in which the theoretical proposition that markets are efficient can be constructed and then empirically tested. Fama suggests that the models can be formally classified as shown below:

(1) Models which assume expected returns are positive.
(2) Models which assume constancy of expected returns.
(3) Tests which assume the market model holds.
(4) Tests which assume an equilibrium risk/return trade-off on portfolio theory lines.[59]

The proposition that all shares at any given time fully reflect available information can be formally stated as follows:

$$s_t^j = f(IS_t) = f(IS_t^M) \tag{4.43}$$

where s_t^j is a vector of equilibrium prices for all shares j ($j = 1, 2, \ldots, n$) at time t, IS_t is the total information set available to investors at time t, IS_t^M is the information set actually used by investors in the market determining equilibrium prices at time t (therefore it follows that $IS_t^M \leq IS_t$), and f is the appropriate function by which information is processed into the determination of an equilibrium set of prices.

Expression (4.43) states that the equilibrium prices determined by investors using information in the market are the same as those implied by the use of all available information. If they were not identical the market would be inefficient. Efficiency implies that no individual investor could devise a trading strategy on the basis of available information and by so doing expect to generate excess returns. The proposition is tautological, but testing it is very difficult as the specification of f is not known; the way in which the market processes information in order to determine equilibrium prices, and therefore the functional form of f, has to be assumed. This means that tests of market efficiency are typically tests of joint propositions – the assumed form of f, and the hypothesis that the market is efficient.

The original most popular method of testing for market efficiency was via the use of random walk models. These assumed that expected returns are constant over time. The model can be developed as below:

$$E[\tilde{r}_t^j(IS_{t-1}^M)] = \frac{E[\tilde{s}_t^j(IS_{t-1}^M)] - s_{t-1}^j}{s_{t-1}^j} \qquad (4.44)$$

where $E[\tilde{r}_t^j(IS_{t-1}^M)]$ is the expected return on security j from holding until time t, as perceived at time $t-1$, on the basis of all information used in the price setting process in the market at time $t-1$; $E[\tilde{s}_t^j(IS_{t-1}^M)]$ is the expected price of security j as perceived at time $t-1$ on the basis of information used by the market in setting prices at $t-1$; and s_{t-1}^j is the actual price of security j at time $t-1$.

Expression (4.44) shows that the expected return on security j at time $t-1$, on the basis of information used in setting prices at $t-1$, is simply equal to the expected change in the share price over the period, divided by the original share price. If the random walk model holds, and the market is efficient, then the expected return, predicted on the basis of information used in the pricing process, should be equivalent to the expected return which would be predicted if all information had been used in the process of setting prices, and both should be equal to a constant. This can be formally stated;

$$E[\tilde{r}_t^j(IS_{t-1}^M)] = E(\tilde{r}_t^j(IS_{t-1})] = \bar{r}^j \qquad (4.45)$$

where $\bar{r}^j$ is the constant return associated with holding security j.

This implies that at time $t-1$ the market sets a current price so that, in terms of the expected future price, the share will yield a constant expected return. It must be borne in mind that the expression refers to *ex ante* expectations; *ex post* the actual returns realized are drawings from a probability distribution, and therefore can have values greater or less than those predicted, but on balance they should conform to the model. This form of testing the efficient markets' hypothesis usually employs a subset of all information available at $t - 1$; the information available in the time series of past returns on the security is utilized for the prediction of future returns. For the applied statistical tests to be valid it has to be assumed that the distribution of successive price changes is independent and that it conforms to a known probability distribution: a stationary normal distribution is the usual assumption. (It is known from section 4.2 that this is not strictly true, and Fama has shown that most models used in finance can be developed from stable non-normal distributions, but it considerably simplifies matters and the deviations from normality are slight.)[60] In an early classic study, Fama tested for autocorrelation in time series of individual security returns.[61] He did find slight evidence of the existence of correlation, but not sufficient to warrant rejection of the efficient markets' hypothesis. His analysis of 'runs', persistent price increases or decreases, also conformed, with slight deviations in the case of daily changes, to what one would expect in an efficient market. An extensive study of UK data by Benjamin and Girmes found evidence that the shares of the larger quoted companies followed a random walk, though the evidence for smaller companies was less clear.[62] This study appeared to give stronger evidence than an earlier study by Kemp and Reid, but whereas their study had the merit of adjusting for non-trading effects, they did not allow for transaction costs, and therefore it is not certain that the evidence of non-random effects in 50 per cent of their sample would be washed out by transaction costs.[63] It would not be appropriate to catelogue the numerous weak form tests of the efficient market hypothesis on the major stock exchanges of the world, but I think it can be safely stated that the bulk of evidence suggests that markets are weak form efficient. Departures from strict randomness do not matter as long as the existence of transaction costs ensures that they cannot be employed to produce profitable trading.

Further evidence in support of the weak form hypothesis has been produced via the use of a less constrained form of the random walk model which merely requires that expected returns be positive rather than constant. Formally:

$$E[\tilde{r}_t^j(IS_{t-1}^M)] = E[\tilde{r}_t^j(IS_{t-1})] > 0. \tag{4.46}$$

This form of the hypothesis can readily be tested against the claims of investment analysts who practise technical analysis or chartism. Basically they work on the premise that the market does not fully appraise all available information and that the adjustment of market prices tends to persist over time. Thus, judicious mapping or charting of historical price movements can establish patterns and therefore be employed for predictive purposes. If the market is efficient and it sets prices to produce positive expected returns, then the optimum policy will be to buy and hold. On the other hand, if the chartists can successfully predict price movements, including downturns in prices, then it might well be profitable at times to go short in securities.

Filter rules have been devised to test a large variety of mechanical trading rules implied by chartism. A filter rule is typified by the following trading strategy: if price moves up x per cent, buy and hold, but if it falls x per cent below its subsequent high, sell and go short, wait, and should the price rise x per cent above the subsequent low, buy and hold again. Ignore intermediate price changes. A pioneering study by Alexander, employing the use of filters on American data, appeared to suggest that filters could produce excess profits, but later corrections by Fama and Blume, in conjunction with their own empirical work, provided evidence that filters do not provide any profitable trading rules.[64] A study of UK data by Dryden provided further evidence that, once transaction costs are taken into account, filter rules do not provide profits in excess of a simple buy and hold strategy.[65] Thus the evidence appears to strongly support weak form efficiency, but it has been pointed out that there is no underlying economic rationale for the assumptions that expected returns are either constant or positive.[66]

From this point of view, semi-strong form tests based on the market model (previously encountered in section 4.14) are more academically respectable in that the model posits a linear relationship between returns on individual securities and those of the market as a whole. Thus there is a hypothesis about returns which has been empirically tested. This model could be expressed as:

$$E[\tilde{r}_t^j(IS_{t-1}^M)R_{M_t}] = E[\tilde{r}_t^j(IS_{t-1})R_{M_t}] = \alpha_j + B_j R_{M_t} \qquad (4.47)$$

where R_{M_t} is the return on the market at time t.

If it is assumed that the relationship is constant over time, the model's parameters can be estimated by regressing returns on the security against returns on a market index (as a proxy for the market) over some historical time period. The model is consistent with a number of different equilibrium conditions, but it is usually assumed that the price distribution of individual security returns is multivariate normal.

The relationship will not hold exactly and therefore it can be described:

$$\bar{r}^j = \alpha_j + B_j R_{M_t} + \tilde{\varepsilon}_t^j \tag{4.48}$$

where $\tilde{\varepsilon}_t^j$ is the error term, which has a mean of zero and is independent of R_M and normally distributed. The relationship is therefore estimated by a normal linear regression but, once again, to be able to estimate the parameters it must be assumed that the distribution of returns is stationary.

Information pertaining to security prices is reflected in the joint distribution of returns and is therefore incorporated in returns on the market, whereas information specific to an individual company is reflected in the distribution of the error term in the regression equation. Therefore analysis of the 'residual' or error term should highlight the adjustment of an individual security to new information:

$$\tilde{e}_t^j = r_t^j - \hat{\alpha}_j - \hat{B}_j R_{M_t} \tag{4.49}$$

where $\tilde{e}_t^j$ is the estimated residual for security j and time t, $\hat{\alpha}_j$ and $\hat{B}_j$ are the estimated regression coefficients for security j, r_t^j is the actual return on security j at time t, and R_{M_t} is the actual return on the market at time t.

A pioneering study by Fama, Fisher, Jensen and Roll applied this methodology to an investigation of stock splits which, as they involve a mere 'accounting' change in the number of shares issued per shareholder, should display no information effects.[67] Examination of the cumulative average residual of the 622 securities in their study showed that in the months prior to the split the residuals were distinctly positive, but after the split they displayed a normal relationship with the market. They interpreted this as evidence that there is typically considerable improvement in the earnings prospects of a company prior to a split, and this is reflected in the behaviour of the residuals, which return to a normal relationship after the split. In point of fact they found different post-split residual behaviour for those firms which subsequently increased or decreased their dividends, but again felt this was consistent with semi-strong form efficiency. A similar type of study was carried out by Ball and Brown with respect to firms with increased or decreased earnings announcements, and again the behaviour of the residuals was consistent with the market successfully anticipating the changes revealed in annual earnings announcements.[68] More recently Marsh has employed a similar methodology, though with sophisticated adjustments, to examine the informational impact of UK equity rights issues.[69] He found evidence of the persistence of positive returns after the announcement, but considered that this was probably tied up with a second factor in some way related to company size which was not fully reflected in his single-factor market model regression. The effect, though persistent, was small, and would have been washed out by transaction costs, and therefore he interpreted his results as being consistent with semi-strong form efficiency.

The tests of strong form efficiency usually employ a version of the capital asset pricing model that was encountered in section 4.13. From the theoretical, methodological point of view, this type of test is the most appropriate in that it is based on an explicit equilibrium pricing model, and therefore does not involve any *ad hoc* assumptions about the return generating process. The basic model could be defined as:

$$E(\tilde{r}^j) = E(\tilde{R}_z) + [E(\tilde{R}_M) - E(\tilde{R}_z)]\beta_{jM} \qquad (4.50)$$

where $\tilde{R}_z$ is the return on any asset or portfolio which is uncorrelated with the return on the market portfolio; this is equivalent to the riskless asset in the Sharpe–Lintner formulation. The empirical methodology is similar to that employed in applying market model tests. The parameters are estimated via linear regression, and the tests of market efficiency can be based upon examination of the behaviour of the computed residuals.

Strong form efficiency suggests that no investor could use any existing information to achieve a superior return. One type of test can be based upon the examination of the performance of the investment managers of mutual funds. If, by superior analysis, the investment managers can consistently achieve superior returns, then this would be a violation of strong form efficiency. The tests of fund performance encountered in section 4.15 are all consistent with strong form efficiency. However, the weighty criticisms of tests of the CAPM have already been noted, and in point of fact the whole approach is troubled by errors in the variables and other econometric difficulties. The evidence is not all one sided either. Jaffe found evidence that the market ignored potentially profitable trading opportunities signalled by insider dealing, and Lorie and Neiderhoffer have provided similar evidence.[70] Thus there are doubts about strong form efficiency, but in the case of the other two, less restrictive, definitions the weight of empirical evidence carries the day.

4.21 CONCLUSION

The rather lengthy material in this chapter has been concerned, first and foremost, with developing a model of investor portfolio behaviour. In the one-period context the model developed is remarkably robust in that it is consistent with risk aversion and therefore 'explains' diversification. It has also important implications for the equilibrium security pricing process, as portrayed in the CAPM. The model has also been extended, as was seen, to the multiperiod context, though the results at the moment can perhaps best be described as being less successful, but promising. There are also the extreme current doubts about the testability of the model. Nevertheless it would be no exaggeration to describe these theoretical developments as important landmarks in the extension of financial economics. They have provided important insights into the 'macro' financial workings of capital markets, and into the 'micro' context of individual firm and investor decisions. These will be returned to frequently in later stages of this text.

What is also remarkable is that these theoretical advances have been remarkably well supported by empirical evidence. The market model has been subject to extensive confirmatory testing, and the happy marriage between theory and empirical tests is nowhere better represented than in the efficient markets' literature. Thus the material just considered, though it still leaves many questions open, marks a remarkably rapid advance in the understanding of financial behaviour. This advance is epitomized in one of the subject areas considered in the next chapter: option theory.

TEST QUESTIONS

1. (a) Draw up a list of three companies whose securities are likely to have high standard deviations of returns, and three companies whose security returns are likely to have low standard deviations of returns.
   (b) List two companies whose security returns are likely to be highly correlated and two that are likely to have low correlation.

2. You are an investor with equal amounts of your funds invested in the following three securities, whose returns, variances, and covariances are as follows:

Security	Expected return	Variance/covariance matrix		
			A	B	C
A	10%	A	12	−5	8
B	15%	B	−5	36	12
C	7%	C	8	12	10

(a) What is the expected return and the risk of your equally weighted portfolio?
(b) Suppose you put 50 per cent of your funds in B and 25 per cent in A and C. What would be the expected returns and the risk of your portfolio now?
(c) Is there any way you could reweight your portfolio and get higher returns for less risk?

3. The two random variables $\tilde{R}_X$ and $\tilde{R}_Y$ represent the possible returns on two securities X and Y.

Probability	R_X	R_Y
0.25	−5%	2%
0.25	0%	5%
0.25	6%	9%
0.25	12%	16%

(a) Calculate the expected return, the standard deviation of return, and the covariance of returns on the two securities.
(b) Calculate the standard deviation and expected return of the following portfolios made up of the two securities:

	Portfolio weights			
X_i	1.25	1.00	0.50	0.25
Y_i	−0.25	0	0.50	0.75

4. A risk measurement service suggests that companies A, B, and C have the following characteristics:

Company	Beta	Specific risk
A	0.48	35
B	0.98	21
C	1.12	30

The risk-free rate is 12 per cent, the return on the market port-folio is 21 per cent and the standard deviation of returns on the market portfolio is 24 per cent.

(a) Calculate the expected return and the risk of a portfolio invested equally in the three companies.

(b) What proportion of the total portfolio risk is unsystematic?

5. Determine which of the following cases contravene the concepts of market efficiency:

(a) Stock Exchange investors are expected to earn a positive return on their investments this year. Some will do better than others.

(b) Managers who deal in their own company's securities make consistently higher risk-adjusted returns than the market as a whole.

(c) A unit trust claims in its advertising material that it out-performed the average rate of return on the market by 50 per cent last year.

(d) Your stockbroker has developed a complex computer program which he claims enables him to earn a return of 3 per cent above the market risk-adjusted rate.

APPENDIX 4.1

ALTERNATIVE PORTFOLIO SELECTION CRITERIA

This appendix will briefly survey, though by no means exhaustively, some of the alternative portfolio selection criteria. In his original monograph Markowitz discussed various alternative criteria and, in particular, favoured the use of semi-variance (defined in chapter 2).[71] This stemmed from the observation that investors are likely to fear downside risk (below-mean returns), but will obviously have no qualms about the possibility of above-average returns. He suggested, as an alternative to the standard quadratic form, a hybrid form of utility curve in association with this risk measure, which would behave like a standard quadratic curve below a critical level of wealth and be linear above it. This suggests risk aversion below the critical level and risk neutrality above it. In the case of non-symmetric distributions this criterion, as it is more sensitive to 'left' – skewed distributions, would probably lead to selection of a different efficient set from the standard criteria.

Roy's 'safety-first' criterion

Simultaneous with the publication of Markowitz's original paper on portfolio theory, Roy published a paper involving an alternative portfolio selection criterion which was concerned with minimizing the probability of a disastrously low return.[72] Suppose there exists a distribution of portfolio or asset returns and estimations of the mean $\bar{r}$ and standard deviation σ_r of these returns. The investor is supremely concerned that his return should not fall below some minimum critical value d. Then, following the assumption that there is not full information available concerning the probability density function of portfolio or asset returns, Roy employs the Bienaymé–Tchebycheff inequality. It follows that if the actual return is a random variable r, then:

$$P(|\tilde{r} - \bar{r}| \geq \bar{r} - d) \leq \frac{\sigma_r^2}{(\bar{r} - d)^2}$$

where p is probability. Thus, *a fortiori*,

$$P(\bar{r} - \tilde{r} \geq \bar{r} - d) = P(\tilde{r} \leq d) \leq \frac{\sigma_r^2}{(\bar{r} - d)^2}.$$

The investor does not know the exact probability of $P(\tilde{r} \leq d)$, but as a method of attempting to minimize this probability he can concentrate on either minimizing $\sigma_r^2/(\bar{r} - d)^2$ or equivalently maximizing $(\bar{r} - d)/\sigma_r$. The implications of this for portfolio selection are shown in figure 4.18. The gradient of the line da is equivalent to $(\bar{r} - d)/\sigma_r$. Thus the steeper the slope of this line, the lower the probability of disaster.

The more conservative the investor, the lower the probability of disaster accepted. In figure 4.18, a very conservative investor might adopt disaster level d' and portfolio b, whereas one slightly less timid might opt for d and portfolio a. Given the specification of the disaster level, this criterion suggests risk diversification and the appropriate portfolio choice.

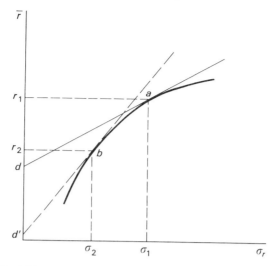

FIGURE 4.18 *Roy's 'safety first' criterion for portfolio selection*

Baumol's gain confidence limit criterion

Baumol built upon the assumption that risk-averse investors are likely to be concerned with downside deviations from the expected return.[73] Portfolios can therefore be ranked according to their expected return $E(\tilde{r})$ and their lower confidence limit defined as:

$$L = E(\tilde{r}) - K\sigma_r$$

where L is the lower confidence limit, σ_r is the standard deviation of return, and K is a positive constant.

The value of K will be greater the more conservative the investor. If the investor will tolerate an 0.5 per cent chance that the return be less than the lower confidence limit, then he can build on the knowledge that 99 per cent of the area under a normal distribution lies within three standard deviations of the mean, and set K equal to 3. It follows that, as both the mean and the standard deviation are taken into account in setting the confidence limit, an increase in the mean may offset an increase in the standard deviation of returns. This means that a 'more' risky security in the Markowitz sense may have a higher lower confidence limit than a 'less risky' security, and therefore be preferred. Thus, hypothetically, the rule leads to the rejection of a small subset of the Markowitz efficient frontier at the lower levels of expected returns; however, it can be seen that the inclusion of a riskless asset in the Markowitz formulation makes it rather redundant.

Stochastic dominance

Hadar and Russell, and Hanoch and Levy, suggested a method of ordering distributions of security and portfolio returns based on a stochastic dominance criterion.[74] The strength of this approach is that it requires few restrictions on investor utility functions – monotonicity in the case of first-degree stochastic dominance – and no specification of the type of probability distribution of returns. Thus the decision rules are much more general than those based upon a specific type of probability distribution (that is, mean–variance analysis). Hadar and Russell initially distinguished two types of stochastic dominance – first and second degree. If $f(R_{P_i})$ and $g(R_{P_i})$ are the probability density functions of returns on portfolios F and G, and their respective cumulative probability distributions are represented by $F(R_P)$ and $G(R_P)$, then the analysis can be developed as follows.

First-degree stochastic dominance. First-degree stochastic dominance holds whenever one cumulative probability distribution lies entirely, or partly, under another. It follows that, in terms of first-degree stochastic dominance, probability function g is said to be at least as large as f, if:

$$G(R_P) \leq F(R_P) \quad \text{for all } R_{P_i} \in R_P.$$

Alternatively, given that the cumulative probability function can be obtained by integrating the original probability density function over the appropriate range (see figure 4.19), the following is obtained:

$$\int_a^{R_P} [g(R_{P_i}) - f(R_{P_i})] \, dR_{P_i} \leq 0$$

for all values of $R_P \in [a, b]$, and with strict inequality holding for at least one value of $R_P \in [a, b]$. As previously mentioned, the only specification for the investor utility function is that it is monotonically increasing.

Second-degree stochastic dominance. This applies when the area under one cumulative probability distribution is equal to, or larger than, the area under the other distribution. Formally, the criterion

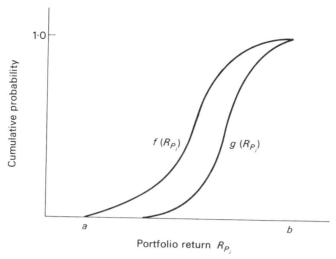

FIGURE 4.19   *Second-degree stochastic dominance*

states that portfolio g dominates portfolio f if:

$$\int_{a}^{R_P} \int_{a}^{R_{P_i}} [g(z) - f(z_i)] \, \mathrm{d}z \, \mathrm{d}R_{P_i} \leq 0$$

for all values of $R_P \in [a, b]$, and again with strict inequality holding for at least one value of $R_P \in [a, b]$. The specification of the investor's appropriate utility of wealth function is slightly more rigorous in that it must be monotonically increasing and concave; that is, $U'(R_P) > 0$ and $U''(R_P) < 0$, but all this means is that it is consistent with risk aversion, and this is the case in most financial decision models.

Equivalence of stochastic dominance and other criteria. Philippatos and Gressis have examined the equivalence between the stochastic dominance criterion and other portfolio selection criteria, and found that it is equivalent to mean–variance for portfolios distributed according to normal and uniform distributions; but its strength is its greater generality.[75] Its great weakness, though, is that, despite providing a general system for ranking existing portfolios or assets the method cannot be easily translated into an algorithm for determining the optimum combination of assets within a portfolio, and until this is further developed its use seems likely to be greatly restricted.[76]

APPENDIX 4.2

THE SELECTION OF EFFICIENT PORTFOLIOS

The basic portfolio problem could be viewed as one involving either maximizing returns at given levels of risk, or minimizing risk at given levels of return. If the latter view is adopted, the need is to minimize the variance of a portfolio given by:

$$\text{var}(R_p) = \sum_i \sum_j x_i x_j \sigma_{ij} \tag{4.51}$$

subject to the constraints written in Lagrangian form, if a calculus solution is to be employed. The first constraint is that the desired level of return must be achieved. This could be written as:

$$\sum_i x_i E(R_i) - ED(R_p) = 0 \tag{4.52}$$

where *ED* is the desired portfolio return. The other constraint is that the portfolio weights must sum to one; this could be written:

$$\sum_i x_i - 1 = 0. \tag{4.53}$$

The risk minimization problem can then be written as follows in terms of the Lagrangian function:

$$Z = \sum_i \sum_j x_i x_j \sigma_{ij} + \lambda_1 \left[\sum_i x_i E(R_i) - ED(R_p) \right]$$
$$+ \lambda_2 \left(\sum_i x_i - 1 \right). \tag{4.54}$$

The solution for determining the minimum variance portfolio can be obtained by setting $\partial Z/\partial x_i = \partial Z/\partial \lambda_j = 0$ for all $i = 1, \ldots, N$ and $j = 1, 2$.

The first term on the RHS of (4.54) is the full matrix for the variance of a portfolio. It could be set out as below:

$$V_p = \begin{cases} x_1 x_1 \sigma_{11} + x_1 x_2 \sigma_{12} + x_1 x_3 \sigma_{13} + \cdots + x_1 x_N \sigma_{1N} \\ x_2 x_1 \sigma_{21} + x_2 x_2 \sigma_{22} + x_2 x_3 \sigma_{23} + \cdots + x_2 x_N \sigma_{2N} \\ \vdots \qquad\qquad \vdots \qquad\qquad\qquad\qquad \vdots \\ x_N x_1 \sigma_{N1} + x_N x_2 \sigma_{N2} + x_N x_3 \sigma_{N3} + \cdots + x_N x_N \sigma_{NN}. \end{cases}$$

For the case where $x_i = x_1$, it can be seen that x_1 appears in the first row and first column of the matrix. Taking the partial derivative $\partial V_p / \partial x_1$:

$$\frac{\partial V_p}{\partial x_1} = 2x_1 \sigma_{11} + x_2 \sigma_{12} + x_3 \sigma_{13} + \cdots + x_N \sigma_{1N}$$

$$+ x_2 \sigma_{21}$$

$$+ x_3 \sigma_{31}$$

$$\vdots$$

$$+ x_N \sigma_{1N}.$$

$$\therefore \quad \frac{\partial V_p}{\partial x_1} = 2x_1 \sigma_{11} + 2x_2 \sigma_{12} + 2x_3 \sigma_{13} + \cdots + 2x_N \sigma_{1N}.$$

There will be an expanded term like this for the derivative of every x_i value.

The differentiation of the second and third terms on the RHS of (4.54) in the case where $x_i = x_1$ is straightforward:

$$\frac{\partial Z}{\partial x_1} = \lambda_1 E(R_1) + \lambda_2 .$$

Thus differentiating (4.54) for values of

$$\frac{\partial Z}{\partial x_i} = \frac{\partial Z}{\partial \lambda_j} = 0$$

yields the following $N + 2$ set of equations:

$$\frac{\partial Z}{\partial x_1} = 2x_1 \sigma_{11} + 2x_2 \sigma_{12} + \cdots + 2x_N \sigma_{1N} + \lambda_1 E(R_1) + \lambda_2 = 0$$

$$\frac{\partial Z}{\partial x_2} = 2x_1 \sigma_{21} + 2x_2 \sigma_{22} + \cdots + 2x_N \sigma_{2N} + \lambda_1 E(R_2) + \lambda_2 = 0$$

$$\vdots$$

$$\frac{\partial Z}{\partial x_N} = 2x_1 \sigma_{N1} + 2x_2 \sigma_{N2} + \cdots + 2x_N \sigma_{NN} + \lambda_1 E(R_N) + \lambda_2 = 0$$

$$\frac{\partial Z}{\partial \lambda_2} = x_1 + x_2 + x_3 + \cdots + x_N - 1 = 0$$

$$\frac{\partial Z}{\partial \lambda_1} = x_1 E(R_1) + x_2 E(R_2) + \cdots + x_N E(R_N) - ED(R_p) = 0.$$

The equations can be set out in matrix form:

coefficient matrix C

$$
\begin{bmatrix}
2\sigma_{11} & 2\sigma_{12} & 2\sigma_{13} & \cdots & 2\sigma_{1N} & E(R_1) & 1 \\
2\sigma_{21} & 2\sigma_{22} & 2\sigma_{23} & \cdots & 2\sigma_{2N} & E(R_2) & 1 \\
\vdots & & & & & & \\
2\sigma_{N1} & 2\sigma_{N2} & 2\sigma_{N3} & \cdots & 2\sigma_{NN} & E(R_N) & 1 \\
1 & 1 & 1 & \cdots & 1 & 0 & 0 \\
E(R_1) & E(R_2) & E(R_3) & \cdots & E(R_N) & 0 & 0
\end{bmatrix}
$$

$$\times \quad x \quad = \quad k$$

$$
\times
\begin{bmatrix}
x_1 \\
x_2 \\
\vdots \\
x_N \\
\lambda_2 \\
\lambda_1
\end{bmatrix}
=
\begin{bmatrix}
0 \\
0 \\
\\
0 \\
1 \\
ED(R_p)
\end{bmatrix}.
$$

There are various ways in which this system may be solved. If C^{-1} is denoted the inverse of the coefficients matrix, then in matrix algebra terms:

$$Cx = k$$
$$C^{-1}Cx = C^{-1}k$$
$$Ix = C^{-1}k$$
$$x = C^{-1}k.$$

This will give a solution in terms of $N + 2$ variables in a portfolio weight vector expressed in terms of the desired level of expected returns $ED(R_p)$. The series of equations will be of the form:

$$x_1 = c_1 + d_1\, ED(R_p)$$
$$x_2 = c_2 + d_2\, ED(R_p)$$
$$\vdots$$
$$x_N = c_N + d_N\, ED(R_p).$$

The portfolio weights are variable, of course, but subject to the constraint that $\sum_i^N x_i = 1$.

The values of c_i and d_i are constants, and the desired level of portfolio return $ED(R_p)$ will be varied, and at each appropriate level of $ED(R_p)$ will generate the optimum security weights for the portfolio.

THE DERIVATION OF THE CAPITAL ASSET PRICING MODEL

It has been established that the equilibrium relationship between the expected return of an efficient portfolio and its risk is determined by the equation of the capital market line. What returns would be expected if an individual security i were combined with the market portfolio M? This situation is shown in figure 4.20.

Suppose a composite portfolio is formed consisting of both security i and the market portfolio M. The proportion of the portfolio invested in security i is denoted x_i, and therefore the weight for the proportion invested in the market portfolio is $(1 - x_i)$.

The expected return of such a portfolio will be:

$$E(R_p) = x_i E(r_i) + (1 - x_i)E(R_M).$$

Differentiation with respect to x_i gives:

$$\frac{\partial E(R_p)}{\partial x_i} = E(r_i) - E(R_M).$$

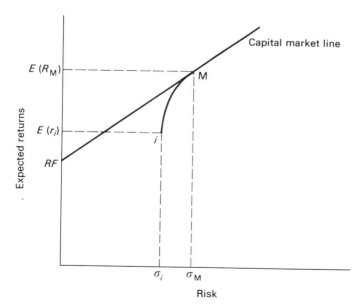

FIGURE 4.20 *Combination of individual security and market portfolio*

Similarly, the risk of this portfolio will be given by:

$$\sigma_p = [x_i^2 \sigma_i^2 + (1 - x_i)^2 \sigma_M^2 + 2x_i(1 - x_i)\sigma_i \sigma_M]^{1/2}.$$

(NB: Remember cov $r_i R_M = \sigma_i \sigma_M$.)
Differentiation with respect to x_i gives:

$$\frac{\partial \sigma_p}{\partial x_i} = \tfrac{1}{2}[x_i^2 \sigma_i^2 + (1 - x_i)^2 \sigma_M^2 + 2x_i(1 - x_i)\sigma_i \sigma_M]^{-1/2}$$

$$\times\; 2[x_i \sigma_i^2 - (1 - x_i)\sigma_M^2 + (1 - 2x_i)\sigma_i \sigma_M].$$

As the first term on the RHS in square brackets is equivalent to $1/\sigma_p$,

$$\frac{\partial \sigma_p}{\partial x_i} = \frac{x_i \sigma_i^2 - (1 - x_i)\sigma_M^2 + (1 - 2x_i)\sigma_i \sigma_M}{\sigma_p}.$$

An expression can be derived to show how expected return will vary with risk in this portfolio by use of the chain rule:

$$\frac{\partial E(R_p)}{\partial \sigma_p} = \frac{\partial E(R_p)}{\partial x_i} \frac{\partial x_i}{\partial \sigma_p}$$

$$\therefore\quad \frac{\partial E(R_p)}{\partial \sigma_p} = \frac{[E(r_i) - E(R_M)]\sigma_p}{x_i \sigma_i^2 - (1 - x_i)\sigma_M^2 + (1 - 2x_i)\sigma_i \sigma_M}.$$

Now consider what happens to the rate of change of expected returns and risk of the composite portfolio at point M, where the whole portfolio consists of M. At this point $x_i = 0$. This means that:

$$\frac{\partial E(R_p)}{\partial \sigma_p} = \frac{[E(r_i) - E(R_M)]\sigma_p}{-\sigma_M^2 + \sigma_i \sigma_M}.$$

Now at point M curve iM, which traces out the locus of the expected return/risk combinations available on the composite portfolio, must be at a tangent to the capital market line. The equation for the capital market line gives a slope equal to $[E(R_M) - RF]/\sigma_M$, and at the point of tangency this must be the same as the slope of the equation for the composite portfolio, which has just been derived:

$$\therefore\quad \frac{\partial E(R_p)}{\partial \sigma_p} = \frac{[E(R_M) - RF]}{\sigma_M} = \frac{[E(r_i) - E(R_M)]\sigma_p}{-\sigma_M^2 + \sigma_i \sigma_M}.$$

But at point M, $\sigma_p = \sigma_M$, and so:

$$\frac{[E(R_M) - RF][-\sigma_M^2 + \sigma_i\sigma_M]}{\sigma_M} = [E(r_i) - E(R_M)]\sigma_M$$

$$\therefore \quad E(r_i) = RF + \frac{[E(R_M) - RF]\sigma_i\sigma_M}{\sigma_M^2}.$$

This is the capital asset pricing model. Sharpe has given an original development of this,[77] and Fama a more advanced treatment.[78]

NOTES AND REFERENCES

1. Marshall, A. *Principles of Economics* (9th edn), Macmillan, London, 1961, vol. 1, p. 613.
2. Markowitz, H. M. 'Portfolio selection', *Journal of Finance* **VII**(1), 1952, pp. 77–91. See also his *Portfolio Selection*, Wiley, New York, 1959.
3. Bachelier, L. B. J. A. *Théorie de la Speculation*, Gauthier-Villars, Paris, 1900.
4. Osborne, M. F. M. 'Brownian motion in the stock market', *Operations Research* **VII**, March–April 1959, pp. 145–173.
5. Mandelbrot, B. 'The variation of certain speculative prices', *Journal of Business* **36**(4), 1963, pp. 394–419.
   Fama, E. F. 'The behaviour of stock market prices', *Journal of Business* **38**(1), 1965, pp. 34–105.
6. Brealey, R. A. 'The distribution and independence of successive rates of return from the British equity market', *Journal of Business Finance* **2**(2), Summer 1970, pp. 29–40.
7. For a discussion of this see: Fama, E. F. and Miller, M. H. *The Theory of Finance*, Holt, Rinehart and Winston, Hinsdale, Illinois, 1972, chapter 6, pp. 215–28.
8. See: Markowitz, H. M. *Portfolio Selection*, Wiley, New York, 1959.
   Or: Sharpe, W. F. *Portfolio Theory and Capital Markets*, McGraw-Hill, New York, 1970, appendices B and C.
   Archer, S. H. and Francis, J. C. *Portfolio Analysis*, Prentice-Hall, Englewood Cliffs NJ, 1971.
   Fama, E. F. *Foundations of Finance*, Basil Blackwell, Oxford, 1977, chapter 7.
9. See: Cohen, K. J. and Pogue, J. A. 'An empirical evaluation of alternative portfolio selection models', *Journal of Business* **40**(2), April 1967, pp. 169–93.
10. Tobin, J. 'Liquidity preference as behaviour towards risk', *Review of Economic Studies* **26**(1), February 1958, pp. 65–86.
    Treynor, J. L. 'How to rate management of investment funds', *Harvard Business Review* **43**(1), January/February 1965, pp. 63–75.
    Lintner, J. 'The valuation of risk assets and the selection of risky investments in stock portfolios and capital budgets', *Review of Economics and Statistics* **47**(1), February 1965, pp. 13–37.
    Sharpe, W. F. 'Capital asset prices: a theory of market equilibrium under conditions of risk', *The Journal of Finance* **19**(3), September 1964, pp. 425–42.

Mossin, J. 'Equilibrium in a capital asset market', *Econometrica* **34**(4), October 1966, pp. 768–83.

Fama, E. F. 'Risk, return and equilibrium', *Journal of Political Economy* **79**(1), January/February 1971, pp. 30–55.

11. Sharpe, W. F. 'Capital asset prices', *The Journal of Finance* **19**(3), September 1964, pp. 425–42.

    Lintner, J. 'The valuation of risk assets', *Review of Economics and Statistics* **47**(1), February 1965, pp. 13–37.

12. This is of course, a very important and potentially very complicated caveat. For an excellent survey of some of the various implications of inflation see: Hamada, R. S. 'Financial theory and taxation in an inflationary world: some public policy implications', *Journal of Finance* **34**(2), May 1979, pp. 347–69.

13. Tobin, J. 'Liquidity preference as behaviour towards risk', *Review of Economic Studies* **26**(1), February 1958, pp. 65–86.

14. For a discussion of short selling see: Fama, E. F. *Foundations of Finance*, Basil Blackwell, Oxford, 1977, chapter 7.

15. Sharpe, W. F. 'Capital asset prices', *The Journal of Finance* **19**(3), September 1964, pp. 425–42.

    Lintner, J. 'The valuation of risk assets', *Review of Economics and Statistics* **47**(1), February 1965, pp. 13–37.

    Treynor, J., in an unpublished paper 'Toward a theory of market value of risky assets'.

16. Fama, E. F. 'Risk, return and equilibrium', *Journal of Political Economy* **79**(1), January/February 1971, pp. 30–55.

17. Sharpe, W. F. 'Capital asset prices', *The Journal of Finance* **19**(3), September 1964, pp. 425–42.

18. Ibbotson, R. G. and Sinquefield, R. 'Stocks, bonds, bills and inflation; simulations of the future', *The Journal of Business* **49**(3), July 1976, pp. 313–38.

19. King, B. F. 'Market and industry factors in stock price behaviour', *Journal of Business* **39**(1), part 2, January 1966.

    Officer, R. R. 'The variability of the market factor of the New York Stock Exchange', *Journal of Business* **46**(3), July 1973, pp. 434–53.

20. Treynor, J. L. 'How to rate management of investment funds', *Harvard Business Review* **43**(1), January/February 1965, pp. 63–75.

21. Blume, M. E. 'On the assessment of risk', *Journal of Finance* **26**(1), March 1971, pp. 1–10.

    Blume, M. E. 'Betas and their regression tendencies', *Journal of Finance* **30**(3), June 1975, pp. 785–95.

22. For an examination of the benefits of risk diversification see: Wagner, W. H. and Lau, S. 'The effect of diversification on risk', *Financial Analysts Journal* **27**, November/December 1971.

23. Cohen, K. J. and Pogue, J. A. 'An empirical evaluation of alternative portfolio selection models', *Journal of Business* **40**(2), April 1967, pp. 169–93.

24. Wallingford, B. A. 'A survey and comparison of portfolio selection models', *Journal of Financial and Quantitative Analysis*, June 1967, pp. 85–106.

25. Elton, E. J. and Gruber, M. J. Estimating the dependence structure of share prices – implications for portfolio selection models', *Journal of Finance* **28**(5), 1973.

26. Roll, R. 'A critique of the asset pricing theories tests', *Journal of Financial Economics* **4**, 1977, pp. 129–76.

27. Jensen, M. C. 'Tests of capital market theory and implications of the evidence', printed in Bicksler, J. L. (ed.) *Handbook of Financial Economics*, North-Holland, 1979.
    Jensen, M. C. 'Capital markets: theory and evidence', *Bell Journal of Economics and Management Science* **3**(2), Autumn 1972, pp. 357–98.
28. Jensen, M. C. 'Tests of capital market theory', in Bicksler, J. L. (ed.) *Handbook of Financial Economics*, North-Holland, 1979.
29. King, B. F. 'Market and industry factors in stock price behaviour', *Journal of Business* **39**(1), part 2, January 1966.
    Blume, M. E. 'On the assessment of risk', *Journal of Finance* **26**(1), March 1971, pp. 1–10.
30. Jensen, M. C. 'Risk, the pricing of capital assets, and the evaluation of investment portfolios', *Journal of Business* **42**(2), April 1969, pp. 167–247.
31. Sharpe, W. F. 'Mutual fund performance', *Journal of Business* **39**(1), part 2, January 1966, pp. 119–38.
    Treynor, J. L. 'How to rate management of investment funds', *Harvard Business Review* **43**(1), January/February 1965, pp. 63–75.
32. Firth, M. 'Unit trusts: performance and prospects', *Management Decision* (3), 1978.
33. Black, F., Jensen, M. C. and Scholes, M. 'The capital asset pricing model: some empirical tests', printed in Jensen, M. C. (ed.) *Studies in the Theory of Capital Markets*, Praeger, New York, 1972.
34. Fama, E. F. and Macbeth, J. C. 'Risk, return, and equilibrium: empirical tests', *Journal of Political Economy* **81**(3), May/June 1973, pp. 607–36.
35. Black, F. 'Capital market equilibrium with restricted borrowing', *Journal of Business* **45**(3), July 1972, pp. 444–55.
36. Brennan, M. J. 'Capital market equilibrium with divergent borrowing and lending rates', *Journal of Financial and Quantitative Analysis* **6**(5), December 1971, pp. 1197–205.
37. Roll, R. 'A critique of the asset pricing theory's tests', *Journal of Financial Economics* **4**, 1977, pp. 129–76.
    Ross, S. A. 'The current status of the capital asset pricing model', *Journal of Finance* **33**(3), June 1978, pp. 885–901.
    Fama, E. F. *Foundations of Finance*, Basil Blackwell, Oxford, 1977, chapter 9.
38. Ross, S. A. 'The current status of the capital asset pricing model', *Journal of Finance* **33**(3), June 1978, pp. 885–901.
    Ross, S. A. 'The arbitrage theory of capital asset pricing', *Journal of Economic Theory* **13**(3), December 1976, pp. 341–60.
39. King, B. F. 'Market and industry factors in stock price behaviour', *Journal of Business* **39**(1), part 2, January 1966.
40. Roll, R. and Ross, S. A. 'An empirical investigation of the arbitrage pricing theory', *Journal of Finance* **35**(5), December 1980, pp. 1073–103.
    Reinganum, M. R. 'The arbitrage pricing theory: some empirical results', *Journal of Finance* **36**(2), May 1981, pp. 313–21.
    For an attempt to rehabilitate Jensen's study of mutual fund performance in an arbitrage framework using a one-factor model, see: Peasnell, K. V., Skerrat, L. C. L. and Taylor, P. A. 'An arbitrage rationale for tests of mutual fund performance', *Journal of Business Finance and Accounting* **6**(3), Autumn 1979, pp. 373–400.
41. See for example: Elton, E. J. and Gruber, M. J. 'On the optimality of some multi-period portfolio selection criteria', *Journal of Business* **47**(2), April 1974.

154   *Theories of Market Valuation*

Fama, E. F. 'Multi-period consumption investment decisions', *American Economic Review* **60**(1), March 1970, pp. 163–174.

Merton, R. 'Optimal consumption and portfolio rule in a continuous time model', *Journal of Economic Theory* **3**(4), December 1971, pp. 373–413.

Mossin, J. 'Optimal multi-period portfolio policies', *Journal of Business* **41**(2), April 1968, pp. 215–29.

Samuelson, P. 'Lifetime portfolio selection by dynamic stochastic programming', *Review of Economics and Statistics* **50**, August 1969, pp. 239–46.

42. This account draws on the excellent treatment by Elton, E. J. and Gruber, M. J. *Finance as Dynamic Process*, Prentice-Hall, Englewood Cliffs NJ, 1975, chapter 7.

43. Mossin, J. 'Optimal multi-period portfolio selection policies', *Journal of Business* **41**(2), April 1968, pp. 215–29.

44. Rubinstein, M. E. 'The strong case for the generalized logarithmic utility model as the premier model of financial markets', *Journal of Finance* **3**(2), May 1976, pp. 551–71.

45. See for example: Fama, E. F. 'Multi-period consumption investment decisions', *American Economic Review* **60**(1), March 1970, pp. 163–74.

Samuelson, P. 'Lifetime portfolio selection by dynamic stochastic programming', *Review of Economics and Statistics* **50**, August 1967, pp. 239–46.

Hakansson, N. 'Optimal investment and consumption strategies under risk for a class of utility functions', *Econometrica* **38**, September 1970, pp. 587–607.

46. Fama, E. F. 'Multi-period consumption investment decisions', *American Economic Review* **60**(1), March 1970, pp. 163–74.

47. Samuelson, P. 'Lifetime portfolio selection by dynamic stochastic programming', *Review of Economics and Statistics* **50**, August 1969, pp. 239–46.

48. Arrow, K. J. 'The role of securities in the optimum allocation of risk-bearing', *Review of Economic Studies* **31**, April 1964.

Debreu, G. *Theory of Value*, Wiley, New York, 1959.

Hirshliefer, J. 'Efficient allocation of capital in an uncertain world', *American Economic Review* **54**(3), May 1964, pp. 77–85.

Fisher, I. *The Theory of Interest*, Macmillan, New York, 1930.

Hirshleifer, J. 'Investment decision under uncertainty: choice theoretic approaches', *Quarterly Journal of Economics*, **79**(4), November 1965, pp. 509–36.

49. Hirshleifer, J. 'Investment decision under uncertainty: choice theoretic approaches', *Quarterly Journal of Economics*, **79**(4), November 1965, pp. 509–36. See also: Hirshleifer, J. *Investment, Interest and Capital*, Prentice-Hall, Englewood Cliffs NJ, 1970.

50. For a full account see: Hirshleifer, J. *Investment Interest and Capital*, Prentice-Hall, Englewood Cliffs NJ, 1970 part II, chapters 8, 9, 10 and 11.

51. Myers, S. C. 'A time-state preference model of security valuation', *Journal of Financial and Quantitative Analaysis* **3**(1), March 1968, pp. 1–33.

However, Hakansson has provided an interesting potential solution to the problem of incomplete markets with his concept of the 'superfund'. See: Hakansson, N. H. 'The superfund: efficient paths towards efficient capital markets in large and small countries', printed in Levy, H. and Sarnat, M. (eds) *Financial Decision Making under Uncertainty*, Academic Press, New York, 1977, pp. 165–201.

52. Hirshleifer, J. *Investment Interest and Capital*, Prentice-Hall, Englewood Cliffs NJ, 1970, p. 308.

53. Rubinstein, M. E. 'The fundamental theorem of parameter preference security valuation', *Journal of Financial and Quantitative Analysis* **8**(1), January 1973, pp. 61–9.

Kraus, A. and Litzenberger, R. H. 'Market equilibrium in a multiperiod state preference model with logarithmic utility', *Journal of Finance* **30**, 1975, pp. 1213–27.

Cass, D. and Stiglitz, J. E. 'The structure of investor preferences and asset returns, and separability in portfolio allocation: a contribution to the pure theory of mutual funds', *Journal of Economic Theory*, June 1970, pp. 122–60.

Ross, S. A. 'The arbitrage theory of capital asset pricing', *Journal of Economic Theory*, December 1976, pp. 341–60.

54. For a development of the linkage between portfolio theory and corporation finance see: Hamada, R. S. 'Portfolio analysis, market equilibrium, and corporation finance,' *Journal of Finance* **24**(1), March 1969, pp. 13–31.

55. Fama, E. F. 'Efficient capital markets: a review of theory and empirical work', *Journal of Finance* **25**(2), May 1970, pp. 383–417.

Fama, E. F. *Foundations of Finance*, Basil Blackwell, Oxford, 1977, chapter 7.

56. Cowles, A. and Jones, H. E. 'Some a posteriori probabilities in stockmarket action', *Econometrica* **5**, July 1937, pp. 280–94.

Kendall, M. G. 'The analysis of economic time series, part 1: prices', *Journal of the Royal Statistical Society* **96**, part 1, 1953, pp. 11–25.

57. Fama, E. F. 'The behaviour of stock market prices', *Journal of Business* **38**(1), 1965, pp. 34–105.

Granger, C. W. J. and Morgenstern, O. 'Spectral analysis of New York Stock Market prices', *Kyklos* **16**, 1963, pp. 1–27.

58. Samuelson, P. A. 'Proof that properly anticipated prices fluctuate randomly', *Industrial Management Review* **6**, Spring 1965, pp. 41–9.

59. Fama, E. F. *Foundations of Finance*, Basil Blackwell, Oxford, 1977, chapter 5.

60. ——— Ibid, chapter 1.

61. Fama, E. F. 'The behaviour of stock market prices' *Journal of Business* **38**(1), 1965, pp. 34–105.

62. Girmes, D. H. and Benjamin, A. E. 'Random walk hypothesis for 543 stocks and shares registered on the London Stock Exchange', *Journal of Business Finance and Accounting* **12**(1), Spring 1975, pp. 135–45.

63. Kemp, A. G. and Reid, G. C. 'The random walk hypothesis and the recent behaviour of equity prices in Britain', *Economica* **38**, 1971, pp. 28–51.

64. Alexander, S. S. 'Price movements in speculative markets: trends or random walks', *Industrial Management Review* **2**, May 1961, pp. 7–26.

Fama, E. F. and Blume, M. E. 'Filter rules and stock market trading', *Journal of Business* **39**(1), Part II, January 1966, pp. 226–41.

65. Dryden, M. M. 'A statistical study of UK share prices', *Scottish Journal of Political Economy*, November 1970, pp. 369–89.

66. Hess, P. J. and Reinganum, M. R. 'Efficient capital markets', reading in Bicksler, J. L. (ed.) *Handbook of Financial Economics*, North-Holland, 1979.

67. Fama, E. F., Fisher, L., Jensen, M. C. and Roll, R. 'The adjustment of stock prices to new information', *International Economic Review*, **10**, February 1969, pp. 1–28.

68. Ball, R. and Brown, P. 'An empirical evaluation of accounting income numbers', *Journal of Accounting Research* **6**, Autumn 1968, pp. 159–78.

69. Marsh, P. 'Equity rights issues and the efficiency of the UK Stock Market', *Journal of Finance* **34**(4), September 1979, pp. 839–62.
70. Jaffe, J. F. 'Special information and insider trading', *Journal of Business* **47**, July 1974, pp. 410–28.
    Lorie, J. H. and Neiderhoffer, V. 'Predictive and statistical properties of insider dealing', *Journal of Law and Economics*, April 1968, pp. 35–61.
71. Markowitz, H. M. *Portfolio Selection*, Wiley, New York, 1959.
72. Roy A. D. 'Safety-first and the holding of assets', *Econometrica* **20**, July 1952, pp. 431–49.
73. Baumol, W. J. 'An expected gain-confidence limit criterion for portfolio selection', *Management Science*, October 1973, pp. 174–82.
74. Hadar, J. and Russell, W. R. 'Rules for ordering uncertain prospects', *American Economic Review*, March 1969, pp. 25–34.
    Hanoch, G. and Levy, H. 'The efficiency analysis of choices involving risk', *Review of Economic Studies*, July 1969, pp. 335–46.
75. Philippatos, C. G. and Gressis, N. 'Conditions of equivalence among E-V, SSD, and EH portfolio selection criteria: the case for uniform, normal, and lognormal distributions', *Management Science* **21**(6), February 1975, pp. 617–25.
76. Nevertheless, considerable progress has been made. See: Markowitz, H. M. 'An algorithm for finding undominated portfolios', printed in Levy, H. and Sarnat, M. (eds) *Financial Decision Making under Uncertainty*, Academic Press, 1977, pp. 3–10.
77. Sharpe, W. F. 'Capital asset prices', *The Journal of Finance* **19**(3), September 1964, pp. 425–42.
78. Fama, E. F. *Foundations of Finance*, Basil Blackwell, Oxford, 1977, chapter 7.

CHAPTER 5

Option theory

The validity of a particular theory is a matter of its logical derivation from the assumptions which it makes. But its applicability to a given situation depends upon the extent to which its concepts actually reflect the forces operating in that situation.[1]

This is well illustrated in the recent development of option theory in financial economics, which has largely developed from work by Black and Scholes.[2] The theory has the singular merit of being built upon very limited and exceedingly realistic assumptions, and yet its applications are potentially so varied that it would not be an exaggeration to claim that it has implications for most financial decision areas.

5.1 THE NATURE OF AN OPTION

The discussion will be concerned first with options written on company shares, and their valuation, and then with more generally defined examples of options. An option contract, written against a company share, gives the holder the right to purchase or sell the share (depending on the type of option) at a specified price within a specified period. The option holder may choose whether or not to exercise this right, and this will depend on whether or not it is in his interest. A call option gives the right to buy at a prescribed price – the exercise price (or striking price as it is sometimes termed) – whereas a put option gives a right to sell at the exercise price. There are two broad classes of options: a European option, which can only be exercised on a specified date; and an American option, which can be exercised at any time during a specified period. Options markets are relatively recent innovations; a tremendously successful one was set up in Chicago in 1973, and within the last few years options markets on an initially modest scale have been set up in Amsterdam and London.

5.2 THE DETERMINATION OF OPTION VALUE AT THE EXPIRATION DATE

First consider the value of a European call and put at their expiration dates (ET). It can be seen that, at this point in time, the options have a worth equal to the maximum of the difference between the underlying share price, against which they are written, and the exercise price, or zero, as follows:

$$c = \max(s - EP, 0) \text{ and } p = \max(EP - s, 0) \qquad (5.1a)$$

where c is an European call option, p is an European put option, s is the share price, and EP is the exercise price.

The option does not have to be exercised by its holder; he will do so only if it is worth his while, and therefore the lowest return it can offer is zero (ignoring for the moment any price paid for the right to the option itself). Thus the value of the option is closely related to underlying movements in the share's price; if the share price moves above the exercise price, in the case of a call, or below it, for a put, then the option will be valuable, otherwise it is worthless. It follows that an option is a contingent claim, written against a separate asset, and that its value is relative; it depends fundamentally on the value of the underlying asset. It also follows that at any given point in time the total number of 'long' and 'short' positions in options must balance, since there is no point in writing an option unless it has a 'purchaser'. Furthermore, the value of the underlying asset is unlikely to be affected by the existence of an options market, as the relationship is one way, with the option value dependent on the asset value.[3] The options market can therefore be viewed as a zero sum game, all gains to the writer being matched by losses to the purchaser or vice versa. The relationship between the return on European puts and calls and the underlying share price can easily be shown as in figure 5.1.

It can readily be appreciated from this figure that the greatest loss that the holder of the option can suffer is the loss of the premium paid originally for the purchase of the option. The position of the writer of the option, on the other hand, is the mirror image or

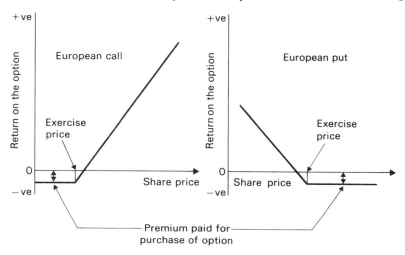

FIGURE 5.1 *The relationship between changes in the share price and the return to the holder of a European call and put option*

reverse of that of the holder (figure 5.2). If events run favourably, he merely stands to gain the premium, but if fortune is unkind he can make quite considerable losses.

5.3 SOME STRATEGIES FOR COMBINING INVESTMENT IN OPTIONS WITH SHARE PURCHASE

There is a very wide range of investment positions which can be achieved by writing or purchasing options and combining them either with purchase of the shares against which they are written, or with investment in a low-risk bank deposit or government security. An option writer is said to be writing 'naked' options if he writes options without prior possession of the appropriate stocks, whereas the writer of 'covered' options has appropriate possession. The inherent riskiness of these joint positions can be varied from being absolutely risk free to a position of extreme exposure. The ability to achieve a riskless or 'fully hedged' position is of crucial importance in the theoretical determination of option values, but some intermediate matters will be considered further to help prepare the ground before proceeding to option valuation formula.

If the investor merely purchased a share his return would vary

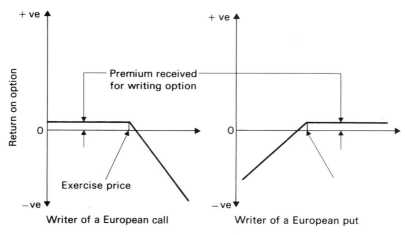

FIGURE 5.2 *The relationship between changes in the share price and the return to the writer of a European call and put option*

with the share price as shown in figure 5.3. Some of the more involved investment strategies can now be considered.

It was demonstrated by Stoll that a combination of investment in a European call, plus an investment in a 'riskless' asset equal to the present value of the exercise price, would yield an investment posi-

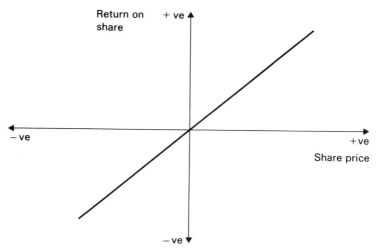

FIGURE 5.3 *The return available to the purchaser of a share*

tion identical to that available from purchasing a put on the same stock, plus the stock itself (assuming identical exercise prices).[4] Formally:

$$c + EP\, e^{-RFt} = p + s \tag{5.2}$$

where e^{-RFt} is the appropriate exponential discount rate (assuming continuous time), RF is the risk-free rate if the asset is considered riskless, and the other symbols are as before.

As this is not immediately obvious an illustrated numerical example will help demonstrate the point. An exercise price of £1 will be assumed throughout. First consider the LHS of (5.2). The purchaser of a call receives a premium for any rise in the share price above $EP = £1$ after paying EP from his funds, equal to the exact amount required, which has been arbitrarily assumed to be invested in a riskless asset. If the share price falls below EP his call is useless, but he still receives a return on his unused funds which has been set to yield a total value of EP on the date the option expires.

The RHS alternative combined position, of an investment in a put plus the share itself, runs as follows. If the share price rises above EP the put is worthless, but the share yields a premium equal to the excess of the share price over EP. If the share price falls below EP, the put comes into play and the investor is guaranteed the sale of his share at $EP = £1$. Thus the two positions are identical. This can be shown diagramatically as in figure 5.4.

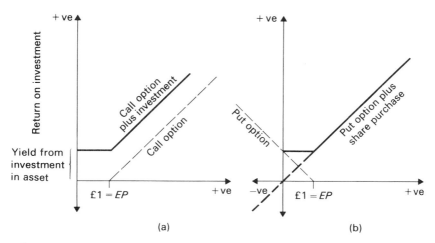

FIGURE 5.4 *The equivalence of (a) investing in a call plus the appropriate amount in a safe asset and (b) investing in a put plus the share*

This result is reassuring in that it demonstrates the 'completeness' of options markets. If puts were not available it would be possible to 'manufacture' them by adopting the appropriate position of investing in a call plus a safe asset.

5.4   RESTRICTIONS ON THE VALUATION OF CALL OPTIONS ON THE BASIS OF STOCHASTIC DOMINANCE

Merton extended the type of approach considered in section 5.3 to determine relative call option valuation on the basis of stochastic dominance.[5] His results are further enhanced in that they involve no assumptions with respect to the nature of the probability distribution of the return-generating process. (It will be seen in section 5.6 that this is one of the few assumptions required in the Black–Scholes valuation model.) The argument is couched in terms of state preference theory. One asset dominates another if, over some period, it offers a return equal to that available on the other across all states, but in addition if in one or more states it offers a higher return. Just a few of Merton's results will be considered (for a more extensive review, see Smith's account).[6]

In the analysis which follows, C is an American call and $T = ET - t$ is the time until expiration of the option.

It can be appreciated from reconsideration of (5.1a) that both European and American calls must have a positive price since the very lowest return they can offer is zero. That is, the following hold:

European call: $c(s, T; EP) \geq 0$

American call: $C(s, T; EP) \geq 0$
$\qquad\qquad\qquad\qquad\qquad\qquad\qquad\qquad\qquad\qquad\qquad$ (5.3)

Consider the case of identical American and European calls. The American call must have a value greater than, or at least as great as, that of the European call, since it offers everything that the European call offers plus the possibility of earlier conversion. In this earlier conversion period there will exist some states of the world in which the exercise price is below the share value, and therefore:

$$C(s, T; EP) \geq c(s, T; EP). \qquad (5.4)$$

By similar logic, two American calls which are identical except in their maturity, or time until expiration, must be so valued that the one with longer maturity has a value equal to or greater than the one with shorter maturity. Therefore if $T_1 > T_2$:

$$C(s, T_1; EP) \geq C(s, T_2; EP). \qquad (5.5)$$

Investment in a share must be at least as valuable as a perpetual call with an expiration date at $ET = \infty$ and a zero exercise price, $EP = 0$.

$$s \geq C(s, \ T = \infty \ ; \ 0). \tag{5.6}$$

The share could be more valuable because of attached voting rights, divided payments etc. This relationship can be turned round to state that, if the complication of dividend payments is ignored, a perpetual call option on a share which does not pay dividends must be worth the same value as the share. It is known from (5.1a) that at expiration the option, if it has a value, is worth the difference between the share value and the exercise price EP, but if the period to expiration is infinitely long, the present value of the future exercise price, $EP \, e^{-RFT}$ (where $T = \infty$), is zero. Therefore

$$C(s, \ T = \infty \ ; \ EP) = s, \tag{5.7}$$

as it is already known from (5.6) that the call cannot be more valuable than the share. Boundaries have now been set on the valuation of call options which will be useful in appreciating the construction of option valuation models, and which are shown in figure 5.5.

In figure 5.5 the line AB relates the value of the option directly to the value of the share on which it is written. Expression (5.7) showed

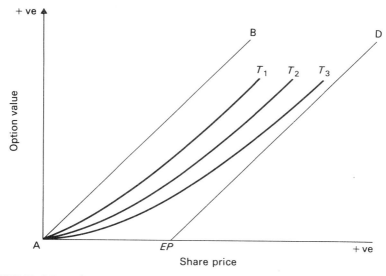

FIGURE 5.5 *The restrictions on the value of a call option in terms of the share price*

that with an infinite time to expiration, the option cannot be more valuable than the share, so AB sets the upper bound on the call option's value. The line *EP–D* sets the lower bound, since at the expiration date the value of the option cannot be greater than the difference between the share price and exercise price. Strictly speaking the exercise price should be expressed in present value terms, $EP\,e^{-RFT}$. This will be equivalent to EP at $T = 0$, but for positive values of T will shift to the left. Thus the lines joining A to T_i ($i = 1$, 2, 3, ...) show the values of options with some time left to their expiration date: $T > 0$, with $T_1 > T_2 > T_3$. The value of these options will asymptotically approach the line $\text{Max}[0, s - EP\,e^{-RFT}]$, and the greater the value of T the more valuable the option.

5.5   A RISKLESS HEDGE

In the treatment of the achievement of a riskless hedged position via combinations of share purchase and the writing of options, the approach followed will be that developed variously by Sharpe, Rubinstein, Rendleman and Bartter amongst others.[7] The treatment will begin by considering a simple example of a two-state world with two periods – the present or period 0, and period 1 when the return on our investment will be realized. The two states are distinguished by the fact that the value of the share under consideration will rise above its current value, should state 1 occur, and fall below this reference point should state 2 occur. The following notation will be employed:

Current share price in current state: $s_{0,0}$
Share price in period 1 state 1: $s_{1,1}$
Share price in period 1 state 2: $s_{1,2}$
The value of a call option in state
   1 at exercise date: $c_{1,1}$
The value of a call option in state
   2 at exercise date: $c_{1,2}$
Relative proportion of the amount of
   a hedged portfolio placed in options
   to the amount placed in a share: x.

It is desired to construct a portfolio consisting of positions in the share and in options that will guarantee a certain return whatever state occurs. If the above notation is employed and the assumption is made that the relative position required in options for a riskless hedge is denoted by x, the following identity is obtained:

$$s_{1,1} + xc_{1,1} = s_{1,2} + xc_{12}. \tag{5.8}$$

This holds by definition. By manipulation of terms:

$$x(c_{1,1} - c_{1,2}) = s_{1,2} - s_{1,1}$$

$$\therefore \quad x = \frac{s_{1,2} - s_{1,1}}{c_{1,1} - c_{1,2}}. \tag{5.9}$$

This shows the riskless hedge proportions as a function of the period 1 share and option values, and a negative value of x would indicate a short position in the options. This can be illustrated by the following numerical example. Assume that:

$s_{0,0} = 50\text{p}$	$EP = 70\text{p}$
$s_{1,1} = 100\text{p}$	$c_{1,1} = 30$ (to the holder)
$s_{1,2} = 50\text{p}$	$c_{1,2} = 0$ (to the holder).

The substitution of these values in (5.9) gives

$$x = \frac{50 - 100}{30 - 0} = -\frac{5}{3}.$$

This indicates that, to achieve a fully hedged position, five call options should be written (short in options) for every three shares purchased (long position in shares). A similar result could be achieved by going long in options and short in shares. Given the figures, what returns would result in period 1 in the two states?

Period 1 position if state 1 occurs

Value of shares	Value of options	Total return
$3 \times 100\text{p} = 300\text{p}$	$5 \times -30 = -150$	150p

Period 1 position if state 2 occurs

Value of shares	Value of options	Total return
$3 \times 50\text{p} = 150\text{p}$	$5 \times 0 = 0$	150

This is exactly required, as the same return is achieved whatever state occurs. Black and Scholes made their breakthrough in the determination of option pricing by utilizing the fact that the return from the hedged position is certain.[8] This being the case, it should offer a return equal to the riskless rate, and this therefore implies a solution to the option problem. Each 'unit' of funds invested in the hedged portfolio at time $t = 0$ should earn the riskless rate RF, which implies the following relation:

$$[s_{0,0} + (x \times \text{premium})](1 + RF) = s_{1,1} + xc_{1,1}$$

$$s_{1,2} + xc_{1,2}. \qquad (5.10)$$

By using (5.10) the value of the premium in the example can be determined, given an assumption of the value of the risk-free rate, which will be assumed to be 10 per cent. Using the numbers previously adopted:

$$\left[50\text{p} + \left(\frac{-5}{3} \times \text{premium} \right) \right](1.1) = 100\text{p} + \frac{-5}{3}(30\text{p})$$

$$\therefore \quad \tfrac{5}{3} \text{ premium} = 4.5\text{p}$$

$$\therefore \quad \text{premium} = 2.7\text{p}.$$

This means that 2.7p should be received for each option sold. The implied relation is that the equity or capital employed should earn a return of 1.1 per cent; the risk-free rate. It is known that writing $\tfrac{5}{3}$ call options for each share invested in guarantees a return of 1.1 per cent or a value of 50p for the terminal holding. As the current amount of equity at stake is the current value (period 0) of the share, minus what is received in premiums for selling the call, the current equity at stake is $50\text{p} - (\tfrac{5}{3} \times 2.7\text{p}) = 45.5\text{p}$; a holding in period 1 worth 50p is guaranteed, so the return is

$$\frac{50 - 45.5}{45.5} + 1 = 1.1\%.$$

The essential mechanisms of option valuation have now been covered, but in a very simplistic two-state world. However, this world does provide an approach to the more realistic model considered in the next section.

5.6   THE BLACK–SCHOLES CALL OPTION PRICING MODEL

Black and Scholes built their call option pricing model on the basis of the following assumptions:

(1) No transaction costs or taxes.
(2) There is a fixed short-term interest rate, and it is possible to borrow any fraction of the price of a security at this rate.
(3) The options considered are European and so they are only exercisable at maturity.
(4) The stock pay no dividends.

(5) There are no imperfections in the market or restrictions on selling short, in the case of either options or stock.
(6) The distribution of potential stock prices at the end of any finite time period is log-normal. This is consistent with stock prices following a random walk in continuous time. The variance of the rate of return on the stock is constant.[9]

The approach developed by Merton referred to in section 5.4 had set limits to the valuation of options without any assumptions about the distribution of returns, but the generality of the approach, though remarkably robust, does not produce finite solutions. The major additional assumptions required to produce a determinate pricing model are remarkably few. It can be seen from the list that those imposed by Black and Scholes are the existence of a perfect market and a log-normal distribution of returns. The familiar caveats with respect to investor preferences and the nature of their utility functions are noticeably absent.

The argument proceeds on lines similar to those discussed in the previous section and basically involves the investor maintaining a continuous hedge to eliminate risk. The previous notation is maintained: c is option price, s is share price and t is time. Then the value of the option can be expressed as a function of time and the share price: $c(s, t)$. Then, suggest Black and Scholes, the number of call options to be written against each share held is given by the reciprocal of the partial derivative of the value of the call option, with respect to the share price and time. The hedge ratio should be set to $1/\partial c(s, t)$. This perhaps can be appreciated intuitively by consideration of figure 5.6, which could crudely be interpreted as an enlarged section of one of the lines AT_i in figure 5.5.

Suppose the share price is 12p, as at point D in figure 5.6, and in the next very small interval of time it is going to move to either point A or point B. The gradient of the line $\partial c(s)$ is 1/2 and therefore the hedge ratio should be $1/\partial c(s) = 2$. Therefore two call options should be written for every share held. For example, if the share rose 2p in value there would be a loss of 1p on each of the options sold short, and therefore the overall position would be unchanged; this would also be the case for a 2p fall in share price. However this is a very rough and ready exposition, as mere persual of figure 5.5 shows that time to expiration will affect option value, and so the line AB would be moving to the right with the passage of time and its gradient would be changing. This means that the hedge ratio holds for very small slices of time and very small price changes, and therefore should be continuously adjusted.

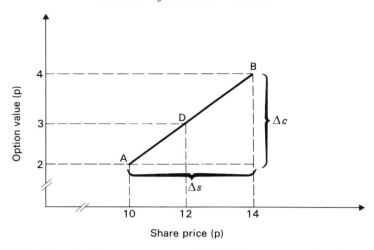

FIGURE 5.6   *Crude representation of the hedge ratio ignoring time effects*

The hedged position involves a ratio of one share long and $1/\partial c(s, t)$ options short. The equity of the investor involved in this is therefore:

$$s - \frac{c}{\partial c(s, t)}. \tag{5.11}$$

The change in value of the investor's equity over a very short instant of time is:

$$\Delta s - \frac{\Delta c}{\partial c(s, t)}. \tag{5.12}$$

The assumptions made about the distribution of returns means that the change in value of the call, Δc, can be expanded by stochastic calculus (see appendix 5.1). This gives:

$$\Delta c = dc = \frac{\partial c}{\partial s} \, ds + \frac{\partial c}{\partial t} \, dt + \frac{1}{2} \frac{\partial^2 c}{\partial s^2} \, \sigma^2 s^2 \, dt \tag{5.13}$$

Where σ^2 is the variance rate of the return on the stock. Substituting (5.13) into (5.12) gives (writing ds for Δs);

$$ds - \frac{\partial s}{\partial c} \left(\frac{\partial c}{\partial s} \, ds + \frac{\partial c}{\partial t} \, dt + \frac{1}{2} \frac{\partial^2 c}{\partial s^2} \, \sigma^2 s^2 \, dt \right). \tag{5.14}$$

NB: $\partial s/\partial c$ has been written for $1/\partial c(s, t)$.

The first two terms in (5.14) cancel out and the remainder is a change in value of the equity, or the hedged portfolio, equal to:

$$- \frac{\partial s}{\partial c} \, dt \left(\frac{\partial c}{\partial t} + \frac{1}{2} \frac{\partial^2 c}{\partial s^2} \, \sigma^2 s^2 \right). \tag{5.15}$$

Expression (5.15) which shows the change in value of the investor's equity, or his hedged portfolio, has become riskless. The only stochastic term in (5.14) was the change in the share price ds, but the hedged portfolio is so constructed that the first two terms in (5.14) cancel out, thus removing the stochastic term. Let dHP be (5.15) which represents the change in value of the hedged portfolio, and HP be the value of the investor's equity, or the hedged portfolio, as represented in (5.11). It follows that if the market is in equilibrium, the return offered must equal the risk-free rate:

$$\frac{dHP}{HP} = RF \, dt. \tag{5.16}$$

The values from (5.15) and (5.11) can then be substituted into (5.16):

$$RF \, dt = \left(\frac{\partial c}{s \, \partial c - c \, \partial s} \right) \left(- \frac{\partial s}{\partial c} \, dt \right) \left(\frac{\partial c}{\partial t} + \frac{1}{2} \frac{\partial^2 c}{\partial s^2} \, \sigma^2 s^2 \right)$$

which simplifies to a differential equation of the form:

$$\frac{\partial c}{\partial t} = cRF - sRF \frac{\partial c}{\partial s} - \frac{1}{2} \frac{\partial^2 c}{\partial s^2} \, \sigma^2 s^2. \tag{5.17}$$

It is known from the discussion in section 5.4 that, at the date of the expiration of the option ET, the option is worth the maximum of the difference between the share price and the exercise price EP or zero. Expression (5.1a) can be rewritten as:

$$c(s, ET) = \max(s - EP, 0). \tag{5.1b}$$

Black and Scholes then solved the differential equation in (5.17), subject to the boundary conditions of (5.1b), by transforming it into the physics heat exchange equation which has a known solution. Their solution is:

$$c(s, t) = sN(d_1) - EP \, e^{-RF(T)} N(d_2) \tag{5.18}$$

where $T = ET - t$ and

$$d_1 = \frac{\ln \dfrac{s}{EP} + (RF + \frac{1}{2}\sigma^2)T}{\sigma\sqrt{T}}$$

$$d_2 = \frac{\ln \dfrac{s}{EP} + (RF - \frac{1}{2}\sigma^2)T}{\sigma\sqrt{T}} = d_1 - \sigma\sqrt{T}.$$

The solution involves just five variables: the share price, the exercise price, the risk-free rate, the length of time until expiration of the option, and the variance of the rate of return on the share. The first four variables are all directly observable, and only the variance needs to be estimated, usually from historical data. The value of the option is positively related to increases in the share price, the time to maturity and the risk-free rate (since both reduce the present value of the exercise price), and to an increase in the variance. This is because an increase in the variance means there is an increased probability of high share values; as the distribution is assumed to be log-normal there is also an increased probability of low share values, but this does not matter as the option has a bounded lower value of zero. There is a negative relation with the exercise price, since an increase in the exercise price will decrease the option value. In (5.18) $N(d_i)$ stands for the cumulative normal density function. Black and Scholes point out that the hedge ratio $\partial c/\partial s$, which is obtained from (5.18), is:

$$\frac{\partial c}{\partial s} = N(d_1). \tag{5.19}$$

Furthermore, the ratio $[s(\partial c/\partial s)]/c$ will always be greater than one, as can be seen from inspection of (5.18) and (5.19). This implies that the relative return on the option will always be greater than the underlying return on the share, and thus the option has greater volatility.

The application of the Black–Scholes formula is quite straightforward. Suppose that $s = 40$, $EP = 45$, $T = 0.25$ (three months or a quarter of a year), $RF = 0.10$ (10 per cent continuously compounded), and $\sigma = 0.30$ (the standard deviation of the continuously compounded annual rate of return on the share is 30 per cent). Most of these variables are readily available, and an estimate of the standard deviation of the rate of return can be obtained from a risk measurement service (such as that offered by the London Business School).

The substitution of these numbers in (5.18) gives an indication of d_1 and d_2, as follows:

$$d_1 = \{\ln(40/45) + [0.10 + 0.5(0.30)^2]0.25\}/0.30\sqrt{0.25}$$
$$d_2 = \{\ln(40/45) + [0.10 - 0.5(0.30)^2]0.25\}/0.30\sqrt{0.25}.$$

These give values of $d_1 = -0.5435$ and $d_2 = -0.6936$. $N(d_1)$ and $N(d_2)$ can then be obtained from a table indicating areas under a standard normal distribution, as shown in table 5.1. (This only gives the areas under one tail; to obtain the negative values, the value is looked up, ignoring the sign, and the reading subtracted from 0.5.) This yields a value of $N(d_1) = 0.2946$ and $N(d_2) = 0.2451$.

Returning to (5.18) and substituting in all the required values yields:

$$c = 40(0.2946) - 45(e^{-0.025})(0.2451)$$
$$= 12.768 - 45(0.9753106)(0.2451)$$
$$\therefore \quad c = 1.027 \text{ pence}$$

(assuming all the prices are in pence). Thus the use of the formula is simple given the assumption that the stock does not pay any dividends.

An intuitive interpretation of the Black–Scholes option pricing formula has been suggested by Smith.[10] He suggests that the equilibrium value of a call option is considered, at its expiration, in a world characterized by complete certainty. In these conditions:

$$c_{ET} = s_{ET} - EP \tag{5.20}$$

which is the familiar pricing condition. In a world of certainty there is only one equilibrium rate of return, which will be denoted r. Given this relation:

$$s_{ET} = s\,e^{rT}.$$

The share price at ET must equal the share price T periods previously, compounded at rate r. Therefore the call option value, prior to its expiration date, can be expressed as:

$$c = e^{-rT}(s\,e^{rT} - EP)$$
$$\therefore \quad c = s - EP\,e^{-rT}. \tag{5.21}$$

The only difference between (5.21) and the standard Black–Scholes

TABLE 5.1   *Areas under the standard normal distribution function* $\int_0^z f(z)\,dz$

z	0.00	0.01	0.02	0.03	0.04	0.05	0.06	0.07	0.08	0.09
0.0	0.0000	0.0040	0.0080	0.0120	0.0160	0.0199	0.0239	0.0279	0.0319	0.0359
0.1	0.0398	0.0438	0.0478	0.0517	0.0557	0.0596	0.0636	0.0675	0.0714	0.0753
0.2	0.0793	0.0832	0.0871	0.0910	0.0948	0.0987	0.1026	0.1064	0.1103	0.1141
0.3	0.1179	0.1217	0.1255	0.1293	0.1331	0.1368	0.1406	0.1443	0.1480	0.1517
0.4	0.1554	0.1591	0.1628	0.1664	0.1700	0.1736	0.1772	0.1808	0.1844	0.1879
0.5	0.1915	0.1950	0.1985	0.2019	0.2054	0.2088	0.2123	0.2157	0.2190	0.2224
0.6	0.2257	0.2291	0.2324	0.2357	0.2389	0.2422	0.2454	0.2486	0.2517	0.2549
0.7	0.2580	0.2611	0.2642	0.2673	0.2704	0.2734	0.2764	0.2794	0.2823	0.2852
0.8	0.2881	0.2910	0.2939	0.2967	0.2995	0.3023	0.3051	0.3078	0.3106	0.3133
0.9	0.3159	0.3186	0.3212	0.3238	0.3264	0.3289	0.3315	0.3340	0.3365	0.3389
1.0	0.3413	0.3438	0.3461	0.3485	0.3508	0.3531	0.3554	0.3577	0.3599	0.3621
1.1	0.3643	0.3665	0.3686	0.3708	0.3729	0.3749	0.3770	0.3790	0.3810	0.3830
1.2	0.3849	0.3869	0.3888	0.3907	0.3925	0.3944	0.3962	0.3980	0.3997	0.4015
1.3	0.4032	0.4049	0.4066	0.4082	0.4099	0.4115	0.4131	0.4147	0.4162	0.4177
1.4	0.4192	0.4207	0.4222	0.4236	0.4251	0.4265	0.4279	0.4292	0.4306	0.4319
1.5	0.4332	0.4345	0.4357	0.4370	0.4382	0.4394	0.4406	0.4418	0.4429	0.4441
1.6	0.4452	0.4463	0.4474	0.4484	0.4495	0.4505	0.4515	0.4525	0.4535	0.4545
1.7	0.4554	0.4564	0.4573	0.4582	0.4591	0.4599	0.4608	0.4616	0.4625	0.4633
1.8	0.4641	0.4649	0.4656	0.4664	0.4671	0.4678	0.4686	0.4693	0.4699	0.4706
1.9	0.4713	0.4719	0.4726	0.4732	0.4738	0.4744	0.4750	0.4756	0.4761	0.4767
2.0	0.4772	0.4778	0.4783	0.4788	0.4793	0.4798	0.4803	0.4808	0.4812	0.4817
2.1	0.4821	0.4826	0.4830	0.4834	0.4838	0.4842	0.4846	0.4850	0.4854	0.4857
2.2	0.4861	0.4864	0.4868	0.4871	0.4875	0.4878	0.4881	0.4884	0.4887	0.4890
2.3	0.4893	0.4896	0.4898	0.4901	0.4904	0.4906	0.4909	0.4911	0.4913	0.4916
2.4	0.4918	0.4920	0.4922	0.4925	0.4927	0.4929	0.4931	0.4932	0.4934	0.4936
2.5	0.4938	0.4940	0.4941	0.4943	0.4945	0.4946	0.4948	0.4949	0.4951	0.4952
2.6	0.4953	0.4955	0.4956	0.4957	0.4959	0.4960	0.4961	0.4962	0.4963	0.4964
2.7	0.4965	0.4966	0.4967	0.4968	0.4969	0.4970	0.4971	0.4972	0.4973	0.4974
2.8	0.4974	0.4975	0.4976	0.4977	0.4977	0.4978	0.4979	0.4979	0.4980	0.4981
2.9	0.4981	0.4982	0.4982	0.4982	0.4984	0.4984	0.4985	0.4985	0.4986	0.4986
3.0	0.4987	0.4987	0.4987	0.4988	0.4988	0.4989	0.4989	0.4989	0.4990	0.4990

formulation is the omission of the two $N(d_i)$ terms, the cumulative standard normal terms. These can be interpreted as probability factors reflecting the uncertainty about the terminal share price.

5.7   EARLIER OPTION VALUATION MODELS

Some of the significant earlier work on option pricing (prior to that of Black and Scholes) was done by Sprenkle, Samuelson, and Boness.[11] Of these three, the Boness model probably came the closest to solving the option valuation problem, a decade prior to the emergence of the eventual solution. Boness made the following assumptions:

(1) Capital markets are in equilibrium, and therefore shares in the same risk class have the same expected return.
(2) Investors have linear expected utility of wealth functions; in effect they are risk neutral.
(3) The distribution of expected share price changes is stationary log-normal.
(4) The variance of returns is proportional to time.

Boness develops his model in terms of the expected expiration value of the option. Galai's exposition of the model will be followed here.[12] The expected value of the share at the expiration date is equal to the current price, compounded at an expected rate of return appropriate to its risk class, weighted by the expected value of the portion of the probability distribution representing the share price being above the exercise price EP, as follows:

$$E(s_{ET}) = s \, e^{kT} \, \frac{N(d_1)}{N(d_2)} \tag{5.22}$$

where $N(d_i)$ are the cumulative normal density functions, corresponding to those employed by Black and Scholes, as shown in (5.18), with the crucial difference that whereas they employ the risk-free rate Boness employs k, the expected return appropriate to the share's risk class. It can be noted further that the straightforward probability of obtaining a future share price above the exercise price is given by $N(d_2)$. The expected value of the option at the expiration date is equal to the expected price of the share, minus the exercise price, all weighted by the overall probability that the share price will be above the exercise price. This is shown as follows:

$$E(c_{ET}) = \left[s \, e^{kT} \, \frac{N(d_1)}{N(d_2)} - EP \right] N(d_2). \tag{5.23}$$

Expression (5.23) gives the conditional expected value of the call at the expiration date, but if it is required in current terms, the current conditional expected present value of the call would be equal to (5.23) discounted at the appropriate rate, as follows:

$$E(c) = \left[s \, e^{kT} \, \frac{N(d_1)}{N(d_2)} - EP \right] N(d_2) e^{-kT}$$

$$\therefore \quad E(c) = sN(d_1) - EP \, e^{-kT} N(d_2) \tag{5.24}$$

where

$$N(d_1) = N\left[\frac{\ln \dfrac{s}{EP} + \left(k + \dfrac{\sigma^2}{2}\right)T}{\sigma\sqrt{T}}\right]$$

$$d_2 = d_1 - \sigma\sqrt{T}.$$

The model as shown in (5.24) is very similar to the Black–Scholes formulation given in (5.18), with the crucial difference being, as previously noted, the employment of k, the expected return appropriate to the share's risk class, rather than RF, the risk-free rate, as the discount rate. The employment of k as the discount rate has no economic justification, and it has already been noted that the option has a higher level of risk than the stock. Nevertheless, the model comes very close to the eventual solution.

5.8   THE VALUATION OF A EUROPEAN PUT

The value of a European put can be determined via the use of the identity met previously in (5.2). Manipulation of this yields;

$$p(s, t) = c(s, t) + EP\, e^{-RF(T)} - s. \tag{5.25}$$

Expression (5.18) is available for valuing a European call, $c(s, t)$, and substitution of this gives:

$$p(s, t) = sN(d_1) - EP\, e^{-RF(T)}N(d_2) + EP\, e^{-RF(T)} - s.$$

This expression can be further simplified, since $1 - N(d_i) = N(-d_i)$:

$$p(s, t) = -s[1 - N(d_1)] + EP\, e^{-RF(T)}[1 - N(d_2)]$$

$$\therefore \quad p(s, t) = -sN(-d_1) + EP\, e^{-RF(T)}N(-d_2)$$

$$\tag{5.26}$$

where

$$-N(d_1) = N\left[\frac{-\ln \dfrac{s}{EP} - \left(RF + \dfrac{\sigma^2}{2}\right)T}{\sigma\sqrt{T}}\right]$$

$$d_2 = d_1 - \sigma\sqrt{T}.$$

Once again this is an option valuation formula based on five variables, and examination of (5.26) will suggest their likely individual influences. The value of the put option will be negatively related to increases in the share price, since these will increase the probability that it will not be worth exercising at its expiration. Conversely it will be positively related to increases in the exercise price for reverse reasons. The effect of an increase in time to expiration is more complex and could be in either direction. A longer time to maturity decreases the present value of the exercise price, and therefore the proceeds from exercising the option. On the other hand with a longer time to maturity the dispersion of the share price at the expiration date is likely to increase, raising the value of the put option. The relative predominance of these two effects is likely to be governed by the proximity of the share and exercise price; the greater the proximity the more likely it is that the first effect will prevail. An increase in the variance will increase the value of the put, as there is an increased probability of very low share prices. Finally, an increase in interest rates will diminish the value of the option since the present value of the exercise price will be diminished. So far so good, but it must be remembered that throughout the analysis it has been assumed that the stock pays no dividends. What happens if this unrealistic assumption is dropped?

5.9 DIVIDENDS AND OPTION VALUATION

To assist in isolating the likely effect of dividend payments, Merton's comparison of an American and a European call on a stock without dividend payments will be reviewed first before the introduction of the complication of these payments.[13] Without dividend payments an American call is worth either zero or the difference between the share price and the present value of the exercise price:

$$C(s, t) \geq [\max 0, s - EP\ e^{-RF(T)}] \qquad (5.1c)$$

but if it is exercised prior to maturity it is worth at least the maximum of $[0, s - EP]$. Therefore, as $EP > EP\ e^{-RF(T)}$, it would be better to sell the option rather than exercise it before maturity. Thus, American calls on non-dividend paying stocks will never be exercised before maturity, and therefore they will have the same value as European calls on the same stock.

Once the possibility of dividend payments is admitted the argument becomes indeterminate. The problem arises from the fact that when a share goes 'ex-dividend' the share price drops by the amount of the dividend, since a new purchaser at that stage forfeits the right to the current dividend. If the share is assumed to go ex-dividend at the expiration date, Merton's analysis can again be followed and the value of the American call at expiration denoted as:

$$C(s, t) = \max[0, s - (EP + d)e^{-RF(T)}] \qquad (5.27)$$

where d is the value of the dividend payment.

Merton suggests that in these circumstances it is no longer certain that his previous argument holds, and there is a positive probability that it may be worth while to exercise the option prior to expiration. Formally:

$$\max[0, s - EP] \gtreqless \max[0, s - (EP + d)e^{-RF(T)}] \qquad (5.28)$$

and there is no solution to this.

Merton has provided a modification to the Black–Scholes European call option valuation model by assuming that the stock pays continuous dividends, but this does seem a rather restrictive assumption, and it does not apply to American calls.[14] Roll has also provided a model for analysing unprotected American call options (with no covenants or restrictions on dividend payments), but has to assume that the dividend payments are known.[15] Thus, the problem of dividend payments remains a contentious issue.

5.10 PROBLEMS WITH AMERICAN PUTS

Merton demonstrated that the value of an American put must be at least as great as the value of a European put.[16] Formally:

$$P(s, t) \geq p(s, t). \qquad (5.29)$$

This follows because the American put offers everything that the European put does, plus the right of premature exercise. Furthermore, there is a positive probability that the American put will be exercised prematurely. Consider the case where the share price drops far below the exercise price. If it falls close enough to zero, it will be better to exercise prior to maturity and reinvest the proceeds in riskless assets, rather than wait until maturity and receive only the discounted present value of the exercise price. Given the existence of these complications no one, as yet, has succeeded in exactly valuing an American put.

5.11 EXTENSIONS AND MODIFICATION OF THE BLACK–SCHOLES MODEL

The original option valuation model has proved amenable to exceedingly rapid extension and generalization. It has been suggested that the original assumption that the share price follows a geometric Brownian process (that is, log-normal and follows a continuous Itô process) is unrealistic. This is because new information affecting the share price is likely to arrive at discontinuous intervals and from time to time may have very significant effects. This means that the share price adjustment to this new information may display sharp, discontinuous leaps. The implications of the share price following this 'Poisson driven' process have been examined by Cox, Ross, and Merton.[17] In general if the risk of the jump taking place is specific to the particular company's shares, it is unsystematic (in the sense of portfolio theory considered in chapter 4) and can therefore be diversified away. If this is the case the resultant pricing model will be analogous to that of Black and Scholes.[18] Indeed, Cox, Ross, and Rubinstein have extended the two-state approach to option pricing (a very simplistic version of which was considered in section 5.5), in discrete time, via application of the binomial theorem.[19] They show that options can be priced on the basis of arbitrage considerations. This is possible as long as there exists a portfolio of other assets which completely duplicates the returns available on the option in every possible state of nature. Whereas Black and Scholes began with the assumptions of continuous time and a log-normal distribution of share prices, the above approach is more general and contains the Black–Scholes model as a limiting case. It also encompasses the previously mentioned continuous jump process.

The link between arbitrage considerations, option pricing, and the pricing of any risky asset is most clearly demonstrated by Rubinstein.[20] He provides a general approach to the valuation of uncertain income streams which is consistent with both the existence of equilibrium in financial markets and rational, risk-averse investor behaviour. By building upon state preference foundations he develops a generalized pricing model which, given the appropriate assumptions, is consistent with CAPM (both discrete and continuous time versions), the existence of an unbiased term structure of interest rates, and a discrete time version of the Black–Scholes model. (The demonstration of these links is beyond the scope of this text, but for an intuitive representation of them see figure 4.17).

Other work has been done on adapting the option pricing model to real-world imperfections. Ingersoll has done work on the implications of the differential rates of taxation on capital gains and income.[21]

Thus, the general impression derived from work done so far is that the basic option pricing model is remarkably robust. Even more surprising is the growing number of financial decision areas for which it has potential implications, some of which are reviewed in the next section.

5.12 SOME POTENTIAL APPLICATIONS OF OPTION PRICING THEORY

Implications of option pricing theory for investment policy

In their original paper on option theory Black and Scholes suggested a reconciliation of their option pricing model and the capital asset pricing model along the following lines. The capital asset pricing model (section 4.13) shows that, given the appropriate assumptions, the return on any share is a linear function of its beta coefficient. The return on a share could be defined as the increment in value of the share over the original value ds/s, and the return on the option can likewise be defined as dc/c. If we take an infinitely small slice of time (that is, $dt \to 0$) we know from stochastic calculus and (5.13) that

$$dc = \frac{\partial c}{\partial s}\, ds.$$

This implies the following relationship between the beta of the share and the beta of the option:

$$\beta_c = \left[\frac{s(\partial c/\partial s)}{c} \right] \beta_s \qquad (5.30)$$

where β_c is the beta coefficient of the option, and β_s is the beta coefficient of the share.

Black and Scholes suggest that the term in brackets [ ] in (5.30) could be viewed as η_c, the elasticity of the option price in relation to the share price (where the elasticity measures the ratio of very small percentage changes in option value to percentage changes in the share value, holding t constant).[22] This being the case, they then demonstrate that the option pricing formula can be derived in a capital asset pricing framework. Galai and Masulis build upon this approach to investigate its implications for the investment policy of a geared or 'leveraged' company.[23]

Consider a firm financed by one class of debt and equity. The debt B is discount debt; it offers no interest payments but is issued at a discount, and redeemed at par after the elapse of T periods. There are covenants attached to the debt forbidding the payment of any dividends whilst it is outstanding. If, after T periods, the value of the firm is sufficient, the debt is redeemed at par and any excess value of the firm is payed to the shareholders as a liquidating dividend. Under these admittedly artificial conditions the shareholders could be viewed as possessing a call option, written against the overall value of the firm, with the exercise price the par value of the debt. In effect:

$$S = V N(d_1) - B\, e^{-RF(T)} N(d_2) \tag{5.31}$$

where S is the value of the equity, V is the value of the firm, B is the par value of the debt,

$$N(d_1) = N \left[\frac{\ln \dfrac{V}{B} + \left(RF + \dfrac{\sigma^2}{2} \right) T}{\sigma \sqrt{T}} \right],$$

and

$$d_2 = d_1 - \sigma \sqrt{T}.$$

For the analysis to be strictly valid, it has been assumed that the conditions are appropriate for both the option pricing model and the 'instantaneous' form of the capital asset pricing to hold. Under these rigorous conditions changes in the relative value of the share capital and the value of the debt, assuming the value of the firm is constant, would not worry investors, as they would hold the market portfolio and would therefore have an interest in both the equity and the debt. (The effects of these wealth transference effects are considered again in the next section.) However, if this assumption is modified and it is assumed that such potential transfers can be important, then some very interesting potential implications follow. Galai and Masulis demonstrate that in these circumstances an investment decision or a merger which increase the variance of the firm's returns will increase the value of the equity at the expense of the debt. This follows from the properties of call options discussed in section 5.6 whereby increases in the variance of returns increase the value of a call. Conversely conglomerate mergers, which reduce risk, benefit debt-holders at the expense of the equity interest. Furthermore, any changes in the scale of the firm, unless they are financed by equi-proportionate changes in the debt and equity, will involve these redistributional effects; however, this is leading on to financial policy implications, which are considered in the next section.

For the individual investor, one of the most startling implications of the marriage of these two branches of financial theory is the finding that the instantaneous beta of the equity in a geared company will be far from stable. This is best appreciated via substitution of the appropriate symbols into (5.30), which showed the relation between option beta and that of the stock against which it is written. This yields:

$$\beta_s = \left(\frac{V}{S} \frac{\partial S}{\partial V} \right) \beta_V \qquad (5.32)$$

where β_s is the beta coefficient of the equity of a geared company, and β_V is the beta coefficient of the company. This means that the equity beta will be a function of all the relevant variables in the option pricing model: the face value of the debt, the period to maturity, the risk free rate, the value of the firm, and the variance of the firm's returns.

This also reinforces the doubts that have been expressed about the validity of tests of the CAPM (section 4.15), and the evidence about the stability of beta coefficients is rather undermined.

Financial decision implications of option theory

The analysis can obviously be employed via manipulation of (5.31) to price both the debt and the equity of a geared company. The variables affecting the value of the debt will be the overall value of the firm, the face value of the debt, the period to its redemption, the risk-free rate, and the variance of the firm's returns. An increase in the value of the firm, or an increase in the redemption value of the debt (if possible), would increase the value of the debt. This makes intuitive sense since these changes would respectively increase either the sucurity of the debt or the size of the debt-holder's claim against the firm's assets. On the other hand, an increase in the term of the debt, the risk-free rate, or the variance of the firm's returns would increase the value of the equity and decrease the value of the debt. These wealth transference effects between a firm's security holders reinforce the importance of the 'me first' rules (discussed in chapter 8). They also provide a rationale for the typical restrictions or covenants attached to debt in order to prevent the occurrence of these problems; following the lead given by Black and Scholes, a number of authorities, including Black and Cox, have examined the problem in an option theory framework.[24] More realistically, a debt instrument with fixed interest payments can be regarded as a compound option, and work has been done on both this and on pricing convertible debt.[25] Merton has extended the applications of option theory to providing an explanation of the risk structure of interest rates and to the pricing of insurance.[26] Smith has analysed the pricing of warrants, rights issues, and underwriting contracts in an option theory framework.[27]

This list is far from exhaustive. Brief consideration of the fact that all these developments have taken place in less than a decade shows the incredibly rich potential of option theory, which will doubtlessly produce many more exciting developments in the next few years. Before the conclusion, some of the results of empirical tests of option theory will be briefly considered.

5.13 EMPIRICAL TESTS OF OPTION THEORY

Black and Scholes applied various tests of their option pricing model.[28] They computed the variance of returns on the relevant shares from historical time series, and then formed hedged portfolios, which they rebalanced daily, as a proxy for continuous adjustment. They compared the actual option price quoted on the options market with the theoretical price predicted from their model. Their results were consistent with the market underpricing high-variance securities and their model overpricing them. The results were improved by calculating cotemporaneously the variance on the stock during the life of the option, and then employing the calculated variance in their model, but this adjustment obviously is not feasible in practice. They also tested the options market for efficiency, and found it to be consistent with efficiency in the sense that no excess returns could be generated once transactions costs had been included.

Another line of approach was adopted by Latane and Rendleman who utilized the fact that, given the price of an option, it is possible to calculate the implied standard deviation of returns.[29] They calculated and performed various tests on the weighted average implied standard deviations. Their main finding that the implied standard deviations are unstable led them to suggest that the model does not fully capture the process determining option prices in the market.

This line of approach has been extended by Macbeth and Merville.[30] A priori, it would be expected that if the Black–Scholes option pricing model held, options of different maturity, written against the same stock, should yield the same prediction of stock variance, given the market price of the option. They found that the differences between the predicted variance rates appeared to be systematically related to the difference between the share and exercise price of the option, and the time left until maturity of the option. On the basis of their own findings, and previous evidence, they assumed that 'at the money' options (where $s \simeq EP \ e^{-RF(T)}$) with at least ninety days to expiration are correctly priced by the model. Using this benchmark they found that the Black–Scholes predicted prices were less than market prices for 'in the money' options (where $s > EP \ e^{-RF(T)}$), and were more than the market prices for 'out of the money' options (where $s < EP \ e^{-RF(T)}$). Furthermore, the prediction error appeared to be systematic and decreased as a function of reduction of time to expiration, until a period of ninety days to expiration was reached, whereupon the relation ceased to be systematic. They suggest, however, that the whole basis of this type of empirical approach may be confounded should the stochastic process generating share prices have a non-stationary variance rate.

Finally, work done by Gould and Galai, on the spreads between option dealers' put and call prices, does find some evidence contrary to the hypothesis of option market efficiency.[31] Thus, the results of empirical work on the Black–Scholes pricing model seem rather mixed, but the field is very new, and empirical testing has hardly got off the ground yet. Though not exact, the model certainly provides a good working approximation to the pricing of option contracts, and on the theoretical level it seems beyond doubt that the model, and its subsequent extensions and applications, mark a breakthrough of fundamental importance.

TEST QUESTIONS

1. A call option is written against a share with a current price of 50p. The option, redeemable in the next period, has an exercise price of 50p. Suppose that you know that there are only two possible states of the world in the next period and that in these two states the share will have a value of either 40p in state 1 or 75p in state 2. You also know that the risk-free rate is 10 per cent.

Calculate the following:
(a) The value of the option to its holder in states 1 and 2.
(b) The hedge ratio.
(c) The price or premium paid to the writer of the call option.
2. What is the value, according to the Black–Scholes formula, of a European call option with an exercise price of 50p and three months to run to maturity, written on a share with a current price of 60p, and a standard deviation of its rate of return of 25 per cent, given that the risk-free rate is 10 per cent per annum?
3. Use the Black–Scholes formula to calculate the value of a European put, given that the price of the underlying share is 40p, the exercise price 40p, the standard deviation of its rate of return 30 per cent, the risk-free rate 10 per cent per annum, and there are three months to maturity.
4. Suppose that a company has a value of £1.5 million and is financed by a mixture of discount debt and equity. The discount debt has a face value of £1 million redeemable in five years' time. The standard deviation of the rate of return on the company's assets is 30 per cent and the risk-free rate is 10 per cent. The firm has a policy of not paying dividends. Given these assumptions use the option pricing model to calculate the following:
(a) The implied current values of the firm's debt and equity.
(b) Assume that fears of inflation cause the risk-free rate to rise to 20 per cent. What is the resultant change in value of the firm's debt and equity?
(c) Assume that the firm embarks on risky ventures which raise the standard deviation of the rate of return on its assets to 50 per cent. What is the effect on the value of its debt and equity?
5. Are the following investment policies risky, of low risk, or riskless?
(a) Buy a share.
(b) Buy a debenture.
(c) Write a call.
(d) Write a put.
(e) Purchase a share and write a call on the share.
(f) Purchase a share and buy a put on the share.
(g) Purchase a share, buy a put and sell a call on the share.
6. The following actions could be interpreted in terms of option theory. Classify them according to the type of option involved.
(a) You have entered into an agreement with an insurance company insuring your business premises against fire risk.

(b) A recent promotion qualifies you for a stock option scheme.
(c) The company in which you hold shares has recently borrowed £10 million in the form of a debenture issue.
(d) You are on the underwriting list of an issuing house and have agreed to underwrite a recent share issue.

APPENDIX 5.1

SOME IMPLICATIONS OF STOCHASTIC CALCULUS

The assumption made in obtaining the Black–Scholes call option pricing model is that the share price displays geometric Brownian motion (that is, it follows a log-normal distribution). The particular form of the distribution assumed means that the movement of the share price follows an Itô process (a continuous Markov process, where the process is determined, at most, by the most recent observation).[32] This means that the process can be differentiated by application of Itô's lemma. McKean suggests that differential and integral calculus based on Brownian motion could be considered similar to the normal calculus of smooth functions, except that if an attempt is made to differentiate a smooth function, say of the following Brownian path, then certain adjustments have to be made.[33]

If the call option price is examined and it is assumed to be a function of the share price (a stochastic variable) and time, then as a first move the quadratic approximation from the Taylor series expansion can be employed:

$$c(s + \Delta s, \, t + \Delta t) = c(s, \, t) + \frac{\partial c}{\partial t} \, \Delta t + \frac{\partial c}{\partial s} \, \Delta s + \frac{1}{2} \frac{\partial^2 c}{\partial s^2} \, (\Delta s)^2.$$

It follows that:

$$\Delta c = c(s + \Delta s, \, t + \Delta t) - c(s, \, t)$$

$$\therefore \quad \Delta c = \frac{\partial c}{\partial t} \, \Delta t + \frac{\partial c}{\partial s} \, \Delta s + \frac{1}{2} \frac{\partial^2 c}{\partial s^2} \, (\Delta s)^2. \tag{5.33}$$

In normal circumstances the third term on the RHS, with $(\Delta s)^2$, could be ignored. But this case concerns a stochastic variable following an Itô process, and in very short intervals of time, given the following adjustments, the quadratic approximation for differentiation will be exact. In an Itô process where by definition

$$ds = \mu(s, \, t)dt + \sigma(s, \, t)dZ$$

it can be shown that the following approximation holds:

$(\Delta s)^2 \simeq \sigma^2 s^2 \Delta t.$

Substitution of this in (5.33) and regrouping terms yields:

$$\Delta c = \mathrm{d}c = \frac{\partial c}{\partial s} \, \mathrm{d}s + \left(\frac{\partial c}{\partial t} + \frac{1}{2} \frac{\partial^2 c}{\partial s^2} \, \sigma^2 s^2 \right) \mathrm{d}t. \tag{5.34}$$

Expression (5.34) is the result employed in expression (5.13) in developing the Black–Scholes option pricing model. It must be appreciated that the derivation of (5.34) given is not a 'proof' in any sense of the word, but merely an attempt to indicate some of the complications involved in stochastic calculus. For a relatively straightforward introduction to the complexities of stochastic calculus see Smith.[34]

NOTES AND REFERENCES

1. Robbins, L. *An Essay on the Nature and Significance of Economic Science*, Macmillan, London, 1933, p. 116.
2. Black, F. and Scholes, M. 'The pricing of options and corporate liabilities', *Journal of Political Economy* **81**(3), May–June 1973, pp. 637–54.
3. The existence of an options market might improve the efficiency of information processing in the stock market and help to reduce 'spreads' in the market for the stock, if the insiders trading on information tend to deal on the options market rather than the stock market. This may be the most effective means of trading on information in that it is possible to achieve a higher percentage return for a given outlay in the options market than by directly dealing in the stock, and it may be easier to take a short position. For a fuller discussion of this see: Black, F. 'Fact and fantasy in the use of options', *Financial Analysts Journal* **31**(4), July–August 1975, pp. 36–72.
4. Stoll, H. R. 'The relationship between put and call option prices', *Journal of Finance* **24**(4), December 1969, pp. 802–24.
5. Merton, R. C. 'The theory of rational option pricing', *Bell Journal of Economics and Management Science* **4**(1), Spring 1973, pp. 141–83.
6. Perhaps the two most comprehensive review articles are: Smith, C. W. Jr. 'Option pricing: a review', *Journal of Financial Economics* **3**(1–2), January–March 1976, pp. 3–51; and: Smith, C. W. Jr. 'Applications of option pricing analysis', a reading in Bicksler, J. (ed.) *Handbook of Financial Economics*, North-Holland, Amsterdam, 1979.
   Another excellent survey is provided by: Cox, J. C. and Ross, S. A. 'A survey of some new results in option pricing theory', *Journal of Finance* **31**(2), May 1976, pp. 383–402.
7. Sharpe, W. F. *Investments*, Prentice-Hall, Englewood Cliffs NJ, 1978, pp. 366–73.
   Rubinstein, M. assisted by Cox, J. C. *Options Markets*, Prentice-Hall, Englewood Cliffs NJ, 1979.

Rendleman, R. J. and Bartter, B. J. 'Two-state option pricing', *Journal of Finance* **34**(5), December 1979, pp. 1093–110.

8. Black, F. and Scholes, M. 'The pricing of options and corporate liabilities', *Journal of Political Economy* **81**(3), May–June 1973, pp. 637–54.
9. Ibid.
10. Smith, C. W. Jr. 'Option pricing: a review', *Journal of Financial Economics*, **3**(1–2), January–March 1976, pp. 3–51; p. 23, footnote 20.
11. Sprenkle, C. M. 'Warrant prices as indicators of expectations', reading in Cootner, P. (ed.) *The Random Character of Stock Market Prices*, MIT Press, Cambridge, Mass., 1974, pp. 412–74.
    Samuelson, P. 'Rational theory of warrant pricing', *Industrial Management Review* **6**(2), Spring 1965, pp. 13–69.
    Boness, A. J. 'Elements of a theory of stock option value', *Journal of Political Economy* **72**(2), April 1964, pp. 163–75.
12. For a full comparison of the two models see: Galai, D. 'On the Boness and Black–Scholes models for valuation of call options', *Journal of Financial and Quantitative Analysis*, 1978, pp. 15–28.
13. Merton, R. C. 'The theory of rational option pricing', *Bell Journal of Economics and Management Science* **4**(1), Spring 1973, pp. 141–83.
14. Ibid.
15. Roll, R. 'An analytical valuation formula for unprotected American call options on stocks with known dividends', *Journal of Financial Economics* **5**(2), November 1977, pp. 251–8.
16. Merton, R. C. 'The theory of rational option pricing', *Bell Journal of Economics and Management Science* **4**(1), Spring 1973, pp. 141–83.
17. Cox, J. C. and Ross, S. A. 'The valuation of options for alternative stochastic processes', *Journal of Financial Economics* **3**(1–2), January–March 1976, pp. 145–66.
    Merton, R. C. 'Option pricing when underlying stock returns are discontinuous', *Journal of Financial Economics* **3**(1–2), January–March 1976, pp. 125–44.
18. For a survey see: Cox, J. C. and Ross, S. A. 'A survey of some new results in option pricing theory', *Journal of Finance* **31**(2), May 1976, pp. 383–402.
19. Cox, J. C., Ross, S. A. and Rubinstein, M. E. 'Option pricing: a simplified approach', *Journal of Financial Economics* **7**(3), September, pp. 229–63.
20. Rubinstein, M. E. 'The valuation of uncertain income streams and the pricing of options', *The Bell Journal of Economics* **7**(2), Autumn 1976, pp. 407–425.
21. Ingersoll, J. 'A theoretical and empirical investigation of dual purpose funds: an application of contingent claims analysis', *Journal of Financial Economics* **3**(1–2), January–March, 1976.
22. Black, F. and Scholes, M. 'The pricing of options and corporate liabilities', *Journal of Political Economy* **81**(3), May–June 1973, pp. 637–54; p. 645.
23. Galai, D. and Masulis, R. W. 'The option pricing model and the risk factor of the stock', *Journal of Financial Economics* **3**(1–2), January–March 1976, pp. 53–81.
24. Black, F. and Scholes, M. 'The pricing of options and corporate liabilities', *Journal of Political Economy* **81**(3), May–June 1973, pp. 637–54.
    Black, F. and Cox, J. C. 'Valuing corporate securities: some effects of bond indenture provisions', *Journal of Finance* **31**, pp. 351–67.
25. Geske, R. 'The valuation of corporate liabilities as compound options', *Journal of Financial and Quantitative Analysis* **12**, 1977, pp. 541–52.

Ingersoll, J. 'A contingent claims valuation of convertible securities', *Journal of Financial Economics* **4**, 1977, pp. 289–322.
26. Merton, R. C. 'On the pricing of corporate debt: the risk structure of interest rates', *Journal of Finance* **29**, 1974, pp. 449–70.
Merton, R. C. 'An analytical derivation of the cost of deposit insurance and loan guarantees: an application of modern option pricing theory', *Journal of Banking and Finance* **1**, 1977, pp. 5–12.
27. Smith, C. W. Jr. 'Alternative methods for raising capital: rights versus under-written offerings', *Journal of Financial Economics* **5**, 1977, pp. 273–307.
28. Black, F. and Scholes, M. 'The valuation of option contracts and tests of market efficency' *Journal of Finance* **27**(2), May 1972, pp. 339–417.
29. Latane, H. A. and Rendleman, R. J. Jr. 'Standard deviations of stock price ratios implied in option prices', *Journal of Finance* **31**(2), May 1976, pp. 369–81.
30. Macbeth, J. D. and Merville, L. J. 'An empirical examination of the Black–Scholes call option pricing model', *Journal of Finance* **34**(5), December 1979, pp. 1173–86.
31. Gould, J. P. and Galai, D. 'Transaction costs and the relationship between put and call prices', *Journal of Financial Economics* **1**, 1974, pp. 105–29.
32. Itô, K. and McKean, H. P. Jr. *Diffusion Processes and their Sample Paths*, Academic Press, New York, 1964.
33. See the account given by: McKean, H. P. Jr. *Stochastic Integrals*, Academic Press, New York, 1969.
34. This account draws from the excellent introduction given by C. W. Smith in the appendix to 'Applications of option pricing analysis', reading in Bicksler, J. L. (ed.) *Handbook of Financial Economics*, North-Holland, Amsterdam, 1979, pp. 109–20.

PART III

The Theory of Corporate Investment and Financial Policy

CHAPTER 6

The investment decision

The essential principle is that estimates should be based on the change in the company's total earnings and total costs that will result from the proposed investment. Only incremental effects are relevant, but all increments, including costs and revenues in other parts of the firm, must be brought into the estimate.[1]

Joel Dean's statement sets the boundaries of the problem and the basic principle to be applied in the investment decision. This chapter will be concerned with the various conceptual difficulties which arise in trying to put his advice into practice, and in combining it with the decision criterion of value maximization first introduced in chapter 1. The analysis begins by assuming conditions of certainty, and is then extended to conditions of uncertainty.

Bicksler suggests that there are four aspects to a typical capital investment decision:

(1) Choosing the appropriate set of investment projects to be evaluated.
(2) Estimating the parameters associated with the projects over their respective lives.
(3) Determining the appropriate decision criterion for evaluating the merits of the respective projects, and
(4) Deciding how to apply it in practice.[2]

All of these aspects will be considered at various stages, though it must be admitted that the theory of finance cannot say much about the 'divination' of the most suitable set of projects. However, confidence remains that, in the 'world' of perfect capital markets first considered in chapter 1, shareholder interests are best served by value maximization, and a separation principle holds which means that investment decisions can be considered independently of financing decisions. It also follows that suitable investment appraisal techniques must involve a discounted cash flow approach, such as the previously considered net present value (*NPV*) and internal rate of return (*IRR*) methods ((1.8) and (1.9)).

6.1   THE CASE AGAINST 'TRADITIONAL' METHODS
OF INVESTMENT APPRAISAL

It follows that 'traditional' non-discounting techniques can be ruled out from the start. Of these, the 'payback' method is particularly popular, and involves the ranking of projects by the time they take to pay back their original cost. Fairly obvious theoretical criticisms can be levelled against this method. It does not take into account a project's full useful life, and therefore as it does not consider all the project's returns it may not fully reflect tax and capital allowance effects. It obviously ignores the time value of money since no discounting is involved. On the other hand economists tend to neglect the problems involved in the identification of the relevant set of

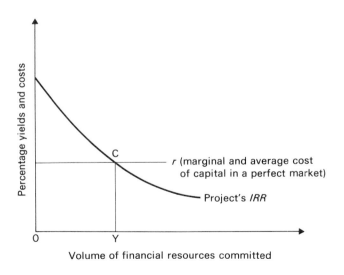

FIGURE 6.1 *Investment decision criteria and equation of marginal yields and costs*

projects to be evaluated and the likely shortage of full information about their respective returns over their entire life. The method may, in part, merely be favoured through the lack of full information.

This excuse cannot be granted to another traditional method – the 'accounting rate of return'. This takes the full accounting returns over the project's entire life, and then puts them over the project's cost to derive a rate of return, but in the process completely ignores the time value of money.

In the context of the 'ideal' conditions assumed in perfect markets both methods are logically indefensible. In the face of market imperfections and lack of information a stronger case might be made in their defence, particularly for the payback method. The extent to which this method might differ, under various conditions, from an 'economic' measure of project worth, has been investigated by Gordon, Weingartner, and Sarnat and Levy.[3] However, this line of approach will not be pursued; instead the emphasis will be on analyzing the extent of the usefulness of the economic-theory-based decision models.

6.2 THE CONSISTENCY OF THE *NPV* AND *IRR* METHODS WITH 'MARGINALISM'

Both the *NPV* and *IRR* methods are consistent with the economist's rule that the optimization of value involves the equation of yields at the margin. This is demonstrated in figure 6.1, in which the descending curve shows projects ranked by their *IRR*s. If a world of certainty and a perfect capital market are assumed the firm's marginal cost of capital is equal to its average cost of capital, which is also the pure rate of interest *r*. Projects would be taken on until the marginal project yield is equated to the marginal cost of capital (point C in figure 6.1). At this point the value of the firm will be maximized, and a total of OY funds will be committed. At point C, by definition, the marginal project will have an *NPV* of zero, and any movement beyond C will reduce the value of the firm, since it will involve the undertaking of 'unprofitable' projects.

Thus there is confidence that in straightforward circumstances where projects can be considered independently, both the *NPV* and *IRR* rules will lead to optimal investment decisions. In practice matters are rarely so straightforward, and some of the likely problem areas will now be considered.

6.3   PROBLEMS ASSOCIATED WITH THE USE OF *IRR*

In the previous section and in chapter 1 it was seen that in the case
of straightforward accept/reject investment decisions the *NPV* and
IRR rules are equivalent, but once some likely 'real-world' complications are introduced then problems arise in the use of *IRR*. Lorie
and Savage drew attention to the problem of potential ambiguity in
the case of *IRR* solution rates.[4] In their famous discussion of the
'pump' problem they noted that where there is more than one
change in sign of the net cash flow over a project's life, there could
well be more than one solution *IRR*.

A simple example of this type of problem is the evaluation of the
project with the cash flows shown in table 6.1. These rather arbitrary
figures could represent an open-cast mining or quarrying venture
which offers two years' returns, after the initial outlay, and then a
further outlay to restore the landscape to its original condition. To
keep matters simple it has been assumed that all cash flows take
place at year ends.

It can be seen from table 6.1 that in the case of this project there
are two *IRR* solutions – approximately 6 per cent and approximately 55 per cent. This is shown graphically in figure 6.2, which
plots the figures from table 6.1.

The problem can be more generally appreciated by considering
the nature of the mathematical solution to an *IRR* problem. If a
four-period cash flow project is taken, as in the example, then the
IRR problem involves finding R^* such that:

$$NCF_0 + \frac{NCF_1}{(1 + R^*)} + \frac{NCF_2}{(1 + R^*)^2} + \frac{NCF_3}{(1 + R^*)^3} = 0.$$

TABLE 6.1   *An investment project with dual IRR solutions*

Discount rate (%)	0	1	2	3	NPV
0	−800	1500	250	−1000	−50
6	−800	1415.1	222.5	−839.6	−2
10	−800	1363.6	206.6	−751.3	+18.9
30	−800	1153.8	147.9	−455.2	+46.9
55	−800	967.7	104.1	−268.5	+3.3
60	−800	937.5	97.66	−244.1	−8.94

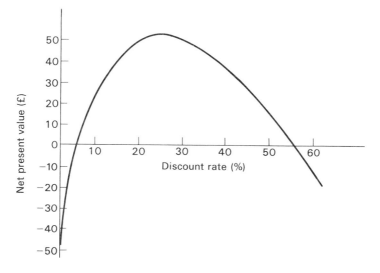

FIGURE 6.2   *A project with dual IRR solutions*

Cross multiplying by $(1 + R^*)^3$ yields:

$$NCF_0(1 + R^*)^3 + NCF_1(1 + R^*)^2$$

$$+ NCF_2(1 + R^*) + NCF_2 = 0. \qquad (6.1)$$

Expression (6.1) is a third-degree polynomial. In general finding the root or *IRR* solution to an investment problem involves solving a polynomial of degree equal to one less than the number of periods of cash flows. Furthermore, the roots could be positive, negative, or involve complex numbers. From an economic point of view, the concern need only be with positive roots or discount rates. In the most straightforward case of an investment problem which involves an initial outlay, a negative cash flow, followed by positive inflows, there will be only one positive root or *IRR* solution. This follows from Descartes's change of sign rule, which says that there can be as many positive roots as there are changes in the sign of the cash flow. In the example given in table 6.1 there were two changes in the sign of the cash flow, and hence two positive roots. The problem is one of how to make sense of multiple *IRR* solutions of the type shown in figure 6.2. The diagram suggests that in the cases where the firm's marginal cost of capital is between 6 per cent and 55 per cent, the project should be accepted as being profitable, but with any marginal costs of capital without those limits it should be rejected as being unprofitable.

If it is likely that a multiple-root problem exists it is sensible to drop the use of *IRR* and utilize *NPV*.

6.4   THE REINVESTMENT RATE

The *NPV* rule assumes that the internal reinvestment rate of the project's cash flows is equal to the discount rate employed – the firm's marginal cost of capital. This is integral to the mechanics of the method. Thus, any early positive cash flows are assumed to accrue interest at this rate. Of course this may be unrealistic in that the only practical options open to the firm for the reinvestment of the project's early cash flows may be a short-term deposit rate, which could be very different from its marginal cost of capital. The assumption does have the merit of consistency at least, and all projects under consideration at the same point in time will have the same assumed reinvestment rate, and the condition holds in a perfect capital market.

The *IRR* rule, on the other hand, assumes that all early positive cash flows are reinvested at the *IRR* solution rate. Thus, projects under consideration at the same point in time, but with different *IRR* solution rates, will be assumed automatically to have different reinvestment rates. This is surely an even more serious violation of reality. As a corollary of this, when it comes to the ranking of a group of projects, it may be found that the two methods give different rankings because of the different assumptions with respect to the reinvestment rate.

6.5   MUTUALLY EXCLUSIVE DECISIONS

Samuelson was one of the first to draw attention to the shortcomings of the *IRR* method.[5] These are particularly apparent in the case of two mutually exclusive investment decisions. As the *IRR* is simply a yield or rate of return it can take no account of differing project scales even when they have the same length of life; this case can be properly handled by *NPV*. The *IRR* can only be trusted in mutually exclusive decisions if the projects concerned have identical scales and project lives. To overcome the problem of different scales, given

TABLE 6.2 *Two mutually exclusive projects with differing length of life*

Year	0	1	2	3	NPV at 10% discount rate
Project A cash flows (£)	−100	65	65	—	£12.8
Project B cash flows (£)	−100	46	46	46	£14.38

equal lives, Merrett and Sykes suggested the use of an 'incremental' *IRR* which involves working out the *IRR* on the difference between the two projects' cash flows, period by period, and comparing this yield with market alternatives.[6]

In situations where mutually exclusive projects have both different scales and lives, both methods fall down. Suppose that a company is faced with the choice between the two mutually exclusive projects shown in table 6.2. Project B has the higher *NPV* yet project A looks intuitively more appealing since it recovers its cash more quickly. Straightforward application of the *NPV* rule will not resolve the dilemma since the projects have differing lengths of life and like is not being compared with like. They have to be translated on to a common basis. One approach is to put them both on to an annual equivalent basis via the use of the annuity formula introduced in chapter 1.

In this approach, it is required to know what would be the constant annual payment or periodic rent, over the life of the project, which when discounted at the test discount rate would give a present value of an annuity equivalent to the *NPV* of the project. From (1.6) the present value of an annuity is given by:

$$PV_a = \frac{A[1 - (1 + k)^{-n}]}{k}.$$

In the case of project A:

$$NPV_A = 12.8 = \frac{A[1 - (1.1)^{-2}]}{0.1} = A(1.7355)$$

$$\therefore \quad A(A) = £7.375.$$

And in the case of project B:

$$NPV_B = 14.38 = \frac{A[1 - (1.1)^{-3}]}{0.1} = A(2.487)$$

$$\therefore \quad A(B) = £5.78.$$

As the periodic rent or payment on an annuity over the life of project A at the test discount rate required to produce the project's *NPV* is greater than that required over the life of B, project A is to be preferred.

In the case of a number of mutually exclusive projects (perhaps they cannot all be taken on because of some constraint on available funds) with identical length of life, recourse can be made to the present value index (*PVI*). This involves ranking the projects according to their *PVI*, obtained by dividing the present value of all the cash inflows associated with a project by the present value of their outflows.

However, once restraints on funds begin to be considered then market imperfections are being introduced, since in a perfect market funds are always readily available. The introduction of market imperfections weakens the basis of the *NPV* rule, as was seen in chapter 1 when the implications of the existence of different borrowing and lending rates were considered. In the case of the existence of absolute limits on the amounts of funds available, a situation of capital rationing, straightforward application of the *NPV* rule is inappropriate and recourse has to be made to the mathematical programming techniques considered in the next section.

6.6   CAPITAL RATIONING AND THE USE OF MATHEMATICAL PROGRAMMING

Weingartner has been in the forefront of the development of the use of mathematical programming decision techniques in theoretical capital rationing situations, but he has also been very careful to point out some of the pitfalls of this area of the literature.[7] He draws a clear distinction between situations in which the restraint on funds is of the self-imposed, internal management policy variety, and those where it is supposed to be externally imposed by the capital market. There may be various reasons, of varying validity, for the existence of self-imposed constraints. A small, tightly controlled company might have an ownership which preferred retention of the existing control structure, and might be prepared to forgo more rapid, externally financed, growth in order to maintain it. This, in turn, suggests that in these situations decision models which assume an objective function of the maximization of the utility of multiperiod consumption, on the part of the ownership, may not be entirely valid.

The case for assuming that absolute limits on funding are externally imposed by the capital market seems even more dubious. Usually funds can be had at a price. The marginal cost of capital may vary considerably over time, or even perhaps be a function of the volume of funds raised in a given time period, but situations of 'strong' capital rationing are likely to be rare. At worst these are likely to be temporary phenomena.

Now that these strict reservations have been noted the type of model frequently employed will be briefly examined.[8] The following notation will be used:

c_{it} is the amount of funds required by the ith project in period t, where projects $i = 1, \ldots, n$ and time periods $t = 1, \ldots, T$.

p_i is the net present value of project i.

B_t is the constraint, or absolute amount of funds to be invested in period t.

x_i is an integer representing the proportion of project i taken on. It is usually constrained to equal 0 or 1; the project is either accepted or rejected.

The normal, unconstrained, maximization of net present value, capital budgeting decision model could be written as:

$$\max \sum_{i=1}^{n} p_i x_i. \tag{6.2}$$

But in a situation of capital rationing there are the added constraints on funds in each period. Thus (6.2) is maximized subject to:

$$\sum_{i=1}^{n} c_{it} x_i \leq B_t \quad (t = 1, \ldots, T)$$

$$x_i = 1 \quad \text{or} \quad 0 \quad (i = 1, \ldots, n).$$

In the constrained maximand form NPV is maximized but account is also taken of each project's use of limited funds and the fact that taking on one project may rule out others. The technique is logically consistent but requires, as a basic data input, estimates of the NPVs of all the projects concerned. If there is a market-determined marginal cost of capital which can be used as a discount rate for determining NPVs, then it seems unlikely that external capital rationing is present. On the other hand, the NPV rule itself has its theoretical origins, as has been seen, in perfect capital markets and the maximization of the utility of final consumption.[9] The use of this rule seems

logically inconsistent in the case of self-imposed constraints on funds
that run counter to its spirit. It was also seen in chapter 1 that in the
face of very weak constraints on funds in the form of different borrowing and lending rates, the separation theorem and the foundations of the *NPV* rule fell down. Thus, in situations of capital
rationing, both the use of the *NPV* rule and the choice of the appropriate discount rate to employ in determining project *NPV*s seems
very problematic. The actual programming technique is very powerful, but there remain serious doubts about the appropriate circumstances in which it can be applied as a decision tool, though in
circumstances where the constraints are managerial or technological
as opposed to financial it may be more justifiable.

6.7   CONCLUSIONS: INVESTMENT APPRAISAL UNDER CERTAINTY

The review of investment decision models under conditions of certainty has now been completed. The basic decision rules have been
derived and then tested under various types of market imperfection.
It has to be admitted that they have not coped particularly well with
market imperfections. In the next sections they will be developed to
accommodate the existence of uncertainty.

6.8   INVESTMENT APPRAISAL UNDER UNCERTAINTY; THE INDIVIDUAL RISKY PROJECT

The remaining sections of the chapter will be concerned with extending the investment decision models to conditions of uncertainty. The
reader will be relieved to discover that most of the relevant concepts
have already been introduced in either chapter 2 or chapter 4.
Nevertheless, applying them in an investment appraisal context has
its own particular difficulties. First the argument will concentrate on
the adjustments that can be made to an individual project's returns
to allow for the existence of uncertainty; it will then proceed to the
application of CAPM to capital budgeting, problems involved with
the market value rule, the complications involved where investment
and financing decisions are interrelated, the interaction of production and investment decisions, and finally the impact of inflation
on capital budgeting.

The use of certainty equivalents

The Lutzs were early advocators of the use of certainty equivalents for the purposes of risk adjustment.[10] In the case of discounting streams of returns the method could be applied in two different ways: it could be used to adjust either the numerator or the denominator of the return streams. If the numerator of the cash flows is adjusted the present value formula can be expressed as follows:

$$PV = \sum_{t=1}^{\infty} \frac{a_t \overline{NCF_t}}{(1 + RF)^t} \tag{6.3}$$

where a_t is the certainty equivalent adjustment for the net cash flow in period t, RF is the riskless rate of interest (applicable as the cash flow has been adjusted for risk), and NCF_t is the expected value of the net cash flow in period t.

Alternatively, the risky cash flows could be left as they are, and the denominator or discount rate could be inflated to adjust for the presence of risk. This gives:

$$PV = \sum_{t=1}^{\infty} \frac{\overline{NCF_t}}{(1 + k)^t} \tag{6.4}$$

where k is a discount rate appropriate for the riskiness of the stream of returns NCF_t.

The logic of the method is identical to that of the 'certain money equivalents' already met in chapter 3, but Robichek and Myers showed that the seductive simplicity of the adjustments masked a number of thorny theoretical issues.[11] They showed that as the method of inflating the discount rate involves only one adjustment for the effects of both time and risk – two logically distinct influences – it necessarily presupposes the nature of their interrelation. Their argument runs as follows. If CCF_t is an equivalent certain cash flow in period t, then:

$$\frac{CCF_t}{(1 + RF)^t} = \frac{a_t \overline{NCF_t}}{(1 + RF)^t} = \frac{\overline{NCF_t}}{(1 + k)^t}. \tag{6.5}$$

This holds by definition. Inspection of (6.5) shows that:

$$a_t = \frac{(1 + RF)^t}{(1 + k)^t}. \tag{6.6}$$

It follows that the adjustment for period $t + 1$ would be:

$$a_{t+1} = \frac{(1 + RF)^t(1 + RF)}{(1 + k)^t(1 + k)} = a_t \frac{(1 + RF)}{(1 + k)}. \tag{6.7}$$

This means that, as the risk-adjusted discount rate $k > RF$, a_t will not be equal to a_{t+1}, and typically $a_t > a_{t+1}$. This means that the use of a constant inflated discount rate as a means of adjusting for risk is strictly valid only when the riskiness of the streams is increasing over time. If the streams were regarded as having constant levels of risk, the discount rate employed would have to decline as a function of time.

Another way of viewing the problem is to consider it in terms of the resolution of uncertainty over time.[12] The use of a constant inflated discount rate implies that the more distant cash flows are the more risky, and also that uncertainty is resolved at a constant rate over time. This may or may not be appropriate. It will be seen in later sections of this chapter that analogous problems concerning the resolution of uncertainty over time arise in certain circumstances when the capital asset pricing model is applied to capital budgeting in a multiperiod context.

It is relatively straightforward to express certainty equivalents in a capital asset pricing model form. As CAPM is an equilibrium one-period pricing model, an initial simplifying assumption may be made that all the firm's existing activities and the new project under consideration have the same level of beta (as defined in chapter 4) or systematic risk.

By definition, the rate at which a cash flow is discounted, in a one-period context, determines the ratio of the value of the net cash flow to its present value, as follows:

$$(1 + k) = \frac{\overline{NCF}}{PV}.$$

But it is known that CAPM shows the equilibrium relationship between discount rates, or 'required rates of return', and levels of risk. Thus:

$$(1 + k) = 1 + RF + [E(R_M) - RF]\beta. \tag{6.8}$$

It follows that:

$$\frac{\overline{NCF}}{PV} = 1 + RF + \left\{ [E(R_M) - RF] \mathrm{cov}\left(\frac{\overline{NCF}}{PV}, R_M \right) \middle/ \sigma_M^2 \right\} \tag{6.9}$$

(by adoption of the appropriate definition of β).

Expression (6.9) can be simplified by writing λ for $[E(R_M) - RF]/\sigma_M^2$:

$$\frac{\overline{NCF}}{PV} = 1 + RF + \lambda \, \text{cov}\left(\frac{\overline{NCF}}{PV}, R_M\right).$$

Rearrangement of terms, plus the fact that PV is a constant which is uncorrelated with market returns, gives:

$$\frac{1}{PV}\left[\overline{NCF} - \lambda \, \text{cov}(\overline{NCF}, R_M)\right] = 1 + RF.$$

$$\therefore \quad PV = \frac{\overline{NCF} - \lambda \, \text{cov}(\overline{NCF}, R_M)}{1 + RF}. \tag{6.10}$$

Just to recap, RF is the risk-free rate of interest, PV is present value, $\overline{NCF}$ is the expected value of the risky cash flow, $E(R_M)$ is the expected return on the market portfolio, and $\text{cov}(\overline{NCF}, R_M)$ is the covariance of the risky cash flow with returns on the market portfolio.

Expression (6.10) shows the certainty equivalent adjustment in a CAPM form. The risky cash flow is reduced by the appropriate amount and then discounted at the risk-free rate; most important, the adjustment is determined by an equilibrium pricing model, CAPM. The risk-adjusted discount rate can be derived in similar fashion. It is already known that:

$$\frac{\overline{NCF}}{PV} = 1 + RF + \lambda \, \text{cov}\left(\frac{\overline{NCF}}{PV}, R_M\right).$$

$$\therefore \quad PV = \frac{\overline{NCF}}{\left[1 + RF + \lambda \, \text{cov}\left(\frac{\overline{NCF}}{PV}, R_M\right)\right]}. \tag{6.11}$$

Expression (6.11) shows how the discount rate is inflated in accordance with CAPM.

This adjustment also has the apparent attraction of being 'market determined' and therefore, under the appropriate circumstances, could be empirically derived by use of the market model as a proxy, rather than being a purely subjective adjustment. However, further consideration reminds us that its formal derivation depends on the existence of all the conditions required by CAPM – in effect, perfect capital markets, homogeneous expectations, and so forth. Furthermore, the model has only been considered under extremely restricted circumstances involving a firm whose projects have identical betas, and in a one-period context.

The problems of extending the model to the multiperiod context will be considered first. To be able to apply it in the multiperiod context, either it must be assumed that the relevant beta is constant over time, or an attempt must be made to estimate the appropriate betas. In chapter 4 some of the empirical work that has been done on assessing beta constancy was encountered, but in chapter 5 it was seen that the theoretical integration of CAPM and the option pricing model suggests that, in the typical case where a company has fixed interest borrowings, beta will not be constant. The problems of trying to estimate future betas seem formidable to say the least, but they will be returned to later.

On the other hand, the original assumption that all the firm's projects have the same beta is unnecessarily restrictive and can be dispensed with. It also leads on naturally to the consideration of the value additivity principle, which is the subject of the next section.

6.9   THE VALUE ADDITIVITY PRINCIPLE AGAIN

In certain circumstances, particularly in the case of the smaller quoted companies whose activities could be concentrated in serving one particular market, it might not be unrealistic to view its projects as having similar beta levels. On the other hand, in the case of the large conglomerate one of the *raisons d'être* of its operations is risk diversification, and therefore its various projects are likely to have differing levels of both systematic and unsystematic risk. If the assumptions are retained that the capital market is composed of rational, risk-averse investors who hold diversified portfolios, and that CAPM holds, then the firm can concentrate on the beta of each project under consideration rather than the firm's risk. This follows since all unsystematic risk has been diversified away from investors' portfolios and the only relevant risk is systematic risk. (Paradoxically, much of the logic behind the risk diversification justification for the activities of conglomerates is also undermined, but this is not of concern at present).[13] Under the perfect capital market conditions assumed, the value of the firm is simply the sum of the value of the streams of returns promised by all the projects which independently add up to that group of projects which make up the firm. This 'intuitive' explanation of the value additivity principle, first introduced in chapter 1, is shown again:

$$V = \sum_{i=1}^{n} P_i \tag{6.12}$$

where V is the value of the firm or corporation, and P_i is the value of the projects which make up the firm $(i = 1, \ldots, n)$.

The present value of all the individual projects which make up the firm will be calculated along the following lines:

$$P_i = \sum_{t=0}^{T} \overline{NCF_t} \left/ \left[1 + RF + \lambda \, \text{cov}\left(\overline{\frac{NCF_t}{PV_0}}, R_M \right) \right]^t \right. \tag{6.13}$$

where $\overline{NCF_t}/PV_0$ is a rate of return, implicit in the equilibrium relationship between an expected cash flow received in period t, NCF_t, and its present value, PV_0, produced by discounting at this appropriate rate. If different projects undertaken by the firm have different levels of risk, then this rate of return and the overall risk-adjusted discount rate will vary.

In effect (6.13) is a multiperiod version of (6.11) but assumes the existence of a flat term structure; the risk-free rate, RF, is assumed constant.[14] However, to assume that (6.13) holds it has to be assumed that a multiperiod version of CAPM holds, and this involves some very difficult issues which for the moment are ignored but which will be returned to later (see section 6.11). On the face of it, the value additivity rule is very reassuring, since it suggests that even when risk is introduced into the capital budgeting framework, in the context of perfect markets at least, present values can be simply added, and it reaffirms faith in the present value rule.

However, in the introduction of certainty equivalents and risk-adjusted discount rates, the treatment of their relation to CAPM, and the brief discussion of value additivity, the existence of perfect capital markets and their concomitant, perfect knowledge, have necessarily been assumed. Yet obviously, in practice, one of the major difficulties encountered in any investment appraisal exercise is estimation of the parameters of a project's future cash flows. In the next section are briefly considered some techniques which may be of assistance in meeting this problem.

6.10 ESTIMATING THE PARAMETERS OF A PROJECT'S RISKY CASH FLOWS

Hertz pointed out that the expected values of the probability distribution of net returns which is employed to summarize estimates of a project's profitability is dependent upon a number of underlying economic factors, all of which are uncertain.[15] As an example he cited the following potential influences on project returns under the general headings of market, investment, and cost analysis: size of market, sales price, market share and market growth rate, investment size and residual value, fixed and variable operating costs and project life. A probability distribution could be estimated for each of these factors. These probability distributions can then be combined in a large number of computer simulation trials to produce an overall probability distribution of project returns. The logical analysis involved in this procedure should sharpen and refine the management's estimation of project returns.

If a project involves sequential investment decisions, then decision trees can be utilized to generate a probability distribution of present values.[16] Hillier has utilized insights developed from portfolio theory to analyse those cases where a firm's project's cash flows can be assumed to be either perfectly serially correlated or perfectly independent, and provides formulae for estimating project risk.[17] Indeed, there have been attempts to apply portfolio theory directly at company level to the selection of groups of a company's projects, but if it is assumed that investors hold diversified portfolios then this is ruled out, since CAPM applies.

This concludes the very brief review of some techniques which may help in the estimation of a project's risk and return and leads back to one of the central theoretical problems of the chapter – the application of CAPM to capital budgeting problems in a multi-period context.

6.11   THE APPLICATION OF CAPM TO CAPITAL BUDGETING

In section 6.8 the application of CAPM to capital budgeting problems was introduced. In this section some of the more problematic issues associated with it will be examined in greater depth. The discussion which follows draws heavily on the work of Myers and Turnbull.[18] The crux of the problem is that in applying CAPM to corporate investment decisions a bridge has to be built between real and financial variables; this follows since a company's beta is determined in financial markets yet its underlying determinants lie in the sphere of the company's operating and investment decisions. The results of empirical work addressed to this problem are varied, though they do seem to support the common-sense notions that earnings' variability and cyclicality, together with financial leverage (see chapter 8), have a major impact.[19]

There is a considerable literature concerned with the application of CAPM to the valuation of assets in a multiperiod context.[20] Central to the problem is the fact that CAPM is essentially a one-period model (this type of problem was first encountered in the discussion of multiperiod portfolio theory in chapter 4). It is required to value the stream of uncertain returns $\widetilde{NCF}_t$ from a real asset or investment project for its working life over periods $t = 0, 1, 2, \ldots, T$. It follows that if CAPM holds, its value at time t, PV_t, is given by:

$$PV_t = [E(\widetilde{NCF}_{t+1} + \widetilde{PV}_{t+1} \mid IS_t^M)$$

$$- \lambda \operatorname{cov}(\widetilde{NCF}_{t+1} + \widetilde{PV}_{t+1}, \tilde{R}_{M_{t+1}})]/(1 + RF) \qquad (6.14)$$

where $E(\widetilde{NCF}_t)$ is the expected value of the probability distribution, written in place of the equivalent NCF_t, IS_t^M is the information sequence used in the market in setting prices at time t (as previously used in section 4.20), and the other notation is as before.

Expression (6.14) utilizes the certainty equivalent form of CAPM, which was first met in (6.10). All it says is that the value of the asset at t is determined by its expected price at $t + 1$, plus the cash stream earned over the period, reduced by the appropriate certainty equivalent adjustment, and then discounted at the risk-free rate. Again, a flat term structure is assumed – RF is constant. The expression also shows the 'recursive' nature of CAPM when applied in a multiperiod context (as considered in section 4.17). The asset's value or price at period t cannot be set without a probability distribution of the value at $t + 1$. As a further simplification, λ, the market price of risk (as defined in section 6.9) is also assumed constant over time.

Myers and Turnbull model the influence, discussed previously, of the cyclicality of earnings on beta by assuming that investors forecast future cash flows on the basis of current information, as follows:

$$\widetilde{NCF}_t = E(\widetilde{NCF}_t \mid IS_{t-1}^M)(1 - \tilde{\varepsilon}_t) \qquad (6.15)$$

where $\tilde{\varepsilon}_t$ is a random error term representing the difference between the forecast and the actual cash flow.[21] They assume that the disturbances represented in this term can be divided between those which are specific to the firm and those which relate to unanticipated factors affecting the entire economy. Formally:

$$\tilde{\varepsilon}_t = \alpha \tilde{I}_t - \tilde{z}_t \qquad (6.16)$$

where α is a constant associated with that part of the disturbance term which is directly related to changes in a general economic index, $\tilde{I}_t$ is a general economic index, subject to unanticipated changes, and $\tilde{z}_t$ is that part of the disturbance term which is purely related to the firm.

It is then assumed that the project's cash flows show no systematic growth trend, and that expectations are revised on the basis of an adaptive expectations model of the type:

$$E(\widetilde{NCF}_{t+1} \mid IS_t^M) = E(\widetilde{NCF}_t \mid IS_{t-1}^M)(1 - \eta \tilde{\varepsilon}_t) \tag{6.17}$$

where η is the elasticity of expectations (normally $0 \le n \le 1$).

Armed in this fashion, rather than worrying about asset beta, one can now switch attention to focus on that part of the cash stream which systematically covaries with the economic index I. A general valuation formula can now be derived, in recursive fashion, by beginning in period $T - 1$ and working backward to period t. Value at $T - 1$ is given by;

$$PV_{T-1} = E(\widetilde{NCF}_T \mid IS_{T-1}^M)(1 - \lambda\alpha \operatorname{cov}_{I, R_M})/(1 + RF) \tag{6.18}$$

where $\operatorname{cov}_{I, R_M}$ is the covariance of the economic index with the market portfolio (assumed constant). Part of the 'risk' or disturbance of the cash flows is linked to the market index by α, its systematic link to changes in the economic index I.

At $T - 2$, the value of the cash flow will depend on both the expected cash flow over the period and the expected price at the end of the period, as follows:

$$PV_{T-2} = [E(\widetilde{NCF}_{T-1} \mid IS_{T-2}^M)(1 - \lambda\alpha \operatorname{cov}_{I, R_M})/(1 + RF)]$$

$$+ [E(\widetilde{NCF}_{T-1} \mid IS_{T-2}^M)(1 - \lambda\eta\alpha \operatorname{cov}_{I, R_M})/(1 + RF)^2]. \tag{6.19}$$

In (6.19) the first term represents the cash flow over the next period and the second term the present value of the end of period price, PV_{T-1}. This price can be expressed in terms of the $\widetilde{NCF}_{T-1}$ rather than $\widetilde{NCF}_T$, because of the adaptive expectations mechanism; notice that η has entered the second term of (6.19), via the relationship between price and cash flows given in (6.18). By working backwards in this manner the price at the first period $t = 0$ can be obtained, and a general valuation formula is obtained as follows:

$$PV_0 = \frac{E(\widetilde{NCF}_1 \mid IS_0^M)(1 - \lambda\alpha \operatorname{cov}_{I, R_M})}{(1 + RF)} \sum_{t=0}^{T-1} \left(\frac{1 - \lambda\eta\alpha \operatorname{cov}_{I, R_M}}{1 + RF} \right)^t. \tag{6.20}$$

Expression (6.20) gives the formula which should be applied, under the conditions assumed by Myers and Turnbull, for evaluating investment projects according to CAPM in a multiperiod context. The expression shows, via the two separately discounted terms on the RHS, that there are two separate sources of risk in this model. One source is the risk associated with the actual size of the next period's cash flow, represented by the first discounted term in (6.20). The other, represented by the multidiscounted term, shows the risk associated with revision of expectations.

Expression (6.20) shows that, even in an extremely restricted model, the determination of beta in a multiperiod context is extremely complicated. As consolation, Myers and Turnbull suggest that calculations show that, where a project's one-period beta is known, discounting multi-period returns with it will not lead to serious biases. However, they have assumed, to get this far, that both the market price of risk, λ, and the risk-free rate, RF, are constant. This is very unlikely, but dropping these assumptions opens a veritable Pandora's box of difficulties.[22] Fama draws attention to the fact that the assumptions of the Sharpe–Lintner version of CAPM, with which we are concerned, rule out any uncertainty about the two market determined parameters mentioned previously.[23] If such uncertainty does exist, Merton has shown that there is an incentive for investors to use their portfolio decisions in one period to hedge against uncertainty about the market portfolio opportunities in the next.[24] If this happens the pricing process which emerges is not consistent with the Sharpe–Lintner version of CAPM.

6.12 PROBLEMS WITH THE MARKET VALUE RULE

This leads on to another troublesome area. In the application of CAPM for the determination of the 'hurdle rate' for the selection of viable capital budgeting proposals, it has been assumed that the objective on the part of the company's decision-makers is the maximization of the company's value. Unfortunately, it has been demonstrated that the investments selected according to this policy are not necessarily Pareto optimal, nor in the best interests of final shareholders (assuming continuous trading is taking place.[25] Baron provides a comprehensive review of this difficult area of the literature, which is beyond the scope of this text, though a crude idea of the difficulties can be given.[26] Again the problem revolves around the revision of expectations. If shareholders, instead of behaving as price-takers, behave strategically and take into account the potential effects of company investment decisions on market parameters, then they will not necessarily favour a policy of value maximization on the part of the company. There are various relatively arbitrary ways of avoiding this problem – for example, by assuming that each individual company is so small that its investment policy will have negligible effect.

At the moment it is probably no exaggeration to claim that there is no general theory of investment for the corporation under conditions of uncertainty. Value maximization holds under very restricted conditions and there are major problems concerning the revision of uncertainties. Once realistic imperfections are admitted into the model, like the fact that firms frequently have oligopolistic positions in their markets, then the whole edifice collapses.[27]

6.13 CIRCUMSTANCES IN WHICH THE INVESTMENT AND FINANCING DECISIONS MAY BE INTERRELATED

In the discussion so far it has been implicitly assumed that the investment decision and the financing decision can be separated (which is acceptable in perfect capital markets, as will be seen via Modigliani and Miller's arguments considered in chapter 8). Thus any potential difficulties associated with gearing or leverage have been ignored and in effect, the firm has been treated as if it were all equity financed. This section will examine more closely possible interaction between the investment and the financing decision.

Again the discussion draws heavily on the work of Myers who, in following the lead given by Modigliani and Miller, has developed extensions to the conventional investment decision criteria which can take into account the 'side-effects' of taking on investment projects, and in particular their contributions to a company's 'debt capacity'.[28] In their 'correction' to their original paper Modigliani and Miller demonstrated that if tax effects were correctly integrated into their original scenario then the tax-saving element on debt interest would lead to an incentive to substitute debt for equity capital (see (8.13)) until a target debt/equity ratio is achieved.[29] They believed that companies maintain 'untapped borrowing powers' because of the limitations imposed by lenders and other factors such as a wish to maintain flexibility. Myers suggested the use of an 'adjusted present value' method of project appraisal which would take into account the potential contribution to 'corporate debt capacity' – the additional borrowing powers conferred by taking on an investment project.[30]

The procedure he suggested runs as follows. First calculate the NPV of the project at a rate suited to all equity financing; this is referred to as NPV_0. Then add to this the adjusted present value APV, which is the present value of the tax shields generated by the project's addition to debt capacity. Myers adds that any other costs associated with the funding of the project, as well as benefits, can also be taken into account. (Incidentally, the logic of the analysis parallels that involved in the lease versus purchase decision; see appendix 6.1). In the analysis which follows:

APV_t is a project's adjusted present value at time t.
  B is the market value of the company's debt.
  S is the market value of the company's shares.
  V is the company value $= B + S$.
  TD is the target debt ratio $= B^*/V^*$ (where * indicates optimal proportions).
  k_i is the interest rate on debt $= r$ (pure interest rate if debt is riskless).
  TS_t is the tax shield in period t.
  CT is the corporate tax rate.
  r_0 is the cost of capital to an all equity financed company.

The analysis would be simplified if the target debt ration was considered in terms of book values, but market values are more realistic. If a Modigliani–Miller world is assumed, the tax shields on the interest payments in any one period could be expressed as:

$$TS_t = \frac{CTr}{(1 + r)^{t+1}}. \tag{6.21}$$

NB: The tax shields are discounted at a factor of $t + 1$ because it is assumed there is a delay of an accounting year before they become available.

Myers writes the additions to debt capacity ΔDC in any period as:

$$\Delta DC_t = TD(APV_t - NCF_t). \tag{6.22}$$

In any one period, the addition to the firm's debt capacity is a fixed proportion of the project's adjusted present value in the period, following the receipt of the project's cash flow for that period. Thus, over the entire project:

$$APV_0 = NPV_0 + \sum_{t=0}^{T-1} \frac{CTrTD(APV_t - NCF_t)}{(1 + r)^{t+1}}. \tag{6.23}$$

But in any individual period, the adjusted present value at that point in time will be a function of APV in all subsequent periods up to the termination of the project at $t = T$. This suggests the following relation:

$$g = \frac{CTrTD}{(1 + r)}.$$

It follows that:

$$APV_{T-1} = NPV_{T-1} + g(APV_{T-1} - NCF_{T-1}). \tag{6.24}$$

Once the APV_{T-1} is calculated, then APV_{T-2} can be calculated:

$$APV_{T-2} = NPV_{T-2} + g(APV_{T-2} - NCF_{T-2})$$

$$+ \frac{g}{(1 + r)}(APV_{T-1} - NCF_{T-1}).$$

Therefore, in this backward recursive fashion, APV_0 could be calculated. Myers suggests that his method is methodologically superior to the 'textbook' weighted average cost of capital formulation (see (8.5)). He argues that that approach is correct where the project is a perpetuity making permanent additions to debt capacity, and where it does not change the risk of the firm's activities. Furthermore, the firm is assumed to be operating with an optimal debt level, and taking on the project is not assumed to affect that target debt level. On the other hand the APV method is more flexible, is not burdened by these assumptions, and can readily accommodate changes in all these factors.

In a subsequent paper, Myers concentrated his attention on some of the factors which may contribute to the determination of a firm's target debt level.[31] The suggestion was that the present value of a company could be viewed as comprising two components – the present value of assets already employed, and the present value of any options the company may possess to make associated additional investment in the future. The implication is that the market for real assets is not perfect and in continuous equilibrium but that the company, either through its own initiative or through the existence of patents etc., has the opportunity to undertake further investment and earn 'quasi-rents' in the near future. This could be written formally as:

$$V = V_{AE} + V_{AF} \tag{6.25}$$

where V is the present value of the company, V_{AE} is the present value of assets already employed, and V_{AF} is the present value of options to make future investments.

Myers then demonstrates that the existence of risky debt as part of the company's funding can lead to suboptimal investment decisions. Consider first the case of an all equity financed company. In the hypothetical example it is assumed that initially the firm has no assets and it is considering investing in an asset in the next period, $t = 1$. The investment involves an outlay of I. If the analysis is couched in state preference terms (as considered in section 4.18) then in each possible state of nature the value of the investment could be denoted Vp_s which would represent its possible state contingent values at $t = 1$. The investment is only worthwhile if:

$$Vp_s \geq I. \tag{6.26}$$

A decision variable could be defined D_s, and assigned a value of 1 when $Vp_s \geq I$ (the investment is taken on) and a value of 0 when $Vp_s \leq I$ (the investment opportunity is forgone). If markets are complete (in the sense considered in chapter 4) the value of the all equity financed firm at $t = 0$ could be written as:

$$V_E = \int_0^\infty \pi_s D_s(Vp_s - I) \, ds \tag{6.27}$$

where V_E is the value of an all equity financed firm, and π_s is the price of £1 delivered at $t = 1$ in state s.

Myers then suggests that the situation is considered of a geared firm which has issued risky debt which matures after the investment option has lapsed, in effect after the investment decision has been made. The face value of the debt which is to be redeemed is B. He then draws up the balance sheet in table 6.3. In these circumstances the investment decision rule, when considered from the shareholders' point of view, will change. They will want the investment to be undertaken only if:

$$Vp_s \geq I + B; \quad \text{in this situation } D'_s = 1.$$

TABLE 6.3 *Balance sheet at period $t = 1$ given that the investment has been undertaken*

Value of asset	Vp_s	Value of debt:	$\min(Vp_s, B)$
		Value of equity:	$\max(0, Vp_s - B)$
Value of firm	Vp_s		Vp_s

But if;

$$Vp_s \leq I + B; \quad \text{then } D'_s = 0.$$

The value of the geared firm at $t = 0$ could be written:

$$V_G = \int_0^\infty \pi_s D'_s (Vp_s - I) \, \mathrm{d}s. \tag{6.28}$$

But clearly $V_E \geq V_G$, since there are likely to be some states in which $Vp_s \geq I + B$, and therefore in this situation the existence of risky debt undermines the incentive to undertake some future investments. From the shareholders' point of view, the optimum policy is all equity financing.

However, this neglects the previously considered tax advantages of debt financing, which would add to the value of the firm. Thus, the optimal policy is likely to avoid a trade-off between these two factors, and provides one explanation (others will be considered in chapter 8), of the existence of a target debt ratio. Myers develops further insights from his analysis. It would make sense for those firms whose value is mainly made up of existing investments to have higher gearing than those with many valuable investment options, and the practice of matching assets and liabilities seems to have a firmer theoretical underpinning. Significantly, the only imperfections assumed in the analysis are tax effects. The whole argument casts strong doubt on the existence of realistic circumstances in which it is possible to separate investment and financing decisions.

6.14 THE INVESTMENT AND THE PRODUCTION DECISION

The discussion so far has concentrated on capital market theory and its implications for company investment decisions, without any consideration of production and output decisions on the part of the company. On the other hand, there is an extensive micro-economics literature which concentrates on the latter whilst neglecting the former. However, there has been a growth in the literature in recent years which spans both areas.[32] The literature is only in its infancy and its potential scope is vast. As the interrelationship of the investment and financing decision has been examined, concentration will be on the work of Hite, who has examined the links between financing and production decisions.[33]

In a very restricted model, Hite looks at the single-period case of a firm which produces for this one period and then goes into liquidation. Capital assets are assumed to be priced according to the Sharpe–Lintner CAPM and the firm is assumed to have a simple production function relating output to homogeneous inputs of capital and labour, and it is a price-taker in factor markets. It faces a downward-sloping stochastic demand curve, and determines production plans after forecasting demand. All its production is placed on the market at a particular date, and price then adjusts until the market is cleared. The object of the firm is assumed to be the maximization of shareholder wealth. By application of the appropriate first-order conditions for maximizing the firm's value and employing comparative statistics he derives the following results. A company with gearing will not have the same capital/labour ratio as that which would be optimal for an all equity financed company, and gearing will have a positive effect on the size of the optimal capital stock employed and on optimal output. The analysis extends the treatment of tax effects. Therefore, if productive effects are considered, gearing changes the value of the firm in a more complex fashion than just by the pure tax effects on interest payments traditionally considered. This very brief reference will perhaps serve to give an impression of the far-reaching implications of this branch of the literature.

6.15   INFLATION AND THE CAPITAL BUDGETING DECISION

In chapter 1 was introduced the 'Fisher effect' (see (1.19)), which distinguishes between the real and the nominal rate of interest as follows:[34]

$$r_i \simeq i - PI \tag{6.29}$$

where r_i is the real rate of interest, i is the nominal rate of interest, and PI is the rate of change of prices according to an appropriate price index. Obviously the existence of inflation, coupled with 'money illusion' (confusion between real and nominal rates) on the part of decision-makers, has serious implications for the capital budgeting process.

Van Horne drew attention to the potential biases in the capital budgeting decision which are likely to result from incomplete adjustment for inflation.[35] If both the nominal discount rate, employed as the discount factor, and the project's estimated net cash flows contain adjustments for inflation, then no bias will result. He suggested that there is a likelihood that whereas nominal interest rates are likely to contain an adjustment for expected inflation, the project's estimated future cash flows are likely to be in current price terms with no adjustments for expected inflation. If this is the case, the project's profitability will tend to be seriously underestimated.

This type of approach has been further extended by Nelson, who analysed the effects of inflation under conditions of certainty, concentrating on tax effects, under the assumption that depreciation charges are calculated on a historical cost (original price) basis.[36] Appropriate inflation accounting adjustments would avoid this problem by introducing appropriate revisions of depreciation charges in line with inflation.[37] Without this revision, the depreciation tax shields will have diminished value (the longer the period over which they are written off, the more accentuated the effect), though the UK provision for 100 per cent write-offs in the first year will diminish these effects). However, given the existence of these effects, the optimal investment level will be smaller and its reduction will be positively linked to the level of inflation. Nelson also demonstrates that, given the appropriate assumptions, the existence of inflation could affect the firm's choice of productive techniques, with higher rates of inflation associated with lower capital/labour values. The ranking of mutually exclusive projects would also be biased, the bias being dependent upon the relative distribution of depreciation charges over the two projects' lives. The bias would be in favour of projects with shorter lives, or durability, since their depreciation charges would be less devalued. Finally, replacement decisions would tend to be deferred, since the tax-saving element from future depreciation charges on new projects would be further reduced the higher the rate of inflation.

The analysis has been extended to a treatment of the effects of uncertain inflation by Chen and Boness.[38] The analysis is framed in the context of the certainty equivalent form of CAPM (first met in section 6.8), which they derive from the following general single-period equilibrium relationship between an asset's risk and return:

$$E(\widetilde{nr_i}) = r_f + \lambda[\text{cov}(\widetilde{nr_i}, \tilde{R}_M) - \text{cov}(\widetilde{nr_i}, \tilde{r}_a)] \tag{6.30}$$

where $E(\widetilde{nr_i})$ is the expected value of the random nominal return on asset i, r_f is the risk-free rate in nominal terms, r_a is the rate of inflation, λ is the market price of risk and is equal to

$$\frac{[E(R_M) - r_f]}{\text{var}(\tilde{R}_M) - \text{cov}(\tilde{R}_M, \tilde{r}_a)},$$

$\mathrm{Cov}(\widetilde{nr}_i, R_M)$ is the covariance between the nominal returns on asset i and the market portfolio R_M, and $\mathrm{cov}(\widetilde{nr}_i, \widetilde{r}_a)$ is the covariance of nominal returns on asset i and the rate of inflation.

In (6.30) there are two components of systematic risk: the 'normal' association between the return on the asset and returns on the market portfolio, plus an inflation element, the covariance of the nominal returns on the asset with the rate of inflation. When this model is applied in its certainty equivalent form as a capital budgeting hurdle rate, it is found that the 'traditional' model without adjustment for inflation leads to the following biases. It understates an asset's systematic risk if its returns are negatively correlated with inflation, and overstates them if its returns are positively correlated with inflation. When Chen integrates tax effects into the analysis it becomes apparent that there is likely to be a link between financing and investment decisions, given the presence of uncertain inflation.[39] Hamada has provided a general taxonomy of the likely implications for the theory of finance of the existence of inflation, under various assumptions, and Lintner has made the first steps towards the consideration of the dynamic effects of inflation on prices and returns in equity markets.[40] However, impressive as these first steps are, the literature in this area is still in its infancy.

6.16 CONCLUSION

This chapter has reviewed the theory of corporate capital budgeting decisions under the assumption that decisions are taken with a view to maximizing shareholder wealth. The appropriate decision rules, even under conditions of certainty, were not found to be particularly robust once realistic market imperfections were admitted to the analysis. When uncertainty was introduced into the framework it was found that there are still major unresolved difficulties in the literature, particularly in the application of the Sharpe–Lintner CAPM to capital budgeting in a multiperiod context. The tax system and the existence of inflation all serve to further complicate matters and it was seen that, in practice, the investment and the financing decision are unlikely to be separable. Thus in this area, as in most others in the theoretical literature, understanding is still incomplete and there exist only 'working guidelines' for application to the capital budgeting decision.

1. You have to choose between two machines X and Y which will both perform the required task. They are expected to produce the following cash flows:

	Cash flow in period t			
Machine	0	1	2	3
X	−100	150	150	—
Y	−150	110	130	130

   (a) Calculate their respective *NPV*s, assuming a 15 per cent interest rate.
   (b) Which machine is to be preferred?
2. Are the following statements true or false?
   (a) The *IRR* of net cash flows of £900 for six years with an initial investment outlay of £4,166 is 8 per cent.
   (b) The *IRR* methodology is superior to the *NPV* methodology because the assumption about the reinvestment rate has greater realism.
   (c) The *IRR* and *NPV* methods of investment appraisal are superior DCF techniques which will always result in optimal investment decisions.
3. Comment on the following statements:
   (a) We avoid the risks associated with inflation by inflating the discount rate used to deflate future cash flows.
   (b) We avoid the risks associated with inflation by working in real rather than nominal terms.
4. A project which involves an outlay of £100 has estimated cash flows of £220 in year 1 and £250 in year 2. The project has a beta of 0.8. The risk-free rate is 8 per cent and the risk premium on the market is 12 per cent. Assuming a constant risk-adjusted discount rate, calculate
   (a) The certainty equivalent cash flows for years 1 and 2.
   (b) The *NPV* of the project.
5. Assume an opportunity cost of capital of 10 per cent. Indicate which of the following four projects has the highest *PVI*. Would the same project have the greatest impact on shareholder wealth?

Project	0	1	2	3	4
		Year end cash flows			
A	− 1000	750	750	750	—
B	− 2000	1000	1000	1000	1000
C	− 500	750	750	—	—
D	− 3000	4000	1500	—	—

APPENDIX 6.1   LEASING

In recent years there has been a remarkable growth in the popularity of leasing on both sides of the Atlantic.[41] It is the normal convention to distinguish between financial and operating leases. Financial leases are usually categorized as those contracts in which the lessor can expect to receive payments which fully amortize his expenditure on the asset from the lessee. Operating leases, on the other hand, frequently give the lessee the option to terminate the contract at short notice, and may have various associated non-financial benefits such as economies in the costs of the maintenance service where provided by the lessor, reduced exposure to technological obsolescence on the part of the asset, and so on. Miller and Upton provide a comprehensive analysis of operating leases.[42]

The concern here will be with the analysis of financial leases. The focus will be on the analysis provided by Myers, Dill, and Bautista, since it follows the 'adjusted present value' methodology already considered in this chapter.[43] They follow the assumption that entry into a financial lease contract on the part of the lessee uses up some of that company's 'debt capacity', and so the fiction that, because leasing is 'off balance sheet' it does not have these effects, is immediately discarded. It is assumed that the lease payments are tax deductible, but that the asset's residual value at the end of the contract, and the depreciation tax shields associated with asset ownership, are forfeited by the lessee.

The value of a lease contract is defined as the advantage of leasing an asset over financing the purchase of the asset by normal means, shown in the following expression:

$$V_L = 1 - PV[L_t(1 - T)] - PV(DP_t T) + PV(k_i TDD_t) \quad (6.31)$$

where V_L is the advantage of lease financing over standard funding, L_t is the lease payment in period t per £ of leased asset, T is the company's marginal corporate tax rate, DP_t is the depreciation per £ asset leased in period t, k_i is the company's borrowing rate, DD_t is the amount of the company's debt displaced in period t as a consequence of leasing per £ of asset leased, and PV is present value. (NB: As borrowing capacity is reduced, DD_t is negative.)

By leasing the firm incurs the cost of the present value of the lease payments, reduced by its marginal tax rate, and the depreciation tax shields forgone by not owning the asset – the first two terms on the RHS of (6.31). If it is assumed that the company is financed by a mixture of debt and equity, it loses some of the interest payment tax shields as a result of reducing its debt capacity. The authors then make a number of assumptions – that dividend policy is irrelevant, that the sole advantage of debt financing is the tax deductibility of interest payments, and that the value additivity principle holds. From the last assumption it follows that any stream of cash flows can be valued independently, and thus the stream of benefits associated with leasing can be valued as follows, using the firm's borrowing rate as a first approximation for capitalizing the streams:

$$V_L = 1 - \sum_{t=1}^{N} \frac{L_t(1 - T)}{(1 + k_i)^t} - \sum_{t=1}^{N} \frac{DP_t\,T}{(1 + k_i)^t} + \sum_{t=1}^{N} \frac{k_i\,TDD_{t-1}}{(1 + k_i)^t} \qquad (6.32)$$

where it is assumed that the length of the lease contract is given by $t = 1, \ldots, N$. Unfortunately (6.32) involves something of a tautology in that the lease value depends on the amount of debt displaced and, *vice versa*, the debt displaced is a function of lease value. By the introduction of an expression to represent the company's optimal debt capacity, and assuming that the company utilizes all of the debt capacity available, they derive the following expression via the use of the appropriate first-order conditions and backward recursive method:

$$V_L = 1 - \sum_{t=1}^{N} \frac{L_t(1 - T) + DP_t\,T}{(1 + k_i - k_i\,T)^t}. \qquad (6.33)$$

This expression shows the value of the lease to the lessee. As the lessor's position is the mirror image of the lessee's, the lessor's position is given by reversing the signs of (6.33). For the lessor

$$V_L = -1 + \sum_{t=1}^{N} \frac{L_t(1 - T) + DP_t\,T}{(1 + k_i - k_i\,T)^t}.$$

(NB: The adjusted discount rate allows for the loss of interest tax shields on the debt displaced.)

However, this expression assumes that leasing displaces debt on a one-for-one basis which implies that the lessor is entirely financed by debt. The authors then introduce a proportionality factor λ, which allows for the fact that debt is not displaced on a one-for-one basis. (This implies that an optimum capital structure exists, and I am not certain about the nature of a market in which both this and the value additivity principle hold. The authors also discuss likely values of λ, and admit to uncertainty over its value and to the possibility that it may differ for lessee and lessor.)

The following adjusted expression is then derived for the value of the lease to the lessor:

$$V_{\mathrm{L}} = -1 + \sum_{t-1}^{N} \frac{L_t(1-T) + DP_t\,T}{[1 + k_{\mathrm{i}}(1 - \lambda T)]^t} \tag{6.34}$$

where λ is the proportionality factor representing £ of debt displaced per £ of assets leased. Expression (6.34) shows that in the absence of any difference in corporate borrowing rates or λ, the most likely source of any mutual advantage from leasing is via the lessee or lessor having different tax positions. This is particularly likely to be the case in the UK where the lessee may well be in a position of tax exhaustion, in which he does not have sufficient profits against which to offset the tax shields. A profitable leasing company, perhaps a bank's subsidiary, will be in a position to utilize the tax shields and pass on some of the benefits to the lessee. Thus both parties gain. There seems little doubt that in competitive markets the most likely reason for the popularity of leasing are these tax effects, though as has been seen there are still doubts about the exact specification of the gain.

In this account the mathematical difficulties asociated with the derivation of the valuation formula have been avoided by omitting a full 'proof'. However, Franks and Hodges have provided a clever graphical demonstration of the result which follows.[44] They manage this by concentrating on the actual cash flows associated with the various alternative strategies rather than their present values. In the following representation of their analysis the original notation will be retained and the assumption made that the asset costs £1 (since all the original values were in terms of £s of assets leased). It is also assumed that $\lambda = 1$. The debt displaced by the lease can be considered as equivalent to the amount required to make all the respective cash flows associated with the purchase of the asset plus borrowing identical to those associated with leasing. Thus the lease

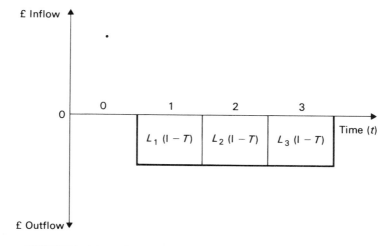

FIGURE 6.3 *The after-tax cash flows associated with leasing*

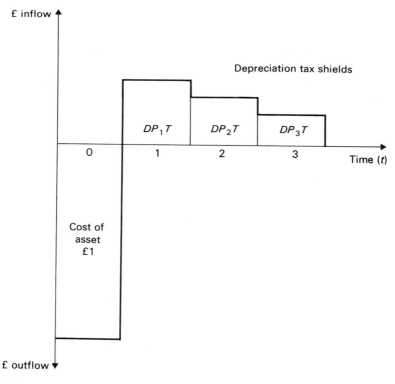

FIGURE 6.4 *The after-tax cash flows associated with purchase of the asset*

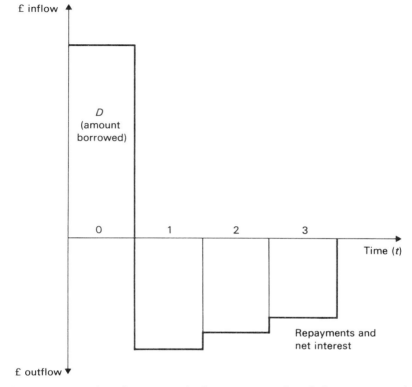

FIGURE 6.5 *The after-tax cash flows associated with borrowing to fund the asset*

is analysed by means of a lease versus buy and borrow strategy, in which the borrowing is chosen to make the resultant cash flows from the two strategies the same. The following set of diagrams illustrate their argument. Figure 6.3 shows the profile of cash streams associated with leasing the asset.

Figure 6.4 shows the after-tax cash flows associated with the purchase of the asset assuming no borrowing is undertaken. There is an initial outflow equal to the cost of the asset (£1 in this case, since the discussion is in terms of £s of assets leased) and subsequent inflows from the depreciation tax shields $DP_t T$.

Figure 6.5 shows a set of cash flows associated with borrowing and repayment. Finally, figure 6.6 demonstrates that the repayment schedules associated with borrowing have been tailored to give an identical set of cash flows to those associated with leasing the asset.

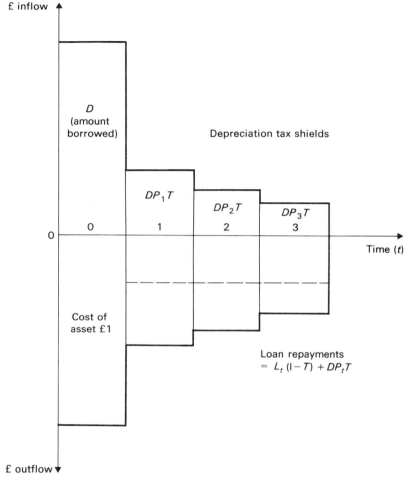

FIGURE 6.6   *A scheme of borrowing plus purchase which gives streams of after-tax cash flows identical to those involved with asset leasing (figure 6.3)*

Franks and Hodges then suggest that the value of the amount borrowed (D) is equivalent to the present value of the stream of repayments:

$$D = \sum_{t=0}^{N} \frac{L_t(1 - T) - DP_t T}{[1 + k_i(1 - T)]^t}$$

where all notation is as previously employed. The difference between the asset cost of £1 and the amount borrowed, D, is the gain to leasing in the initial period, since in all subsequent periods the cash flows are identical. Therefore:

$$V_L = 1 - D = 1 - \sum_{t=0}^{N} \frac{L_t(1 - T) + DP_t T}{[1 + k_i(1 - T)]^t}$$

which is the required result as given previously in (6.33).

NOTES AND REFERENCES

1. Dean, J. *Capital Budgeting*, Columbia University Press, New York, 1951, p. 35.
2. Bicksler, J. 'Capital budgeting', reading in Bicksler, J. (ed.) *Handbook of Financial Economics*, North-Holland, Amsterdam, 1979, pp. 189–204.
3. Gordon, M. J. 'The pay off period and the rate of profit', *Journal of Business*, October 1955.
   Weingartner, M. 'Some new views on the payback period and capital budgeting decisions', *Management Science* **15**, August 1969.
   Sarnat, M. and Levy, H. 'The relationship of rules of thumb to the internal rate of return: a restatement and generalization', *Journal of Finance* **24**(3), June 1969, pp. 479–90.
4. Lorie, J. H. and Savage, L. J. 'Three problems in rationing capital', *Journal of Business*, October 1955, pp. 229–39.
5. Samuelson, P. A. 'Some aspects of the pure theory of capital', *Quarterly Journal of Economics* **51**, 1937, pp. 469–96.
6. Merrett, A. J. and Sykes, A. *The Finance and Analysis of Capital Projects*, Longmans, London, 1963, pp. 153–4.
7. Weingartner, M. 'Capital rationing: *n* authors in search of a plot', *Journal of Finance* **32**(5), December 1977, pp. 1403–31.
   Weingartner, M. *Mathematical Programming and the Analysis of Capital Budgeting Problems*, Prentice-Hall, Englewood Cliffs NJ, 1963.
8. Ibid., chapter 3.
9. See: Fama, E. F. and Miller, M. H. *The Theory of Finance*, Holt, Rinehart and Winston, New York, 1972, p. 136.
10. Lutz, F. and Lutz, V. *The Theory of Investment of the Firm*, Greenwood Press, Princeton NJ, 1951, chapter 15, pp. 179–92.
    See also: Knight, F. H. *Risk, Uncertainty and Profit* (1921), reprinted by Kelly, New York, 1964.
11. Robichek, A. A. and Myers, S. C. 'Conceptual problems in the use of risk-adjusted discount rates', *Journal of Finance* **21**(5), December 1966, pp. 727–30.
    Robichek, A. A. and Myers, S. C. *Optimal Financing Decisions*, Prentice-Hall, Englewood Cliffs NJ, 1965, chapter 5.
12. For additional discussion, see: Van Horne, J. C. 'The analysis of uncertainty resolution in capital budgeting for new projects', *Management Science* **15**(8), April 1969, pp. 376–86.
13. Levy, H. and Sarnat, M. 'Diversification, portfolio analysis, and the uneasy case for conglomerate mergers', *Journal of Finance* **25**(4), September 1970, pp. 795–802.

Justification on the grounds of enhanced debt capacity is given by: Lewellen, W. G. 'A pure financial rationale for the conglomerate merger', *Journal of Finance* **26**(2), May 1971, pp. 521–37.

14. For a more extended discussion, see: Stapleton, R. C. 'Portfolio analysis, stock valuation and capital budgeting decision rules for risky projects', *Journal of Finance* **26**(1), March 1971, pp. 95–117.
    See also: Rubinstein, M. E. 'A mean–variance synthesis of corporate financial theory', *Journal of Finance* **28**(1), March 1973, pp. 167–81.

15. Hertz, D. B. 'Risk analysis in capital investment', *Harvard Business Review* **42**(1), January–February 1964, pp. 95–106.

16. Magee, J. F. 'Decision trees for decision making', *Harvard Business Review* **42**, July–August 1964, pp. 79–96.

17. Hillier, F. S. 'The derivation of probabilistic information for risky investments', *Management Science* **9**(3), April 1963, pp. 443–57.

18. Myers, S. C. and Turnbull, S. M. 'Capital budgeting and the capital asset pricing model: good news and bad news', *Journal of Finance* **32**(2), May 1977, pp. 321–33.
    Myers, S. C. 'The relation between real and financial measures of return', in Friend, I. and Bicksler, J. (eds) *Risk and Return in Finance*, vol. 1, Ballinger, 1977, pp. 40–80.
    See also: Epstein, L. G. and Turnbull, S. M. 'Capital asset prices and the temporal resolution of uncertainty', *Journal of Finance* **35**(3), June 1980, pp. 627–43.
    Stapleton, R. C. and Subrahmanyam, M. 'A multiperiod equilibrium asset pricing model', *Econometrica* **46**(5), September 1978, pp. 1077–98.

19. Beaver, W. H., Kettler, P. and Scholes, M. 'The association between market determined and accounting determined risk measures', *Accounting Review* **45**, October 1970, pp. 654–82.
    Gonededes, N. J. 'Evidence on the information content of accounting numbers: accounting based and market based estimates of systematic risk', *Journal of Financial and Quantitative Analysis* **8**(3), June 1973, pp. 407–44.
    Pettit, R. and Westerfield, R. 'A model of capital asset risk', *Journal of Financial and Quantitative Analysis* **7**(2), March 1972, pp. 1649–68.

20. Bogue, M. and Roll, R. 'Capital budgets for risky projects with 'imperfect' markets for physical capital', *Journal of Finance* **29**(2), May 1974, pp. 601–13.
    Fama, E. F. 'Risk-adjusted discount rates and capital budgeting under uncertainty', *Journal of Financial Economics* **5**, 1977, pp. 3–24.
    For an attempt to get round some of the difficulties see: Stapleton, R. C. and Subrahmanyam, M. 'A multi-period equilibrium asset-pricing model', *Econometrica* **46**(5), September 1978, pp. 1077–98.

21. Myers, S. C. and Turnbull, S. M. 'Capital budgeting and the capital asset pricing model: good news and bad news', *Journal of Finance* **32**(2), May 1977, pp. 321–33.

22. See: Merton, R. C. 'An intertemporal capital asset pricing model', *Econometrica* **45**(5), September 1973, pp. 867–87.

23. Fama, E. F. 'Risk-adjusted discount rates and capital budgeting under uncertainty', *Journal of Financial Economics* **5**, 1977, pp. 3–24.

24. Merton, R. C. 'An intertemporal capital asset pricing model', *Econometrica* **45**(5), September 1973, pp. 867–87.

25. Jensen, M. C. and Long, J. B. Jr. 'Corporate investment under uncertainty and

Pareto optimality in the capital markets', *Bell Journal of Economics and Management Science* **3**(1), Spring 1972, pp. 151–74.

Leland, H. E. 'Production theory and the stock market', *Bell Journal of Economics and Management Science* **5**(1), Spring 1974.

26. Baron, D. P. 'Investment policy, optimality, and the mean–variance model', *Journal of Finance* **34**(1), March 1978, pp. 207–32.

27. An excellent and readily accessible coverage of the problems is given in: King, M. *Public Policy and the Corporation*, Chapman and Hall, London, 1977, Chapter 5.

28. Myers, S. C. 'Interactions of corporate financing and investment decisions: implications for capital budgeting', *Journal of Finance* **29**(1), March 1974, pp. 1–25.

Myers, S. C. 'Determinants of corporate borrowing', *Journal of Financial Economics* **5**(2), 1977, pp. 147–75.

Modigliani, F. and Miller, M. H. 'Corporate income taxes and the cost of capital: a correction', *American Economic Review* **53**(3), June 1963, pp. 433–43.

Miller, M. H. and Modigliani, F. 'Some estimates of the cost of capital to electric utility industry: 1954–57', *American Economic Review* **56**(3), June 1966, pp. 333–91.

29. Modigliani, F. and Miller, M. 'Corporate income taxes and the cost of capital: a correction', *American Economic Review* **53**(3), June 1963, pp. 433–43.

30. Myers, S. C. 'Interactions of corporate financing and investment decisions: implications for capital budgeting', *Journal of Finance* **29**(1), March 1974, pp. 1–25.

31. Myers, S. C. 'Determinants of corporate borrowing', *Journal of Financial Economics* **5**(2), 1977, pp. 147–75.

Incidentally, for a discussion of some of the problems associated with the 'traditional' capital budgeting literature see: Peasnell, K. V. 'The present value concept in financial reporting', *Journal of Business Finance and Accounting* **4**(2), Summer 1977, pp. 153–68.

Keane, S. M. 'The irrelevance of the firm's cost of capital as an investment decision tool', *Journal of Business Finance and Accounting* **4**(2), Summer 1977, pp. 201–16.

32. For a good general review, see: Nickell, S. J. *The Investment Decisions of Firms*, James Nisbet & Co Ltd and Cambridge University Press, Welwyn, 1978.

Hite, G. 'Leverage, output effects and the M–M theorems', *Journal of Financial Economics* **4**, 1977, pp. 177–202.

Hite, G. 'On the theory of the firm in a capital asset pricing model world', reading in *Handbook of Financial Economics*, North-Holland, Amsterdam, 1979, pp. 163–88.

See also: Leland, H. E. 'Production theory and the stock market', *Bell Journal of Economics and Management Science* **5**(1), Spring 1974.

Merton, R. C. and Subrahmanyam, M. 'The optimality of a competitive stock market', *Bell Journal of Economics and Management Science* **5**(1), Spring 1974, pp. 145–70.

Jensen, M. C. and Long, J. B. Jr. 'Corporate investment under uncertainty and Pareto optimality in the capital markets', *Bell Journal of Economics and Management Science* **3**(1), Spring 1972, pp. 151–74.

Ciccolo, J. and Fromm, G. ' "Q" and the theory of investments', *Journal of Finance* **34**(2), May 1979, pp. 535–46.

Jorgensen, D. W. 'Investment behaviour and the production function', *Bell Journal of Economics and Management Science* **3**(1), Spring 1972, pp. 220–51.

Fama, E. F. 'Perfect competition and optimal production decisions under uncertainty', *Bell Journal of Economics and Management Science* **3**(2), Autumn 1972, pp. 509–30.

33. Hite, G. 'Leverage, output effects and the M–M theorem', *Journal of Financial Economics* **4**, 1977, pp. 177–202.

Hite, G. 'On the theory of the firm in a capital asset pricing model world', reading in *Handbook of Financial Economics*, North-Holland, 1979, pp. 163–88.

34. Fisher, I. *The Rate of Interest*, Macmillan, New York, 1907.

35. Van Horne, J. C. 'A note on biases in capital budgeting introduced by inflation', *Journal of Financial and Quantitative Analysis* **6**(1), January 1971, pp. 653–58.

36. Nelson, C. R. 'Inflation and capital budgeting', *Journal of Finance* **31**(3), June 1976, pp. 923–31.

37. See: Statement of Standard Accounting Practice No. 16 (SSAP 16), March 1980. *Inflation Accounting, Report of the Inflation Accounting Committee*, HMSO, Cmnd 6225, September 1975.

38. Chen, A. H. and Boness, A. J. 'Effects of uncertain inflation on the investment and financing decision of a firm', *Journal of Finance* **30**(2), May 1975, pp. 469–83.

Chen, A. H. 'Uncertain inflation and optimal corporate investment decisions', reading in *Handbook of Financial Economics*, North-Holland, Amsterdam, 1979, pp. 243–56.

39. Ibid.

40. Hamada, R. S. 'Financial theory and taxation in an inflationary world: some public policy issues', *Journal of Finance* **34**(2), May 1979, pp. 347–69.

Lintner, J. 'Inflation and security returns', *Journal of Finance* **30**(2), May 1975, pp. 259–80.

41. For an account of the UK experience, see: Franks, J. R. and Hodges, S. D. 'The role of leasing in capital investment', *National Westminster Bank Quarterly Review*, August 1979, pp. 20–31.

42. Miller, M. H. and Upton, C. W. 'Leasing, buying and cost of capital services', *Journal of Finance* **31**(3), June 1976, pp. 761–86.

43. Myers, S. C., Dill, D. A. and Bautista, A. J. 'Valuation of financial lease contracts', *Journal of Finance* **31**(3), June 1976, pp. 799–819.

44. Franks, J. R. and Hodges, S. D. 'Valuation of financial lease contracts: a note', *The Journal of Finance* **33**(2), May 1978, pp. 657–69.

CHAPTER 7

The valuation of the corporation and dividend policy

A cow for her milk,
A hen for her eggs,
And a stock, by heck,
For her dividends.

Such was the advice given by the farmer to his son, as cited by J. B. Williams.[1] It will be seen shortly that a stock can be valued in terms of both its dividends and its earnings (appropriately defined). It will also become apparent that Williams's observation (cited at the beginning of chapter 1) that prices depend upon estimations of future income is particularly apt.

So, too, are the three questions posed by Solomon, which were also cited in chapter 1. The issues raised there concerned the range of assets to acquire, the volume of funds to commit, and the choice of financial instruments to raise the required funds. This chapter and chapter 8 are concerned with how an enterprise should choose to fund its operations, and the type of considerations which may have to be borne in mind.

Before these matters are discussed, consideration will be given to the type of factor which is likely to influence the valuation of the corporation. Much of the material introduced in Parts I and II should prove useful, and the insights and concepts developed in Part II, in which were considered the various ways in which equilibrium pricing models can be applied in the capital markets, should be of value.

The corporation or, to be more precise, the publicly quoted company, naturally occupies a central position in the theory of finance. This chapter will be concerned with analysing many of the ramifications associated with the problem of valuing the corporation, with particular attention to the financial policy implications of this. The corporation is owned by shareholders who provide risk finance – the equity capital – in the expectation of future returns. These returns could be in the form of future dividends, or future capital gains via share price appreciation, or both. They are, therefore, likely to be very concerned with the market share value of the corporation, and it was seen in chapter 1 that the usual assumption is that the managers of the company, acting on behalf of the shareholders, are concerned with maximizing shareholder wealth. All decisions are assumed to be made with this end in mind.

This recalls the present value rule, and once again the assumption is that financial decisions which maximize the present value of the shareholder's interest are optimal from this point of view.

7.1 THE DIVIDEND DECISION IN A PERFECT MARKET

To begin, a restricted view will be adopted and the assumption made that the corporation is financed entirely by equity shareholders, who receive their income in the form of current and future divided payments. The concern will be with exploring the relationship, given the assumptions, between the corporation's dividend policy and the market value of its equity. The crucial question, which has exercised financial theorists over the past three decades, is whether or not dividend policy can affect the valuation of the corporation. If it does have an effect, then the circumstances and variables linking dividend policy and valuation have to be isolated and examined, and this also raises the issue of what constitutes an optimum dividend policy. But, before these thorny issues are raised, examination of dividend policy in perfect markets will continue.

There are obviously a number of variables, such as changes in investment policies and changes in earnings levels, which can affect the valuation of the corporation. (These will be considered in detail later in this chapter.) In order to concentrate upon the effect of dividend decisions, the effect of these other variables has to be assumed away. Thus in the following analysis it is assumed that the company's production and investment plans for the future periods concerned are given, and that the company's managers and shareholders are equally well informed of their details. This, in effect, implies that the company's future earnings are determined, but the chosen dividend policy will determine both the division and the timing of the distribution of those earnings. The question is, given these assumptions, can dividend policy affect share value?

In the following analysis, dividend per share paid to existing shareholders is denoted by d_t, and the total dividends paid during the period t by D_t. SR_t represents gross sales revenue during t, and W_t stands for expenditure on wages and other bought-in factors of production. I_t represents the company's investment during period t.[2] It thus follows that the company's net earnings available for the shareholders during period t can be defined as:

$$SR_t - W_t - I_t. \tag{7.1}$$

It is still assumed that the analysis takes place within a perfect market. One of the major characteristics of a perfect market which has already been encountered is that there is only one unique rate of return, the pure interest rate, which links income received at different points in time. If any financial security or potential investment offered a rate of return greater than this rate, all investors would know about it (since it is assumed that they have complete access to all information in a perfect market) and there would be a considerable demand for this particular asset, so that in equilibrium its price would be pushed up to the point where it offered a return equal to the pure rate of interest.

7.2 ONE UNIQUE RATE OF RETURN IN PERFECT MARKETS

This establishes the important point that in equilibrium there is only one unique rate of return in perfect markets. This has further important implications for the analysis of dividend policy under perfect market conditions. If the pure rate of interest between period t and period $t + 1$ is denoted $_t r_{t+1}$, then in equilibrium a shareholder in any firm should receive a return on his shareholding equal to this rate. His rate of return will be equal to the difference in value of his shares at the beginning and end of the period, plus the value of any dividends received, all divided by the value of his shares at the beginning of the period, to give a one-period rate of return. This is shown as follows:

$$_t r_{t+1} = \frac{s_{i,\,t+1} + d_{i,\,t+1} - s_{i,\,t}}{s_{i,\,t}} \tag{7.2}$$

where $s_{i,\,t+1}$ is the value of shares held by the ith shareholder at time $t + 1$, $s_{i,\,t}$ is the value of shares held by the ith shareholder at time t (except any dividend in $t - 1$), and $d_{i,\,t+1}$ are the dividends received by the ith shareholder in the period up to $t + 1$.

Expression (7.2) could be rearranged to show the equivalence in present value terms of the value of the shareholding and dividends received by the ith shareholder at time $t + 1$ and the present value of the shareholding at time t, as depicted in the following expression:

$$s_{i,t} = \frac{s_{i,t+1} + d_{i,t+1}}{1 + {}_t r_{t+1}}. \tag{7.3}$$

This analysis applies equally to all shareholders in the company; thus, in general, expressions can be derived with respect to the total value of the company's shares and the total dividends paid. As previously, upper case letters are used to denote total values. Expression (7.3) can be rewritten in terms of total values as shown in (7.4). The discussion is now in terms of the present value of all issued shares of the company, and relates this to the future value of the shares at time $t + 1$ plus the value of dividends paid over the period. As dividends have been allowed for separately, the share values are ex-dividend values.

$$S_t = \frac{1}{1 + {}_t r_{t+1}} (D_{t+1} + N_t s_{t+1}) \tag{7.4}$$

where S_t is the total value of the company's shares outstanding at time t, D_{t+1} are the total dividends paid to shareholders between time t and $t + 1$ (NB: does not include dividends on any new shares, which are assumed to be paid in the next period), s_{t+1} is the value of an individual share of the company at time $t + 1$, and N_t is the total number of the company's shares outstanding at time t.

The important point to note about (7.4) is that the value of the shares at time $t + 1$ is expressed as equal to their price at $t + 1$, s_{t+1}, multiplied by the number of shares outstanding at time t. This is not simply the total value of shares outstanding at time $t + 1$, S_{t+1}. This is to allow for the fact that there could be a change in the total number of shares outstanding if the company made a new issue of shares at the beginning of time $t + 1$. Suppose M stands for the number of new shares issued at the beginning of time $t + 1$ at the ruling price s_{t+1}. Then it follows that the total value of the company's shares at time $t + 1$ is equal to the total number of shares outstanding at $t + 1$ multiplied by their price at that time, and that this must be equal to the number of shares outstanding at time t, plus any change in that number such as would follow from a new issue, multiplied by their price at time $t + 1$. This is shown as follows:

$$S_{t+1} = N_{t+1} s_{t+1} = N_t s_{t+1} + M_{t+1} s_{t+1}.$$

It therefore follows that:

$$N_t s_{t+1} = (N_{t+1} - M_{t+1}) s_{t+1}$$

and therefore

$$N_t s_{t+1} = S_{t+1} - M_{t+1} s_{t+1}.$$

If the above identity is substituted in (7.4) the following expression is obtained:

$$S_t = \frac{1}{1 + {}_t r_{t+1}} (D_{t+1} + S_{t+1} - M_{t+1} s_{t+1}). \tag{7.5}$$

Expression (7.5) can now be used to further explore the influence of dividend decisions, under perfect market conditions, on share value. By definition, as an accounting identity, the total sources of funds must equal the total uses of funds in any given period. An expression can be obtained to represent total sources in terms of time $t + 1$ by rewriting (7.1) in terms of time $t + 1$ and adding a term to represent funds raised from new issues. This, by definition, must equal total uses of funds at time $t + 1$, which will include payment to factors of production W_{t+1}, gross investment I_{t+1}, and dividends D_{t+1}. The identity of sources and uses of funds is shown as follows:

$$SR_{t+1} + M_{t+1} s_{t+1} \equiv D_{t+1} + I_{t+1} + W_{t+1}. \tag{7.6a}$$

It follows from this identity that in any period any difference between gross sales revenue SR and total uses of funds, as represented by the RHS of (7.6a), must be made up by new issues. Therefore it follows that:

$$M_{t+1} s_{t+1} = SR_{t+1} - D_{t+1} - I_{t+1} - W_{t+1}.$$

If the above identity is substituted (7.5), then dividends at time $t + 1$, D_{t+1}, cancel out and the following expression remains:

$$S_t = \frac{I}{I + {}_t r_{t+1}} (S_{t+1} + SR_{t+1} - I_{t+1} - W_{t+1}). \tag{7.7}$$

7.3 THE IRRELEVANCE OF DIVIDENDS

Expression (7.7) shows that the value of the company's shares at time t is completely independent of dividend payments at time $t + 1$ under perfect market conditions, and this is the essence of Miller and Modigliani's famous proposition about the irrelevance of dividends in their 1961 article.[3]

At first sight the proposition that dividends are irrelevant seems rather sweeping, but the rather strict conditions under which it has been put forward must be borne in mind. It has been assumed that the firm's operating and investment policy for all future periods is given and known. Therefore, in the case of (7.7) all shareholders know the value of $SR_{t+1} - I_{t+1} - W_{t+1}$, and as this knowledge extends into the future to all relevant periods, they know the value of S_{t+1}. They therefore have no doubts about the present value of their total shareholding S_t. It follows that the irrelevance of dividends under these assumptions in a perfect market is something of a tautology, but it nevertheless marks an important step forward in the clarification of arguments about the influence of dividend policy on company valuation. The essence of the argument is that the present value of the company's future income is given, and once this is accepted it can be seen that, according to Fisher's analysis (mentioned previously), all the company can do is to alter the timing of the shareholders' receipt of that income by changes in dividend policy; in a perfect market, however, this is of little importance. The only way that the company could benefit the shareholders would be by increasing the present value of their future income, but this is ruled out by the assumption of a given operating and investment policy.

The choice faced by the company is either to pay a higher current dividend and resort to greater use of external finance through a new share issue to help fund investment, or to cut the current dividend to finance the investment by retentions. It can be seen from the following restatement of (7.6a), where bars over symbols have been added to denote variables assumed given, that the two financial policy variables the company can determine in joint consideration are new share issues $M_{t+1} s_{t+1}$ and dividend policy D_{t+1}:[4]

$$\overline{SR}_{t+1} + M_{t+1} s_{t+1} \equiv D_{t+1} + \overline{I}_{t+1} + \overline{W}_{t+1}. \tag{7.6b}$$

The two variables vary directly and the larger the current dividend the larger the external financing requirement. If the company pays a higher current dividend and raises new share capital, the existing shareholders' claim on the company's future income will be diluted by the extent of the new share issue. If the company chooses to pay a smaller current dividend and avoid the need for a new issue, the shareholders' current income will be reduced but they will have a greater claim on the company's future income than under the previous alternative. However, in a perfect market, under the principle of equalization of returns, the two positions will be identical, and their present values will be the same. It is in this sense that dividend policy is irrelevant. The analysis has been undertaken for one period, but the same logic could be applied to the next period, and so on up to N periods, with the same results – that dividend policy is irrelevant under the stipulated conditions.

An analysis of the allocation of income under perfect market conditions has now been considered. This has been employed as a basis for an analysis of dividend policy under the same conditions, and thereby has determined the conditions under which dividend policy is unequivocally irrelevant. Before proceeding to an extension of the analysis, and introducing various modifications and market imperfections which may make dividend policy relevant, it should serve to clarify the issues by engaging in a brief review of some of the major valuation models which may be employed to determine the value of the corporation. This is particularly relevant to the purpose in hand since many of the arguments about the effects of dividend policy stem from the variety of assumptions and types of valuation models employed.

7.4 MAJOR MODELS OF THE VALUATION OF THE CORPORATION

There are two broad approaches to the problem of the valuation of the corporation. It can be argued either that shareholders take up shares in public companies in anticipation of the future dividends they expect to receive, or that they do so with a view to the future earnings that they hope will accrue to their interest. Thus there is the stream of dividends and the stream of earnings approach.[5] Modigliani and Miller demonstrated that the two approaches are basically equivalent, if it is assumed that there is no difference between the tax treatment of retained and distributed earnings.[6] This will be considered after an examination of the two main approaches.

7.5 VALUATION ON THE BASIS OF DIVIDENDS

Under this approach the current market value of the company's shares is determined by the summation of the discounted present value of all future dividend payments up to a chosen time horizon T, plus the discounted present value of the company's shares in the horizon time period T. This is illustrated as follows:

$$S_0 = \sum_{t=1}^{t=T-1} \frac{D_t}{\prod_{t=1}^{t=T-1} (1 + k_t)} + \frac{S_T}{(1 + k_t)^T} \tag{7.8}$$

where D_t is the total dividend payment in every period from $t = 1$ to $t = T - 1$, k_t is the appropriate shareholders' discount rate for every period under consideration, and S_T is the horizon value of the company's shares. (NB: $\prod$ means the multiplicative sum through the brackets.)

If T, the time horizon, is moved far into the future so that $T \to \infty$, then the value of the last term in (7.8) will tend to 0 (as long as the company is not growing more quickly at this stage than the shareholder discount rate k; if this were the case the company would have an infinite value, which would be economic nonsense). If the further simplifying assumption is made that the discount rate k is constant over all the periods under consideration, then (7.8) simplifies to the more familiar expression below:

$$S_0 = \sum_{t=1}^{t=\infty} \frac{D_t}{(1 + k)^t}. \tag{7.9}$$

7.6   VALUATION ON THE BASIS OF EARNINGS

The basis of the earnings approach to valuation is the hypothesis that net future earnings attributable to shareholders are capitalized to determine the current share value rather than future dividends. If the available expression (7.1) for net earnings attributable to shareholders is used, and if the simplifying assumptions are adopted that were employed with the dividend model in (7.9), about the constancy of the discount rate and so forth, then the current market share value is determined as follows:

$$S_0 = \sum_{t=1}^{t=\infty} \frac{SR_t - W_t - I_t}{(1 + k)^t}. \tag{7.10}$$

7.7   EQUIVALENCE OF THE TWO APPROACHES

It is fairly straightforward to demonstrate the equivalence of the two approaches by returning to the accounting identity of sources and uses of funds in any given period. This identity is set out algebraically as follows, where all terms are employed in the same manner as previously and $M_t s_t$ represents new share issues and D_{mt} the dividends payable on new issues:

(sources) $\equiv$ (uses)

$SR_t + M_t s_t \equiv D_t + W_t + I_t + D_{mt}.$

Therefore, rearranging terms:

$$D_t = SR_t + M_t s_t - I_t - W_t - D_{mt}.$$

This suggests that shareholders at time 0 expect the sum total of dividends to be equal to net earnings plus funds raised from new issues minus gross investment and dividends paid to new shareholders. This expression can be modified to make it equivalent to the company's accounting treatment of income. Suppose that the company's accounting procedures generate some figure for depreciation in period t, which will be denoted Z_t. Then Z_t can be added to both sides of the previous equation and the following expression obtained:

$$D_t + Z_t = SR_t + M_t s_t + Z_t - I_t - W_t - D_{mt}.$$

If the terms are regrouped the following expression is obtained:

$$D_t = (SR_t - W_t - Z_t) - (I_t - M_t s_t - Z_t) - D_{mt}. \tag{7.11}$$

But the accounting income of the firm, which will be denoted X_t, is given by:

$$X_t = SR_t - W_t - Z_t$$

and the term $I_t - M_t s_t - Z_t$ is that proportion of gross investment which must be financed by retained earnings, and which are reinvested by definition. If X_r represents this amount of retained earnings which are reinvested, then:

$$S_0 = \sum_{t=1}^{t=\infty} \frac{D_t}{(1+k)^t} = \sum_{t=1}^{t=\infty} \frac{X_t - X_{rt} - D_{mt}}{(1+k)^t}. \tag{7.12}$$

Expression (7.12) shows the equivalence of the two approaches, but Miller and Modigliani's warning must be heeded; they drew attention to the fact that the two approaches are only equivalent if the taxation of retentions and distributions is identical, and if the adjusted figure for earnings is employed. If just a series of earnings figures representing current and future earnings were employed then double counting would occur, since some of the current earnings will be reinvested and will produce future earnings; but the company cannot be valued on the basis of the current value of the earnings committed to the investment, and on the present value of the future earnings the investment generates as well. Thus account must be taken of the fact that in order to maintain earnings levels in the future, current earnings have to be committed to the productive process, whether raised via retentions or new issues, and that these earnings have an opportunity cost. The adjusted earnings figures shown in (7.12) are therefore employed.

7.8   DIVIDEND POLICY AS A FINANCING DECISION IN THE ABSENCE OF A GIVEN INVESTMENT POLICY

The two major approaches employed in valuation models of the corporation have now been established, and the analysis of dividend policy will be continued with reliance on the use of dividend valuation models. So far the irrelevance of dividend policy in a perfect market with a given investment policy has been established. The implications of dropping the assumptions of a given investment policy will now be examined.

The effects of a change in dividend policy on company valuation can be examined by employing the simple dividend valuation model (7.9) and looking at the effect of forgoing a dividend in the first period of returns in order to finance a one-period investment opportunity. The analysis is on the lines suggested by Levy and Sarnat and originally investigated by Walter.[7] Assume that the company is faced with a one-off investment opportunity which will take up all the earnings which would have been available to the shareholders as a dividend in the first period. It can invest these earnings at a rate of return GR for one period only. It then pays out the returns on the investment as extra dividends in the next period. This sequence of events is summarized as follows:

$$S_0 = \frac{0}{(1 + k)} + \frac{D_2 + D_1(1 + GR)}{(1 + k)^2} + \sum_{t=3}^{t=\infty} \frac{D_t}{(1 + k)^t}. \tag{7.13}$$

The increase in company value which stems from taking on this one-period investment opportunity will be found by deducting (7.9), the simple dividend valuation model, from (7.13):

$$\Delta S_0 = (7.13) - (7.9) = \frac{D_1(1 + GR)}{(1 + k)^2} - \frac{D_1}{(1 + k)}$$

$$= \frac{D_1}{(1 + k)} \left(\frac{1 + GR}{1 + k} - 1 \right).$$

$$\therefore \quad \Delta S_0 = \frac{D_1}{(1 + k)^2} (GR - k). \tag{7.14}$$

It is obvious from (7.14) that, in the special case where the rate at which dividends can be reinvested in the company, GR, is equal to the shareholder's required rate of return, k, that changes in dividend policy will have no effect on share value. Otherwise, if $GR > k$ then retaining dividends and reinvesting them will increase share value, and if $GR < k$ then the share value would be optimized by paying out all available earnings as dividends.

From this simple treatment has been excluded, for the sake of brevity, the possibility of the company using new sources of external finance. This means that the dividend decision is directly related to the investment decision and in this approach becomes a passive residual, with the payout ratio varying according to the profitability of available investments. Under these conditions the dropping of the assumption of a 'given investment policy' assumes great importance, and the dividend decision does have an effect on share value.

The examination of investment policy can be taken a stage further by exploring the effects of assumptions about the future growth of dividends and earnings as a result of assumed investment policies. The major theoretical contributions in this area are largely based upon the pioneering work of M. J. Gordon.[8]

7.9 THE GORDON GROWTH MODEL

Gordon developed his model by continuing the assumption that the company's investment is financed entirely by retentions, and by employing a valuation model based upon discounted expected future dividend payments. The model assumes that a constant proportion b of earnings per share y_0 in each period are reinvested at a constant growth rate GR. This means that the company's share value will be determined as follows:

$$s_0 = \frac{(1 - b)y_0}{(1 + k)} + \frac{(1 - b)y_0(1 + bGR)}{(1 + k)^2}$$
$$+ \frac{(1 - b)y_0(1 + bGR)^2}{(1 + k)^3} + \cdots$$
$$s_0 = \sum_{t=1}^{t=\infty} \frac{(1 - b)y_0(1 + bGR)^{t-1}}{(1 + k)^t} \tag{7.15}$$

where y_0 are current earnings per share, b is the fraction of earnings retained, GR is the constant average rate at which earnings are retained and reinvested, k is the shareholder's discount rate, and $(1 - b)y_0 = d_0$ is the current dividend per share.

If the current share value is expressed in terms of dividends on a continuous basis, then the value of the share is given by:

$$s_0 = \int_0^\infty d_t \, e^{-kt} \, dt$$

or its equivalent:

$$s_0 = \int_0^\infty (1 - b)y_0 \, e^{bGRt} \, e^{-kt} \, dt$$

$$\therefore \quad s_0 = (1 - b)y_0 \int_0^\infty e^{-t(k - bGR)} \, dt. \tag{7.16}$$

This expression can only be integrated if $k > bGR$, otherwise the share will have an infinite price.

By integration:

$$s_0 = \frac{(1 - b)y_0}{(k - bGR)}. \tag{7.17}$$

Using this share valuation model, Gordon investigated the effect of alternative retention policies upon share price. Initially he assumed that GR and k, as well as y_0, are independent of b.[9] The effect of alternative retention policies is found by taking the derivative of (7.17) with respect to b. This gives:

$$\frac{ds_0}{db} = \frac{y_0(GR - k)}{(k - bGR)^2}. \tag{7.18}$$

It thus follows that the condition for ensuring that the retention rate has no effect upon share value is to set $GR = k$. In this situation the marginal investment has a zero net present value, and it is only under these circumstances that dividend policy is irrelevant in the context of the Gordon growth model. Whereas Modigliani and Miller neutralized the effect of investment policy by holding investment constant, Gordon achieved the same effect by holding the net present value of investment constant.[10] Otherwise the implications of (7.18) tend to contradict observed behaviour. The suggestion is that in order to maximize share price, all earnings should be retained if $GR > k$ and all earnings should be distributed if $GR < k$, yet few companies seem to follow such extreme policies in practice. Gordon suggested that the most sensible way out of this difficulty is to relax

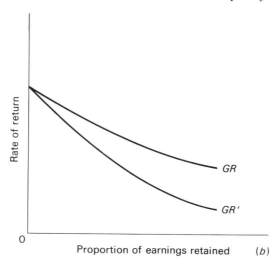

FIGURE 7.1 *The relationship between retentions and rate of return*

the assumption that GR is independent of b. This is intuitively appealing if it is assumed that companies undertake the most profitable investment projects available first, and therefore as more projects are taken on in a given period the profitability of projects at the margin will decline. This means that GR will fall as b is increased. This is shown diagrammatically in figure 7.1.

This figure shows the relationship between the rate of retentions and the average rate of return on projects undertaken (GR), and the marginal rate of return on projects undertaken (GR'). As more projects are undertaken, in a given period, average and marginal profitability decline.

This modification is sufficient to get rid of the extreme implications of the previous approach. If the derivative is taken of (7.17) and it is assumed that GR is a function of b:

$$\frac{ds_0}{db} = \frac{y_0}{(k - bGR)^2}\left[GR - k + b(1 - b)\frac{\partial GR}{\partial b}\right]. \tag{7.19}$$

From (7.19) it follows that if $GR > k$ when $b = 0$, investment is profitable and should be undertaken, but it can be seen from figure 7.1 that as more investment is undertaken (or b is increased) then GR will decline. Investment should be continued up to the point where share price is maximized, which is where the term in brackets [ ] in

(7.19) is equal to 0.[11] Thus, the share price is maximized at some finite value of b where $ds_0/db = 0$. At this point, where the marginal rate of return is equal to the cost of capital, the optimum investment policy and the optimum dividend policy are jointly determined.

A further difficulty with the original Gordon model, (7.17), is that the model only makes sense if $k > bGR$. Otherwise it can be seen from (7.17) that if the value of bGR approaches that of k the share price approaches infinity. A way out of this problem is to assume that k is no longer independent but a function of b. The argument is that an increase in the rate of retentions resulting from an increase in b shifts the timing of expected dividend payments from the projects taken on further into the future. However, dividends expected in the future are regarded as being subject to greater risk than dividends expected in the very near future. Therefore, dividends expected at different future dates will be viewed as having different levels of risk and will be discounted at different discount rates k, the general rule being that the more distant the future dividend the higher the value of k used to discount it. The share valuation model implied is as follows:

$$s_0 = \frac{d_1}{(1 + k_1)} + \frac{d_2}{(1 + k_2)^2} + \cdots + \frac{d_t}{(1 + k_t)^t} \qquad (7.20)$$

where d_t is the expected dividend per share in period t, k_t is the shareholder discount rate appropriate to period t, and $k_t > k_{t-1}$.

7.10   THE RELEVANCE OF DIVIDENDS UNDER THIS APPROACH

The implication of this approach is that dividends are relevant to share valuation in the sense that any change of dividend policy which involves a cut in dividends and an increase in retentions will, other things remaining equal, cause a fall in share value. This is because earnings and consequent receipt of dividends would be shifted further into the future by such a move and would then be discounted at higher rates and so their present value would be less. This can be proved as follows.

If the first derivative of (7.17) is taken and k is assumed to be a function of b, then:

$$\frac{ds_0}{db} = y_0 \frac{\left[GR - k - \frac{\partial k}{\partial b}(1 - b) \right]}{(k - bGR)^2}. \qquad (7.21)$$

Now if GR is set to k so that the rate of return on investment at the margin is equal to the discount rate, or cost of capital k, it still does not follow that dividend policy is irrelevant since:

$$\frac{\mathrm{d}s_0}{\mathrm{d}b} = \frac{-y_0(1-b)\dfrac{\partial k}{\partial b}}{(k - bGR)^2} \neq 0.$$

As this expression is not equal to 0, dividend policy does have an effect on share value unless $\partial k / \partial b = 0$, and it was assumed that, in general, this was not the case. Thus Gordon came to the firm conclusion that dividend policy does affect share value and entered into a dispute with Miller and Modigliani, whose views are considered in the next section.[12]

7.11   DIVIDEND POLICY UNDER RISKY CONDITIONS

The impact of changes in dividend policy under risky conditions will now be examined more closely. This area was broached in the previous section, when Gordon's assumptions about changes in the discount rate to reflect risk in his constant growth model were considered. The most comprehensive and persuasive analysis of the impact of dividend policy under risky or uncertain conditions is that put forward by Miller and Modigliani.[13] They begin by asserting that the share market must display 'imputed rationality' and 'symmetric market rationality'. By this they mean that every trader in the market assumes that all other traders in the market are 'rational' in the sense of preferring more wealth to less, regardless of its form, and that they all impute rationality to all other traders. This is the basis of the second proposition, 'symmetric market rationality', according to which every trader behaves rationally and imputes rationality to the market.

Given these assumptions they suggest that two identical firms (1) and (2) be considered, whose future streams of total earnings and total investment are expected by investors to be identical, and, apart from dividend payments in the first period (period 0), whose future dividend payments are expected to be identical too. The assumptions, adopting the previous notation, are thus:

$$\tilde{X}_{1(t)} = \tilde{X}_{2(t)} \quad \text{for} \quad t = 0, \ldots, \infty$$

$$\tilde{I}_{1(t)} = \tilde{I}_{2(t)} \quad \text{for} \quad t = 0, \ldots, \infty$$

$$\tilde{D}_{1(t)} = \tilde{D}_{2(t)} \quad \text{for} \quad t = 1, \ldots, \infty.$$

where tildes indicate that the variables represent current expectations of future values drawn from probability distributions of expected values.

They then ask the question, what will be the one-period rate of return to existing shareholders in firm 1 in the current period? This one-period expected return is as follows:

$$_0\tilde{r}_1 = \tilde{D}_{1(0)} + N_{1(0)}\tilde{s}_{1(1)} - \tilde{M}_{1(1)}\tilde{s}_{1(1)} \qquad (7.22)$$

where $_0\tilde{r}_1$ is the expected one-period return to shareholders, $\tilde{D}_{1(0)}$ is the expected dividend to be paid by firm 1 in period 0, $N_{1(0)}\tilde{s}_{1(1)}$ is the total value of existing shares at the end of the period, and $\tilde{M}_{1(1)}\tilde{s}_{1(1)}$ is the expected value of new share issues by firm 1 during the period.

Given this, the relationship between new share issues and dividends (in the absence of other sources of funds) is still an accounting identity, as shown in (7.6) and (7.7). Miller and Modigliani write the equivalence as follows:

$$\tilde{M}_{1(1)}\tilde{s}_{1(1)} = \tilde{I}_{1(0)} - (\tilde{X}_{1(0)} - \tilde{D}_{1(0)})$$

and the substitution of this identity in (7.22) gives:

$$_0\tilde{r}_1 = \tilde{X}_{1(0)} - \tilde{I}_{1(0)} + N_{1(0)}\tilde{s}_{1(1)}. \qquad (7.23)$$

Thus they have demonstrated that the one-period payment to shareholders in firm 1 is completely independent of current dividend payments. A similar exercise with identical consequences can be undertaken with regard to the one-period return to existing shareholders in firm 2. Given the original assumptions that the future streams of earnings and investments of the two firms are identical, it follows that the value of the two firms at the end of the period considered, $N_{i(1)}s_{i(1)}$, must depend on the expectations of future earnings, investment and dividends after period 1. But these, too, are identical by assumption. Therefore, the implication of 'symmetric market rationality' implies that every investor expects $N_{1(1)}s_{1(1)} = N_{2(1)}s_{2(1)}$ and, therefore, the one-period return on shares in the two firms must be identical. This means that if the return to shareholders for the period is the same for both firms, it must be independent of any difference in dividend payments in that period. The same analysis, whilst maintainng the assumptions, can be applied to the next period, and so on to future periods. Hence Miller and Modigliani have proved that, given the investment policy, dividend policy is irrelevant in all future periods, even under conditions of uncertainty. The assertion that dividend policy is an unimportant 'mere detail' met with considerable controversy.

Lintner took issue with this viewpoint by defining different types of uncertainty. He agreed that dividend policy was irrelevant under conditions of what he termed 'fully idealized uncertainty' which had the following properties:

(a) all actual and potential shareholders in the market must have identical subjective distributions regarding (b) all relevant aspects of the future, both with respect to (c) the given stock and with respect to (d) all other investments available in the market.[14]

This meant that the relaxation of any one or combination of the above assumptions would make market share price a direct function of the chosen time vector of dividend payments, because the dropping of the assumptions meant shareholders would have a preference for some particular mix of retained earnings and new issues. In general, he argued that existing shareholders would prefer that new investments be financed by retentions as opposed to new issues. This is because a new share issue has to attract new shareholders who are unlikely to hold quite such a favourable view of the company as existing shareholders. This means it would be issued at a discount on current values and this would give a lower market valuation than the alternative of financing by retentions. Therefore, existing shareholders would prefer that investments be financed by retentions. Now in particular types of market conditions, with the addition of market imperfections, Lintner's argument could well hold, but under Miller and Modigliani's original conditions it does not.[15]

Gordon's arguments about the relevance of dividend policy to share valuation were also dismissed by Miller and Modigliani, who argued that his approach 'suffers fundamentally from the typical confounding of dividend policy with investment policy that so frequently accompanies use of the internal financing model.[16] They suggested that shareholders are uncertain about the size of total future returns, but as a change in future dividend payments involves a shift in the future balance of dividends and capital gains, and no change in the expectation of total return, a rational investor should be untroubled by it.

The charge that Gordon's model involves a compounding of the effects of investment and financing decisions is further supported by Brennan.[17] He shows that a change in the retention ratio in Gordon's model from b_1 to b_2 involves not just a one-off change in the amount invested and earned, but a change in investment and earnings in all subsequent periods, which is equivalent to a change in investment policy. It is the net present value of this change in investment policy which has to be examined to determine the influence on share valuation. If the assumption is retained that all investment is financed by retentions and if the increase in investment which follows an increase in the retention ration is denoted by ΔI_t, then the present value of this change in investment policy in period t, which by definition is carried forward into all future periods, is given by:

$$\sum_{z=1}^{z=\infty} \frac{GR \, \Delta I_t}{(1 + k_{t+z})^z} - \Delta I_t.$$

The net present value of all such possible changes in future investment policy is given by:

$$NPV = \sum_{t=1}^{t=\infty} \frac{\Delta I_t}{(1 + k_t)t} \left[-1 + GR \sum_{z=1}^{z=\infty} \frac{1}{(1 + k_{t+z})^z} \right]. \qquad (7.24)$$

Brennan points out that setting $GR = k$ in (7.24) will not cause the expression to be equal to zero unless all the k_t are equal and equal to k, which is precisely the case in which Gordon found dividend policy to be irrelevant. Thus Miller and Modigliani's arguments are upheld.

Brennan also demonstrates that the argument holds under slightly less restrictive assumptions than those implied in 'symmetric market rationality'. He suggests that provided investors accept that the value of a firm at the end of any given period is dependent upon expectations about future earnings, dividends and investment, then a set of assumptions which he terms 'independence of irrelevant information' will lead to the same result. All this requires is that investors are rational in the above sense, that shares are valued on the basis of future prospects, and that at least some investors act on these assumptions. This will be sufficient to ensure that two firms with identical future prospects have the same value, irrespective of dividend policy. In order to reject these findings, one has to argue either that investors are not rational, or that share prices do not depend solely on future events, or that investors generally do not understand the share valuation process. None of these seems very likely.

7.12   THE INFLUENCE OF OTHER MARKET IMPERFECTIONS

Taxation

One of the most important potential influences assumed away in the analysis so far is the impact of taxation. In many countries, including the United Kingdom, capital gains are taxed at a lower rate than tax dividends. Furthermore, cash dividends are taxed at the shareholder's marginal rate of tax, and if it is assumed that most individual shareholders are fairly wealthy, in the surtax bracket, then this would introduce a bias in favour of retentions and a lower payout ratio. The situation is further complicated by the growing influence of the institutions, of which a number, such as pension funds, are not liable to this tax disadvantage.

King has investigated the relationship between the tax discrimination against dividend payments and the payout ratio. He found that the payout ratio was a monotonically increasing function of the existing tax discrimination variable θ ($\theta = 1 - m$, where m is the marginal rate of tax on the shareholder).[18] The elasticity of the payout ratio with respect to θ was not constant but depended on both the optimum payout ratio for the firm and the extent of the tax discrimination. In a more extensive subsequent study, he incorporated an investigation of these effects in empirical tests of a model of dividend behaviour which assumed that dividend payments play an important role in signalling management views to shareholders.[19] (This leads on to issues covered later in section 7.12.) The results, not surprisingly, depended on what marginal tax rate was assumed to be representative of the shareholder's position.

Thus, with taxation, it could be argued that dividend policy is no longer irrelevant, and that an optimum payout policy exists. This leads on to further complications, since it is only shareholders in identical marginal tax positions who will favour a particular payout policy on tax grounds. This has further led to speculation about the existence of a 'clientele effect'. This suggests that firms with particular payout policies will attract shareholders who prefer that type of policy. Elton and Gruber claim to have found evidence of this effect.[20] This does not necessarily have any implications for corporate valuation, however, unless there is a very marked asymmetry in shareholder preferences, since the company's point of view is that one clientele is as good as another.

However, Miller and Scholes have recently demonstrated that, in the American context at least, the attitude towards dividend payments may not necessarily be heavily influenced by individual shareholder tax positions.[21] They demonstrate that, in the appropriate circumstances, the relative tax penalization of dividend payments can be removed by appropriate shareholder action. Their arguments rest upon two features of the American tax system; the possibilities open for the tax-free accumulation of wealth at pre-tax interest rates in certain investments, particularly life insurance, and the limitation of interest deductions to investment income received. The mechanism revolves around 'washing out' the taxable element on the receipt of dividend payments by ensuring the appropriate counterbalancing element of interest payments. This is done by gearing up the individual shareholder's position by borrowing the necessary amount, but any extra financial risk is avoided by reinvesting the proceeds in an insurance policy which, if a riskless rate of interest is assumed, will yield a rate of return equal to the borrowing rate. Thus, the tax-saving element of the interest payments is achieved without any extra risk. The UK tax system does not parallel the American one on this point, and therefore the arguments do not have the same relevance to UK financial markets.

Transactions and flotation costs

The case for the irrelevance of dividends in perfect markets is made under the assumption of zero transactions and flotations costs. In this world, in the absence of differential taxation, the shareholder would be indifferent between current income and capital gains. If he has a capital gain via earnings retentions, and he wants current income in lieu of forgone dividend payments, all he has to do is sell a few shares. But the existence of transaction costs on purchases and sales of securities discriminates against the investor with a preference for current income. This particular shareholder will prefer a company which pays dividends; the sale of a unit of stock is not a perfect substitute for dividend payments, as it bears transactions costs.

Similarly, the existence of flotation costs on new share issues may lead companies to prefer finance by retentions at the expense of dividends, rather than through new issues, as the existence of these costs ensures that each pound's worth of retentions is worth more than a pound's worth of new issues. Indeed, the effect of this, coupled with other influences like the desire to maintain the existing control structure and a reluctance to divulge further information about company operations, have possibly led to the marked preference for finance by retentions displayed by quoted United Kingdom companies.[22] There are further ramifications from this. A number of empirical studies have suggested that companies have been fairly lax in their use of retentions and that, typically, rates of return on assets financed by retentions have been less than on those financed by new issues.[23] Clearly if this is the case, there are important implications for company dividend policies.

The information content of dividend payments

A further complication arises from the fact that capital markets are far from perfect and investors are obviously not in full possession of all relevant information about company activities. A popular argument is that shifts in dividend payments have a major impact upon shareholder expectations. The hypothesis about the 'information content' of dividends is that changes in dividend policy convey to shareholders any revision in the company management's assessment of future earnings prospects. Thus, according to this view, increases in dividend payments are treated gleefully and lead to share price appreciation, whereas cuts in dividends bode ill and lead to a depression of prices. This seems to be a very plausible argument and mere casual observation of securities markets does suggest the existence of such an effect. Empirical evidence provided by Pettit and by Watts provides positive, though varying, degrees of support.[24] In markets with imperfections and various information barriers Lintner's arguments, mentioned previously about the existence of diverse subjective judgemental probability distributions of expected returns could well hold water, and dividend policy could well have an effect upon share value. Nevertheless, it is not dividend policy *per se* which is important but expectations about future levels of income. Dividend policy is only relevant to the extent that it might influence these expectations, and therefore Modigliani and Miller claim that, not withstanding this, their irrelevance of dividends proposition is still inviolate.

However, a recent paper by Hakansson examines the information content of dividends in a general equilibrium framework, and in these circumstances he demonstrates that the Modigliani–Miller irrelevance proposition can be viewed as a special case in a more general framework in which the information content of dividends can render them relevant.[25] In situations in which investors have homogeneous beliefs and time additive utility functions, and where markets are 'complete' in a state preference sense, dividends serve no useful purpose. On the other hand dividends improve investor welfare when beliefs are heterogeneous, utility is not additive, or markets are incomplete, even when there are 'deadweight costs' (unfavourable tax effects, new issue costs, and so on) associated with dividend payments.

Sale of shares at a discount

The conventional arguments about dividend irrelevance assume that, should a company wish to maintain its dividend payments, it can always replace forgone retentions by the issue of new shares at the current market price. This is not necessarily the case. If, as one would expect, there is a downward-slopping demand curve for the company's shares, the shareholders at the margin will have less optimistic expectations about the company's future earnings than the existing shareholders. This means that they will only subscribe to a new share issue at a lower price. This will cause a dilution of the value of all outstanding share capital and, logically, the company should prefer a policy of finance by retention of earnings.

Merrett, Howe and Newbould, in an empirical study of the UK New Issue Market, found substantial evidence that new share issues were at a considerable discount on existing share values.[26]

7.13 CONCLUSION: THE INFLUENCE OF DIVIDEND POLICY ON VALUATION

It is clear that in a perfect market dividend policy is irrelevant, given the investment decision, in that rational investors in these circumstances would be indifferent to the timing or content of their return, be it in the form of dividends or capital gains. In reality, it is also clear that capital markets are manifestly imperfect and that the existence of differential taxation, transactions and flotation costs, different levels of information, and various other imperfections, means that both management and shareholders could have a bias in favour of either dividends or retentions, depending upon the net influence of the various factors mentioned previously. Early studies suggested that dividends have a greater effect upon share value, pound for pound, than retentions.[27] Friend and Puckett disputed this view and also drew attention to the considerable statistical difficulties involved in the empirical investigation of the effects of dividend policy.[28] These are centred around the fact that any empirical study of factors influencing company valuation has to contend with the influence of variables which are not directly observable. Company values are determined by expectations of future returns and estimations of the riskiness of those returns, neither of which are readily available for quantification.

Much of the earlier empirical work could be grouped under the following two headings; partial adjustment models and adaptive expectations models.[29] The classic work on partial adjustment models was done by Lintner who, after conducting interviews with 28 US companies, decided that companies typically had a target payout ratio and that there was a lagged relationship between profit changes and subsequent adjustment of dividends.[30] Brittain also pursued a major study along the same lines.[31]

The essence of the approach is as shown in the following two-equation model:

$$D_t^* = rP_t \tag{7.25}$$

where D_t^* is the optimum level of dividends at time t, r is the target payout ratio, and P_t is the current level of profits.

But dividend payments are not immediately adjusted to their optimum level; they are partially adjusted in each period as in the following expression, which shows the partial adjustment of dividends towards the desired level given in (7.25):

$$D_t - D_{t-1} = a + c(D_t^* - D_{t-1}) + U_t \tag{7.26}$$

where a is a positive constant (this reflects Lintner's finding that firms are reluctant to cut dividends), and c represents the speed of adjustment per period, a reflection of the fact that firms may wish to 'play safe' and not immediately adjust dividends to the desired level.

The statistically estimable reduced form of the model can be obtained by substituting (7.25) into (7.26). This gives:

$$D_t - D_{t-1} = a + c(rP_t - D_{t-1}) + U_t$$
$$\therefore \quad D_t = a + crP_t + D_{t-1}(1 - c) + U_t. \tag{7.27}$$

The adaptive expectations approach assumes that a change in dividends follows in response to a change in the management's perception of long-run profits.[32] This links in with the 'information content' view of dividends. If dividends are raised it is a sign that management's expectations of long-run profits are more favourable. This approach could be expressed as;

$$EP_t - EP_{t-1} = \rho(P_t - EP_{t-1}) \tag{7.28}$$

where EP_t are the expected profits at time t, P_t are the actual profits at time t, and ρ is the 'coefficient of expectations', which reflects the proportion of expectational error assumed to be permanent.

The relationship between dividends and expected profits could be written as follows:

$$D_t = bEP_t \qquad (7.29)$$

where b describes the relationsip between D_t and EP_t, which are as used previously.

The substitution of the solution for EP_t from (7.29) into (7.28) yields the reduced form of the model, suitable for the purposes of statistical estimation once a disturbance term ε_t has been added. Thus:

$$\frac{D_t}{b} - EP_{t-1} = \rho(P_t - EP_{t-1})$$

$$\frac{D_t}{b} = \rho P_t + EP_{t-1}(1 - \rho)$$

$$D_t = b\rho P_t + bEP_{t-1}(1 - \rho)$$

$$\therefore \quad D_t = b\rho P_t + D_{t-1}(1 - \rho) + \varepsilon_t. \qquad (7.30)$$

Waud was the first to point out that the reduced form of the adaptive expectations model, shown in (7.30), and the reduced form of the partial adjustment model, shown in (7.27), are indistinguishable from the standpoint of estimation.[33] One way round the problem is to specify some of the coefficients prior to estimation.

Fama and Babiak tested the partial adjustment model and avoided some of the problems mentioned above by assuming that $\rho = 1$ (in this case the reduced forms of the two approaches are distinct).[34] Their empirical tests derived a value of -0.37 and thus they rejected the adaptive expectations model as being inappropriate and confirmed that the Lintner partial adjustment model performed best. This result was later reaffirmed by Fama in the course of an investigation of the relationship between company dividend and investment decisions.[35] Black and Scholes have tested the effects of dividend yield and dividend policy on share prices and returns utilizing a capital asset pricing model methodology, but could find no evidence of any effects.[36] Thus, there have been numerous empirical studies, some supporting and some opposing the the irrelevance of dividends proposition.[37] The assertion that dividend policy is relevant in imperfect markets is quite plausible, but definite empirical proof, and the discovery, should it exist, of the exact nature of the optimum dividend policy, awaits the development of more sophisticated statistical and econometric techniques.

TEST QUESTIONS

1. Use the Gordon valuation formula to calculate the implied share value in the following cases. Assume the initial earnings per share y_0 are 50p, the discount rate k is 20 per cent, the growth rate GR of reinvested earnings is 15 per cent, and the retention ratio b varies in each case as follows: (a) $b = 0$, (b) $b = 25$ per cent, (c) $b = 50$ per cent, (d) $b = 70$ per cent.
2. Would you expect there to be any difference in the dividend policy of a small, tightly controlled, young company and a large, widely held corporation? Explain fully.
3. When a company increases its dividends, its share price often increases. How would you reconcile this with the Modigliani–Miller dividend irrelevance thesis?
4. Modigliani and Miller demonstrate the conditions under which dividend policy is irrelevant. One assumption they do not make is:
   (a) Capital markets are perfect.
   (b) Transactions costs are non-existent or negligible.
   (c) Investors have homogeneous expectations about future investment policies.
   (d) Tax effects are unimportant.
5. Are any of the following factors likely to have an effect on payout ratios? Explain fully.
   (a) An increase in the rate of income tax.
   (b) An increase in company profits.
   (c) A decline in interest rates.
   (d) A decline in profitable investment opportunities.

NOTES AND REFERENCES

1. Williams, J. B. *The Theory of Investment Value* (1938), reprinted North Holland, Amsterdam, 1964, p. 58.
2. For the original analysis of the effects of dividend policy under these conditions see: Miller, M. H. and Modigliani, F. 'Dividend policy, growth and the valuation of shares', *Journal of Business* **XXXIV**(4), October 1961, pp. 411–33.
   A comprehensive treatment of the subject is available in: Fama, E. F. and Miller, M. H. *The Theory of Finance*, Holt, Rinehart and Winston, Hinsdale, Illinois, 1972.
3. This section draws very heavily on the original article by Miller, M. H. and Modigliani, F. 'Divident policy, growth, and the valuation of shares', *Journal of Business* **XXXIV**(4), October 1961, pp. 411–33.

4. For simplicity equity issues only will be considered. The implication of a new debt issue will be considered in chapter 8, where it will be shown that the debt/equity decision is irrelevant in perfect market conditions.
5. Miller and Modigliani examine four variations:
   (a) the discounted cash flow approach,
   (b) the current earnings plus future investment opportunities approach,
   (c) the stream of dividends approach,
   (d) the stream of earnings approach.
   Miller, M. H. and Modigliani, F. 'Dividend policy, growth and the valuation of shares', *Journal of Business* **XXXIV**(4), October 1961, pp. 411–33.
6. Ibid.
7. See: Levy, H. and Sarnat, M. *Capital Investment and Financial Decisions*, Prentice-Hall, Englewood Cliffs NJ, 1978, p. 302.
   Walter, J. E. 'Dividend policies and common stock prices', *Journal of Finance* **11**(1), March 1956, pp. 24–41.
8. Gordon, M. J. *The Investment, Financing and Valuation of the Corporation*, Irwin, Homewood, Illinois, 1962.
9. Ibid.
10. Brennan, M. J. 'A note on dividend irrelevance and the Gordon valuation model', *Journal of Finance* **26**(5), December 1971, pp. 1115–21.
11. For an investigation of some of the tricky implications of this see: Vickers, D. 'Profitability and re-investment rates: a note on the Gordon paradox', *Journal of Business* **39**(3), July 1966, pp. 366–70.
12. See: Gordon, M. J. 'Optimal investment and financing policy', *The Journal of Finance* **XLVIII**(2), May 1963, pp. 264–72.
13. Miller, M. H. and Modigliani, F. 'Dividend policy, growth and the valuation of shares', *Journal of Business* **XXXIV**(4), October 1961, pp. 411–33.
14. Lintner, J. 'Dividends, earnings, leverage, stock prices and the supply of capital to corporations', *The Review of Economics and Statistics* **XLIV**(3), August 1962, pp. 243–69.
15. Modigliani, F. and Miller, M. H. 'Dividend policy and market valuation: a reply', *Journal of Business* **36**, January 1963, pp. 116–19.
16. Miller, M. H. and Modigliani, F. 'Dividend policy, growth and the valuation of shares', *Journal of Business* **XXXIV**(4), October 1961, pp. 411–33.
17. Brennan, M. J. 'A note on dividend irrelevance and the Gordon valuation model', *Journal of Finance* **26**(5), December 1971, pp. 1115–21.
18. King, M. A. 'Dividend behaviour and the theory of the firm', *Economica*, February 1974, pp. 25–34.
19. King, M. A. *Public Policy and The Corporation*, Chapman and Hall, London, 1977, chapter 6, pp. 166–203.
20. Elton, E. J. and Gruber, M. 'Marginal stockholder tax rates and the clientele effect', *Review of Economics and Statistics* **52**(1), February 1970, pp. 68–74.
21. Miller, M. H. and Scholes, M. S. 'Dividends and taxes', *Journal of Financial Economics*, forthcoming.
22. See: Meeks, G. and Whittington, G. 'The financing of quoted companies in the United Kingdom', Royal Commission on the Distribution of Income and Wealth, Background Paper No. 1, HMSO, 1976.
23. See, for example: Little, I. and Raynor, A. *Higgledy Piggledy Growth Again*, Blackwell, Oxford, 1966.
   Baumol, W., Heim, P., Malkiel, B. and Quandt, R. 'Earnings, retentions, new

capital and the growth of the firm', *Review of Economics and Statistics* **52**(4), November 1970, pp. 345–55.

Whittington, G. 'The profitability of retained earnings', *Review of Economics and Statistics* **54**(2), May 1972, pp. 152–60.

24. Pettit, R. Richardson. 'Dividend announcements, security performance and capital market efficiency', *Journal of Finance* **27**(5), December 1972, pp. 993–1007.

Watts, R. 'The information content of dividends', *Journal of Business* **46**(2), April 1973, pp. 191–211.

25. Hakannson, N. H. 'To pay or not to pay dividends', *The Journal of Finance* **37**(2), May 1982, pp. 415–28.

26. Merrett, A. J., Howe, M. and Newbould, G. D. *Equity Issues and the London Capital Market*, Longmans, London, 1967.

27. See, for example: Gordon, M. J. 'Dividends, earnings and stock prices', *Review of Economics and Statistics* **41**(1), February 1959, pp. 99–105.

28. Friend, I. and Puckett, M. 'Dividends and stock prices', *American Economic Review* **54**(5), September 1964, pp. 656–82.

29. See: Ang, J. S. 'Dividend policy: informational content or partial adjustment?', *Review of Economics and Statistics* **57**(1), February 1975, pp. 65–70.

For an alternative interpretation see: King, M. A. *Public Policy and The Corporation*, Chapman and Hall, London, 1977, pp. 169–71.

30. Lintner, J. 'Distributions of incomes of corporations among dividends, retained earnings and taxes', *American Economic Review* **46**(2), May 1956, pp. 97–113.

31. Brittain, J. A. *Corporate Dividend Policy*, The Brookings Institution, Washington D.C., 1966.

32. See: Prais, S. J. 'Dividend policy and income appropriation', in Tew, B. and Henderson, R. F. (eds) *Studies in Company Finance*, Cambridge University Press, Cambridge, 1959.

Stone, J. R. N. 'Spending and saving in relation to income and wealth', reprint no. 265, University of Cambridge, Dept. of Applied Economics, 1967.

33. Waud, R. N. 'Small sample bias due to misspecification in the 'partial adjustment' and 'adaptive expectations' models', *Journal of the American Statistical Association* **61**, December 1966, pp. 1130–52.

34. Fama, E. F. and Babiak, H. 'Dividend policy: an empirical analysis', *Journal of the American Statistical Association* **63**, December 1968, pp. 1132–61.

35. Fama, E. F. 'The empirical relationships between the dividend and investment decisions of firms', *American Economic Review* **64**(3), June 1974, pp. 304–18.

36. Black, F. and Scholes, M. 'The effects of dividend yield and dividend policy on common stock prices and returns', *Journal of Financial Economics* **1**(1), May 1974, pp. 1–22.

37. See, for example: Walter, J. E. *Dividend Policy and Enterprise Valuation*, Wadsworth, Belmont, California, 1967.

Miller, M. H. and Modigliani, F. 'Some estimates of the cost of capital to the electric utility industry, 1954–57', *American Economic Review* **56**(3), June 1966, pp. 333–91.

CHAPTER 8

The capital structure debate and the cost of capital

> In all the different employments of stock, the ordinary rate of profit varies more or less with the certainty or uncertainty of the returns.[1]

Few commentators would take issue with the accuracy of Adam Smith's observation, but whilst its essential truth remains, the associated analysis has been considerably refined since the original statement appeared in 1776. This chapter will be concerned with the examination of a number of the branches of analysis which have sprung from this original root. The concern will be with the analysis of the nature of the returns required by providers of finance to companies. By and large the discussion will concentrate upon the providers of long-term funds, and the issues will be viewed both from the point of view of the suppliers of the capital ('stock') – the debenture holders and shareholders – and from the point of view of the users – the company itself. Thus the return on capital is a 'profit' or 'required rate of return' from the provider's viewpoint but a 'cost' when regarded from the company's position. It follows that if the assumption is retained that the managers of the company aim to maximize shareholders' wealth, then this is consistent with minimizing the cost of the overall mix of the company's sources of funds.

In the maximization of shareholder wealth, Stiglitz has shown that the company's decisions can be divided into four groups:

(a) How should the company finance its investment?
(b) How should the company distribute its revenue?
(c) How much should the firm invest?
(d) Which projects should the firm undertake (or what techniques of production should the firm employ)?[2]

The first two questions can be viewed as involving financial decisions and the latter two as requiring real decisions in the sense that they involve material factors of production. This chapter is concerned with examining the issues involved in answering question (a); the previous chapter was concerned with question (b). Chapter 6 looked at questions (c) and (d). This adopted scheme immediately poses further questions. Is it 'correct' to distinguish between real and financial decisions? If not, these issues ought to be considered jointly and the three chapters in this part should be regarded as a unit concerned with closely related interdependent issues.

It has already been seen in the previous chapter that under perfect market conditions it is possible to distinguish between real and financial decisions in the case of question (b), and that in these circumstances the chosen distribution/retention policy has no influence upon company valuation. If the previous line is taken, by first considering how the firm should finance its operations under perfect market conditions, then similar conclusions will be reached.

8.1 FINANCING IN A PERFECT MARKET

In perfect markets in conditions of certainty the method a company chooses to finance its activities would be of no consequence. In this situation a debenture would be no different from a share. Investors would know the returns available on both and these would be identical per unit of value; there is only one rate of return in a perfect market, and so both would sell at the same price per unit of return.

8.2 THE PROBLEM OF RISK

If the assumption of perfect markets is retained and risk is introduced into the analysis, then the question of the influence of a company's chosen method of finance, or 'capital structure' in conventional terminology, becomes a much more debatable issue. Indeed, controversies have raged over the last thirty years over whether or not different capital structures have different associated costs of capital. In fact the question is by no means yet resolved, although, as will be seen, there has been considerable clarification of the issues involved and theoretical progress made. But before these matters are considered it will probably help to pause, and 'clear the decks', by considering a few points of method and related matters, before the theoretical fray is joined.

For a start, it must be borne in mind that most of the pioneering work in this area has been framed in the context of semi-static, partial equilibrium analysis.[3] In essence, this approach parallels that adopted in micro-economic analysis and, in many cases, is inspired by micro-economic theory's methodology. In recent years the basic theorems have been generalized in the context of general equilibrium theory, but initially for the sake of clarity the original approach will be followed.[4] Thus the economist's *ceteris paribus* convention (holding all other things equal) is applied, and the effects of variations in the variable of interest are examined in detail.

In the case of the capital structure problem there are a number of other variables which must be taken as given. The fact that the analysis is framed in a perfect market context means that for the moment it is assumed that there are no taxation and transaction costs. It is also obvious from the analysis of valuation models in the previous chapter that any changes in investor expectations of the nature of a company's future earnings can affect its share value, and hence, will be seen, its cost of capital. To avoid this problem it is assumed that the expected values of the subjective probability distributions representing expectations of the future earnings of the company are the same for all investors.

Before further discussion it must be admitted that capital structure is a somewhat 'slippery' concept with a number of possible definitions and hence measures.[5] A convenient comprehensive definition is provided by defining it as the ratio between the total value of fixed and variable interest securities in the balance sheet. But even then further complications arise. Should book or market values be used? On what side of the line do you place hybrids like participating preference shares? For the present purpose, though, the semantics will be ignored and it will be stated that this ratio, however defined, is commonly referred to as gearing (or 'leverage' in American parlance).

One of the central concerns will be the relationship between capital structure and financial risk. It is important to note the distinction between business risk and financial risk. Business risk is broadly defined as the risk which ensues from the very nature of the company's productive operations; it encompasses technical risks, the economic risks in the market it serves, and so forth. Financial risk, on the other hand, is the risk which is purely associated with the capital structure and arises solely from the company's financial structure. Thus 'gearing up', or increasing the proportion of fixed interest securities in the company's capital structure, is regarded as increasing the company's financial risk, particularly from the view-point of the shareholders. This is because debentures are a prior charge against company earnings, and therefore the more highly geared a company the greater the probability that the prior interest charges will eat into earnings available for the shareholders. Even worse, if profits fluctuate markedly, a bad year could mean technical insolvency or bankruptcy.

The analysis which follows has a format on the lines first suggested by Solomon, which provide an object lesson in clarity.[6] For the sake of simplicity it will be assumed that the analysis concerns a company financed purely by long-term debt and equity and the values employed are market values. Thus the total value of the company is given by:

$$V = S + B \tag{8.1a}$$

where V is the company value, S is the market value of the company's shares, and B is the market value of the company's debentures.

As well as the original perfect market assumptions it will also be assumed in the following analysis that:

(a) The expectations of investors in the market about future earnings are the same as those for current earnings; in other words earnings are constant and are not expected to grow.
(b) All existing and future investments are regarded as having the same risk by investors.

In the simplified example the company will generate the following streams of earnings:

X: annual expected net operating earnings.
F: annual debt interest.
Y: annual net earnings on equity.

These three annual earnings streams will be valued or 'capitalized' in the market at three particular capitalization rates. (The assumptions ensure the following simple expressions.)

The equity capitalization rate is given by

$$K_e = \frac{Y}{S} = \frac{\text{earnings available to equity}}{\text{market value of equity}}. \tag{8.2}$$

The debt capitalization rate is given by:

$$K_i = \frac{F}{B} = \frac{\text{debt interest}}{\text{market value of debt}}. \tag{8.3}$$

The overall capitalization rate, also known as the cost of capital, is given by:

$$K_0 = \frac{X}{V} = \frac{\text{net operating earnings}}{\text{total market value of company}}. \tag{8.4}$$

The cost of capital, or overall capitalization rate, K_0, is a weighted average cost of capital. Thus:

$$K_0 = W_1 K_e + W_2 K_i \tag{8.5}$$

where W_1 is the proportion of equity in the capital structure, W_2 is the proportion of debt in the capital structure, and

$$1 = W_1 + W_2.$$

This relationship could also be expressed in terms of its constitutent capital values as follows:

$$K_0 = K_e \frac{S}{(S + B)} + K_i \frac{B}{(S + B)}. \tag{8.6}$$

The crucial question in the examination of the capital structure problem is what happens to K_0, K_e and K_i when the level of gearing, as defined by B/S, is altered? In the approach to this problem, tradition will be followed and the two polar methods of valuing a company's earnings streams will be examined first.[7] These two methods, suggested by Durand, are the net income approach (NI) and the net operating income approach (NOI).[8]

8.3   THE NET INCOME APPROACH

The essential difference between the net income approach and the net operating income approach lies in the different streams of earnings which are capitalized to give the company its market value. In the NI approach it is assumed that both the interest rate on debt and the rate at which shareholders capitalize net earnings available to shareholders are constant, regardless of the level of gearing. This is illustrated in the example which follows. Assume there exists a no-growth firm with annual net operating income (*NOI*) equal to £1,000. Its equity capitalization rate (K_e) is 10 per cent and it is financed entirely by equity. Then:

$$
\begin{aligned}
X = NOI &= \quad £1,000 = \text{net operating income.}\\
F &= \qquad\quad 0 = \text{debt interest.}\\
Y = \quad NI &= \quad £1,000 = \text{net income.}\\
K_e = 10\% &= \quad\ \times 10 = \text{equity capitalization rate.}\\
V &= £10,000 = \text{market value of company.}
\end{aligned}
$$

As net income is capitalized at an equity capitalization rate of 10 per cent the market value of the company is £10,000.

Now assume that the company gears up by replacing some of its equity with £3,000 of debentures. (Strictly speaking it is illegal in the UK to retire equity and replace it with debt, but this will be indulged in for the sake of the example.) If the debentures bear an interest rate of 4 per cent the value of the company and the new cost of capital can be worked out as follows:

$$
\begin{aligned}
X &= \qquad\qquad NOI = \quad £1,000 = \text{net operating income.}\\
F &= 4\% \times £3,000 = \quad\ £120 = \text{debt interest.}\\
Y &= \qquad\qquad NI = \quad\ £880 = \text{net income.}\\
K_e &= \qquad\qquad 10\% = \quad \times 10 = \text{equity capitalization rate.}\\
&\qquad\qquad\quad\ S = \ £8,800 = \text{market value of equity.}\\
&\qquad\qquad\quad\ B = \ £3,000 = \text{market value of debt.}\\
V &= \qquad\quad S + B = £11,800 = \text{market value of company.}
\end{aligned}
$$

The assumption that both K_e and K_i, the capitalization rate on debt, are constant (perhaps a little unrealistic given the increased financial risk that higher gearing involves) means that the company's value increases with increased gearing. This must happen as long as $K_i < K_e$, which is what would be expected in the absence of inflation. Once debt is introduced into the company's capital structure a portion of the company's assets are financed by the relatively cheaper debt. After the deduction of interest charges from net operating income, the net income remaining is still capitalized at the same equity capitalization rate, and net income has not been reduced in the same proportion as the equity funds retired. This means that the value of the smaller amount of equity now required has been increased and this is equivalent to a reduction in the overall cost of

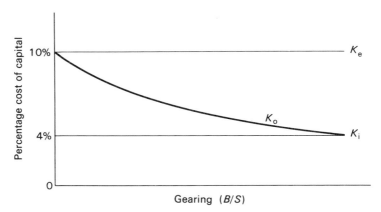

FIGURE 8.1   *The relationship between gearing and cost of capital: the net income approach*

the company's capital. This can be illustrated by the utilization of (8.4):

$$K_0 = \text{cost of capital} = \frac{X}{V} = \frac{\text{net operating earnings}}{\text{market value of company}}$$

$$K_0 = \frac{£1,000}{£11,800}.$$

$$\therefore \quad K_0 = 8.47\%.$$

Thus, the implication of the net income approach is that increases in gearing will continually reduce the overall cost of capital. The relationship between gearing and the cost of capital implicit in this approach is shown in figure 8.1.

8.4   THE NET OPERATING INCOME APPROACH

Different results are obtained with the net operating income approach. The basis of this approach is the assumption that the average cost of capital is constant regardless of the degree of gearing. If it is assumed, as before, that $K_i < K_e$, then the implication is that K_e will have to increase as gearing is increased in order to ensure that the average cost of capital, K_o, is constant. The necessary relationship between K_e and K_o is as follows:

$$K_e = K_o + (K_o - K_i)\frac{B}{S}. \tag{8.7a}$$

The previous example will now be returned to, and a firm will be assumed with a net operating income of £1,000 financed purely by equity with a capitalization rate of 10 per cent. The firm's value, according to the net operating income approach, would be determined as follows:

$$X = NOI = £1,000 = \text{net operating income.}$$
$$K_o = K_e = 10\% = \times\ 10 = \text{cost of capital/equity capitalization rate.}$$
$$V = S = £10,000 = \text{market value of company.}$$

Thus, according to the net operating income approach, it is net operating income, capitalized at the firm's average cost of capital, which determines firm value.

Now, once again, assume that the same firm replaces some of its equity with £3,000 of debentures. The firm's market value, its overall cost of capital, and the rate at which its equity is now capitalized can be determined as shown in the following example:

$$X = NOI = £1,000 = \text{net operating income.}$$
$$K_o = 10\% = \times\ 10 = \text{average cost of capital.}$$
$$V = £10,000 = \text{company value.}$$
$$B = £3,000 = \text{value of debentures.}$$
$$S = V - B = £7,000 = \text{value of equity.}$$

In this approach, by assumption, the average cost of capital is constant and therefore the company value remains constant; but what has happened to the equity capitalization rate? If it is still assumed that the interest rate on debentures is 4 per cent then interest charges are £120, leaving a net income available to shareholders of £880. This means that the equity capitalization rate has risen to the following extent:

$$K_e = \frac{Y}{S} = \frac{NI}{S} = \frac{£880}{£7,000} = 12.57\% \qquad \text{(as predicted in (8.7a)).}$$

This suggests that the gains from gearing up and financing a portion of company assets with cheaper debentures are entirely offset by the accompanying rise in the cost of equity finance. There is a certain logic to this process, in that the shareholders could possibly demand an increase in the equity capitalization rate to compensate them for the increased financial risk of their position, which results from an increase in gearing. The implied relationship between cost of capital and capital structure, according to the net operating income approach, is shown in figure 8.2.

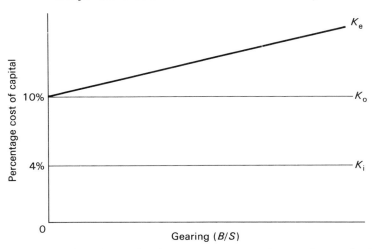

FIGURE 8.2   *The relationship between gearing and cost of capital: the net operating income approach*

Which of the two approaches is correct? Both seem plausible, and it must be admitted that there is no general agreement on the solution to this question. A modified version of the net income approach forms the basis of what is termed the 'traditional' approach to the capital structure problem, which will be examined next. On the other hand, Modigliani and Miller have put forward very powerful theoretical arguments in favour of the net operating income approach.[9]

8.5   THE TRADITIONAL APPROACH

The 'traditional approach' is a generic term used to describe a number of individual approaches to the capital structure problem which share a great deal of commonality. As a general rule traditionalists tend to support a modified version of the net income approach. The essence of the traditional approach is the belief that an optimal capital structure does exist and that careful use of gearing can maximize a company's total value, and therefore minimize its cost of capital.

The argument will begin with the hypothetical case of a company initially financed purely by equity, and it will be assumed, as previously, that $K_i < K_e$ and that any new projects taken on by the company have the same risk and expected returns as existing projects. This means that any change in the perceived riskiness of the company will stem from financial and not business risk. The three stages of shareholder reaction to increases in gearing which are central to the traditional approach are now examined.

Stage 1

The company begins to gear up and introduces some debt into its capital structure. It is usually assumed that at low levels of gearing, the cost of debt, K_i, is constant. This means that, at the margin, a portion of the company's assets are financed by cheaper debt, and that therefore these new assets provide proportionately greater net income for the shareholders than existing assets. In return the shareholders have borne a slight increase in financial risk. Some authorities would argue that the equity capitalization rate, K_e, would remain constant at low levels of gearing, whereas others suggest that it would increase slightly in response to greater financial risk. However, there is agreement that the shareholders would view the higher expected returns as more than compensatory for the increased risk, and that therefore the share price would rise. In figures 8.3 and 8.4 this is illustrated as a movement from A_1 towards B_1.

Stage 2

Further increases in gearing offer the prospect of even greater net income available to shareholders but at the cost of even greater financial risk. The point is reached where the shareholders regard the extra expected returns as only just compensatory for the extra financial risk. This means that there will be no further increase in share value. Company value is therefore maximized and the cost of capital minimized at this level of gearing. This is the optimal capital structure. It is illustrated by point B_1 in figures 8.3 and 8.4.

In figure 8.3 the shareholder's attitudes to risk and expected returns is illustrated by the use of indifference curves. The point of tangency between the line $A_1 C_1$, which represents the risk/return combinations available from gearing up, and the highest attainable indifference curve, marks the optimum capital structure.

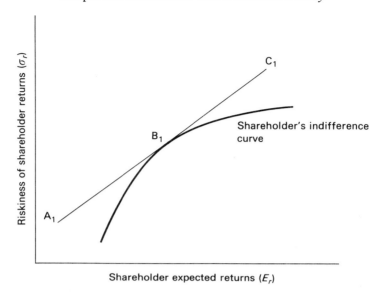

FIGURE 8.3 *The relationship between expected returns and riskiness associated with increases in gearing according to the traditional approach*

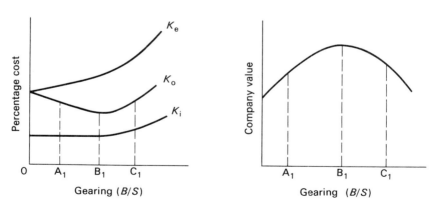

FIGURE 8.4 *The traditional approach, showing the relationship between cost of capital, capital structure, and company value*

Stage 3

If the company persists in gearing up even further, the shareholders will regard the extra potential returns available as not being sufficient to offset the even greater financial risk associated with very high levels of gearing. This will cause the share value to drop and the cost of capital to increase again. This stage is illustrated by point C_1 in figures 8.3 and 8.4.

The general view of the relationship between gearing, cost of capital, and company value adopted in the traditional approach is as illustrated in figure 8.4. There is some disagreement about the average cost of capital curve, K_o. Some authorities regard it as being U-shaped, which suggests that there is a unique optimum, whereas others view it as being saucer-shaped, which suggests a range of optimum gearing levels. For the sake of simplicity I have shown a unique optimum, but whichever view one chooses to adopt matters little in the context of the central arguments involved in this approach.

This then, is the essence of the traditional view. Obviously, riskiness will vary according to the type of industry considered, and some will have more scope for debt finance than others, but all should gain from attempting to gear up to the optimum level for their industry. This appears to be a reasonable argument, but Durand's warning of some of the inherent dangers in this view ought to be heeded. He pointed out that the arguments involved in the net income approach appear to suggest that 'the security holders of a business can raise themselves by their own bootstraps', and he admitted that his own leanings, with some reservations, were towards the net operating income approach. But it was left to Modigliani and Miller to provide the theoretical vindication of this approach, and their arguments will be considered next.

8.6 THE MODIGLIANI–MILLER VIEW

Modigliani and Miller (MM) put forward convincing arguments proving that, given their assumptions, an optimal capital structure does not exist, and therefore that the cost of capital is constant irrespective of the degree of company gearing. Over the years, as a consequence of the controversies and debate provoked by their original article, there have been a number of extensions and slight modifications to their original argument. Nevertheless its essence remains unchanged, and I shall therefore proceed to introduce their ideas by reconsidering their original model, and then subsequently modifying it to take into account later revisions.[10]

The crucial assumptions in their original model are as follows:

(1) The existence of a perfect market with the usual attributes – no transaction costs, rational investors, fully available costless information, infinitely divisible securities, and all buyers and sellers price-takers.

(2) A world of uncertainty in which future profit streams are estimated by investors in the form of subjective random variables. Furthermore, all investors agree in their estimates of these subjective random variables in the case of all companies, and future values are expected to be the same as current values (that is, profit streams are expected to remain constant).

(3) Companies can be grouped into 'equivalent return' classes. All companies within an 'equivalent return' class are homogeneous in the sense that they are subject to the same operating risk. This ensures that the shares of companies in any particular risk class are perfect substitutes for each other.

(4) A world of no taxation.

Modigliani and Miller employ these assumptions to demonstrate that in a perfect market two identical products must sell at the same price. In this case the identical products are the securities of two companies of identical size, earnings capability, and operating risk. The crux of their case is that the net operating earnings of these companies, both identical, would determine their value, and that the financial package funding their operations would have no effect. Thus the companies would have the same value irrespective of differences in their capital structure or degrees of gearing. Modigliani and Miller prove their case by the employment of two propositions.

Proposition 1 is that the market value of any company is independent of its capital structure. If the original notation is retained, and subscript j stands for any firm j in risk class n and a bar over indicates the expected value of a random variable, then this proposition is equivalent to stating that:

$$V_j = (S_j + B_j) = \frac{\bar{X}_j}{K_n} \tag{8.8}$$

where V_j is company value, $S_j + B_j$ is the value of company j's shares and debentures, $\bar{X}_j$ is the expected value of net operating earnings of company j, and K_n is the capitalization rate of equity in risk class n of which company j is a member.

Alternatively, their proposition can be restated in terms of the average cost of capital: the average cost of capital is independent of capital structure and is equal to the capitalization rate of the equity of an ungeared company of the same risk class. This is shown in the following expression, which is an alternative version of proposition 1:

$$\frac{\bar{X}_j}{(S_j + B_j)} = \frac{\bar{X}_j}{V_j} = K_n \quad \text{for all companies in class } n. \tag{8.9}$$

Modigliani and Miller prove that proposition 1 must hold by demonstrating that if it does not there will be scope for 'arbitrage', or switching, by wise investors who will make extra returns until the market returns to an equilibrium where proposition 1 does hold. The arbitrage mechanism works as shown in the following example. First, however, it must be borne in mind that in the perfect capital markets postulated, rational investors are assumed to be indifferent between having a company borrow and gear up on their behalf, and doing the borrowing themselves and producing 'homemade' gearing. Furthermore, in perfect markets investors can borrow at the same rate as corporations. Expressions (8.8) and (8.9) also imply Modigliani and Miller's *proposition 2*, which is simply a restatement of (8.7a) and shows the equilibrium required rate of return on a geared company's equity, as follows:

$$K_j = K_n + (K_n - K_i) \frac{B_j}{S_j} \tag{8.7b}$$

where all symbols are as before and K_j shows the required rate of return on geared company j's shares.

Given all this, suppose there are two companies, company A and company B, both in the same 'equivalent return' class, and both earning £1,000 net operating income. The only difference between the two companies lies in their capital structure, as company A is financed purely by equity whereas company B is geared and has £3,000 of debentures in its capital structure. It will be assumed that the equity capitalization rate, K_e, is 10 per cent and the interest rate is 4 per cent. To illustrate the scope for arbitrage a disequilibrium situation will be assumed in which two companies are valued according to the net income, as opposed to the net operating income, approach:

			company A	company B
X = net operating income	=		£1,000	£1,000
F = debt interest	=		0	£120
Y = net income	=		£1,000	£880
K_e = equity capitalization rate	=		0.10	0.10
S = equity value	=		£10,000	£8,800
B = market value of debt	=		0	£3,000
$V = S + B$ = company value	=		£10,000	£11,800
$K_0 = \dfrac{X}{V}$ = cost of capital	=		10%	8.47%
$\dfrac{B}{S}$ = gearing ratio	=		0	0.375

In this example, according to the net income approach, company B is valued more highly than company A because of the effect of gearing. Modigliani and Miller argue that this situation could not persist because of the scope it presents for the following 'arbitrage' mechanism. Suppose a rational investor owned 10 per cent of company B shares worth £880. He should sell these for £880 and then substitute his own gearing in the same ratio as company B's gearing, so in this case he should borrow £300 at 4 per cent. He now has funds of £1,180. He should reinvest these by spending the £1,180 on 11.8 per cent of company A, as this will make him better off. This can be proved by examining the relative annual income associated with the two positions:

Original income:
A 10 per cent holding of shares in company B yields an annual income of £88.

Income after arbitrage:

An 11.8 per cent holding in company A yields an annual income of	£118
Less interest at 4 per cent of borrowing of £300	−£12
His new income after arbitrage	£106

Clearly he is much better off after engaging in this 'arbitrage' operation.

Opportunities for gain resulting from this 'arbitrage' operation will continue to exist until the market value of the geared company has been pushed down by these activities to the same value as the company financed purely by equity. This is the equilibrium price level. To continue with the example, if company A and company B are to have the same value and assuming that B's debentures are valued at £3,000, then B's share capital must be valued at £7,000. To demonstrate that this is the equilibrium price level the 'arbitrage' process will be examined once again, assuming these prices.

An investor with a 10 per cent holding of company B's equity could sell his shares for £700. To substitute a comparable level of 'home-made' gearing for corporate gearing, he would borrow £300 at 4 per cent, as previously. He would now possess £1,000 of funds which he would reinvest in company A, purchasing 10 per cent of its equity. His relative income from the two investment positions is as follows:

Original income:
Annual income from a 10 per cent holding of company B shares is
   £88.

Income after arbitrage:

A 10 per cent holding in company A yields an annual income of	£100
Less interest at 4 per cent on borrowings of £300	−£12
His new income after 'arbitrage'	£88

Clearly, at the equilibrium price, by definition, there is no further gain to be made by engaging in the 'arbitrage' operation.

Once granted their assumptions, Modigliani and Miller have indisputably proven their case. The question was, and still is, to what extent can their assumptions be relaxed, real-world imperfections be readmitted, and yet their conclusions remain valid? In point of fact, as will be seen in the remainder of this chapter, their conclusions have proved in the following years of argument and discussion, to be much more general and far more robust than most would have originally imagined.

Durand in an early reply conceded their theoretical case but attacked the 'subtle and restrictive' nature of their assumptions.[11] The next concern will be with the way their arguments have been modified and extended over the years to counter this type of criticism.

8.7   THE INFLUENCE OF CORPORATE TAXATION

The existence of corporate taxation is a market imperfection which is obviously going to influence both company and investor earnings, and hence have an influence on company cost of capital. In their original paper Modigliani and Miller briefly referred to the influence of taxation and stated that the 'arbitrage' process would ensure that the market values of companies in each 'equivalent return' class, in equilibrium, must be in proportion to their net of tax, expected return. This ignores the tax-saving element on the interest payments of geared companies, an error of omission which they amended in a subsequent paper.[12]

If taxation is included, the after-tax earnings of a company can be expressed as:

$$X^t = (1 - t)(X - F) + F \qquad (8.10)$$

where X^t are after-tax earnings gross of interest payments, and t is the corporate tax rate. Expression (8.10) simplifies to:

$$X^t = (1 - t)X + tF. \qquad (8.11)$$

Expression (8.11) represents the company's net of tax returns. The effect of the introduction of company tax considerations on the cost of capital will depend on how net of tax returns are capitalized to determine company value. If K^t is the capitalization rate of the net of tax returns of an ungeared company, then its cost of capital will be given by:

$$K^t = \frac{(1 - t)}{V_u} \bar{X} \qquad (8.12)$$

where $\bar{X}$ is the expected value of after-tax earnings, K^t is the capitalization rate for net of tax returns, and V_u is the market value of a company without gearing. However, what happens in the case of a geared company with the extra tax-saving element in its earnings of tF? Its value will obviously be greater, and the extent of this gain in value will once again depend on how the excess earnings tF are capitalized. Modigliani and Miller originally suggested that if the company's debt was permanent and riskless, then this element could be capitalized at the pure rate of interest.[13] However, whether the pure rate of interest, or a higher rate to allow for risk, is adopted, it does not effect the essential logic of the argument. In either case the geared company will be worth more, as can be seen from the following expression:

$$V_L = \frac{(1 - t)}{K^t} \bar{X} + \frac{tF}{r} = V_u + tB \qquad (8.13)$$

where V_L is the value of a geared company, and

$$\frac{tF}{r} = \frac{trB}{r} = tB$$

(because the debentures are assumed to be riskless). This cuts across Modigliani and Miller's earlier finding that capital structure is irrelevant. Expression (8.13) shows that the value of a geared company is always greater than that of an ungeared company. Therefore its cost of capital is less. As its gain in value increases with increases in gearing, it also implies that the cheapest form of capital structure is 100 per cent debt. In practice, Modigliani and Miller suggest that considerations such as the personal tax positions of investors (which we will turn to shortly), limitations imposed by creditors, and other real-world imperfections and costs, prevent companies from choosing 100 per cent debt capital structures. This concession though, as Van Horne suggests, is a little puzzling in that it suggests that after a certain level of gearing the cost of capital rises; is this a return to the traditional view?[14] Even without these tax considerations there are difficulties with the theoretical implications of their arguments with respect to very high levels of gearing.

8.8 THE COST OF CAPITAL AT EXTREME LEVELS OF GEARING

Further problems arise concerning the possible behaviour of the debt and equity capitalization rates at very high levels of gearing. If it is assumed that debt-holders are risk averse, presumably one of the principal reasons for holding debt, then the increased level of financial risk associated with high gearing will probably cause them to demand recompense via an increase in the debt capitalization rate. Modigliani and Miller accept this but argue that their first proposition still holds and the average cost of capital remains constant. This can only be the case, though, if the increase in the equity capitalization rate correspondingly diminishes at very high levels of gearing.[15] If this is the case, why should investors place a higher value on shares subject to a greater level of financial risk than at previous levels of gearing? Modigliani and Miller rejoin that some investors are not averse to risk, and are gamblers who are willing to pay a premium for very risky shares. This is a little confusing if, at lower levels of gearing, investors try to avoid taking on greater financial risk without recompense. It must be admitted that this is a

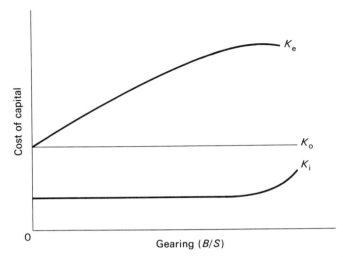

FIGURE 8.5   *The Modigliani–Miller model: cost of capital and capital structure*

puzzling though minor theoretical point, as in practice companies do not gear up to these very high levels. The implied behaviour of capitalization rates in the Modigliani–Miller model is as shown in figure 8.5.

8.9   A SUGGESTED RECONCILIATION OF THE MODIGLIANI–MILLER AND TRADITIONAL APPROACHES

Robichek and Myers suggested a possible reconciliation of the two views.[16] They argued that common sense and mere observation reveal that companies, despite the tax advantages, do not gear up to very high levels. Gearing has remained at relatively conservative levels for decades. Why is this so? They argue that the assumption that investors do not think that higher gearing has an effect on the company's expected net operating income is unrealistic. In a multi-period context company valuations reflect investor expectations about future investment activities. They suggest that highly geared companies in imperfect markets, if faced with temporary earnings setbacks, may find themselves unable to proceed with planned investment. The existence of market imperfections may limit the availability of funds at the company's cost of capital. The risk that this will happen increases with gearing and thus they suggest that the investor's estimate of average earnings $\bar{X}$ may well be a declining function of gearing.

Given this assumption they take (8.11) and rewrite it as:

$$X^t = (1 - t)\bar{X}(\lambda) + tiB \tag{8.14}$$

where $\bar{X} = \bar{X}(\lambda)$ is assumed to decline with high levels of gearing.

If (8.14), representing the expected income of a geared company is then capitalized to give the value of a geared company, the following expression is obtained:

$$V_L = \frac{(1 - t)\bar{X}(\lambda)}{K^t} + tB. \tag{8.15}$$

Rearrangement of (8.15) shows that if:

$$\frac{(1 - t) \, d\bar{X}(\lambda)}{K^t \, dB} > t$$

then the value of a geared company will be a declining function of leverage. Robichek and Myers then argue that if we knew the specification of $\bar{X} = \bar{X}(\lambda)$, then the optimal capital structure would be determined by the following condition:

$$\frac{(1 - t) \, d\bar{X}(\lambda)}{K^t \, dB} = t. \tag{8.16}$$

A reconciliation of the two views on similar lines can also be achieved if bankruptcy costs are introduced, and this will be examined in a later section of this chapter.

8.10 THE IMPACT OF PERSONAL TAXATION

Although the impact of personal taxation was alluded to in earlier articles it was only recently that Miller elucidated the impact of personal taxation upon the Modigliani–Miller thesis.[17] His analysis runs as follows, the value of an all equity financed company (assuming perpetual streams) will be equal to its after-tax (personal and corporate) earnings, capitalized at the appropriate rate. This is given by:

$$V_E = \frac{X(1 - t)(1 - t_{ps})}{K^t}$$

where t_{ps} is the personal tax rate on income from shares and all other notation is as used previously. If the firm is geared with debt outstanding its cash earnings after payment of debt interest will be given by:

$$(X - rB)(1 - t)(1 - t_{ps})$$

and its payment to debtholders will be $rB(1 - t_{pB})$, where t_{pB} is the personal tax rate on income from debentures. The total payments to suppliers of capital can be written:

$$X(1 - t)(1 - t_{ps}) - rB(1 - t)(1 - t_{ps}) + rB(1 - t_{pB}).$$

The value of a geared company V_G will be equivalent to these perpetual streams capitalized at the appropriate rates. Thus:

$$V_G = \frac{X(1 - t)(1 - t_{ps})}{K^t} - \frac{rB(1 - t)(1 - t_{ps})}{r} + \frac{rB(1 - t_{pB})}{r}$$

(assuming the debt is riskless). This means the value of a geared company is equal to the value of an all equity financed company plus a premium.

$$V_G = V_E + B\left[1 - \frac{(1 - t)(1 - t_{ps})}{(1 - t_{pB})}\right]. \tag{8.17}$$

If the tax rates are set equal to zero in (8.17) then the result is the standard Modigliani–Miller finding of no gains from gearing in the absence of taxation. If the personal tax rate on income from shares is the same as that on income from debentures, then the gain from gearing is equal to tB, the standard finding which has already been met in (8.13).

The really interesting results are in the range where $t_{pB} > t_{ps}$, which is the case for most investors in the UK since the 1973 introduction of the imputation system of corporate taxation. In this range the gains from gearing will be less than tB, and in some cases, depending on the relative tax rates, could be zero or even negative. Furthermore, Miller suggests that as investors are interested in net of tax returns, to finance their consumption, debenture holders will have taken this tax disadvantage into account when assessing the yield on the debentures they hold. Thus, although the interest payable on debentures is tax deductible, from a corporate point of view the interest paid, or yield to investors, will have been grossed up to allow for the unfavourable tax treatment from the investor's point of view. Thus, much of the gain is illusory.

The differences in personal tax rates will ensure that where the interest offered on fixed interest securities is the pure interest rate, then only tax-exempt individuals, or securities which offer non-taxable returns, such as some Government securities, will be active in the market. Investors paying taxes will only be enticed into the market where higher security yields offer compensation for their tax position. This suggests, states Miller, that there will be an equilibrium level for aggregate corporate debt, but there will be no optimum debt level for individual companies. Instead there will be a clientele effect. Companies with high gearing will attract a clientele of investors in low tax brackets and the reverse will apply for companies with low gearing. But from the individual company's point of view, one clientele is as good as another, and hence there will be no effect on company value. This suggests that even granted the existence of favourable tax treatment of debentures, the original Modigliani–Miller thesis concerning the absence of an optimum structure still holds.

However, DeAngelo and Masulis extended the approach in a state preference context, and took into account the existence of non-debt corporate tax shields such as depreciation allowance and investment tax credits.[18] The implication is that as a company expands its debt issues there is a greater probability that it will not be able to fully utilize all available tax shields. The introduction of these considerations implies that each company will have a unique optimal capital structure in equilibrium even after all Miller's 'supply-side' effects are taken into consideration. The inclusion of other debt-related costs such as bankruptcy costs further reinforces their findings.

Modigliani has recently added further weight to this view by means of an analysis conducted in a mean–variance framework.[19] He shows that gearing will have a positive value, though its advantages will be more modest if the tax-saving element is regarded as being subject to risk, rather than a perpetuity as in the previous arguments by Miller and Modigliani and Miller. Thus, the tax implications of debt are still a moot point, but opinion does seem to be swinging back to a 'traditional' viewpoint.

8.11 'ME FIRST' AND 'EQUAL ACCESS' RULES

It was seen in (8.1) that maximizing a company's value V is equivalent to maximizing the combined sum of the values of its equity S and debentures B. However, it may be possible to maximize overall value by taking decisions which involve a shift in the component values of B and S in favour of either the debenture or the equity holders. Thus, one can think of three possible subsidiary maximizing criteria within the context of maximizing overall value V:

Maximize overall value V whilst at the same time maximizing:

either   (a)   the individual values of B and S,
or   (b) S at the expense of B,
or   (c) B at the expense of S.

To avoid this problem and any possible ambiguities, Fama and Miller suggested 'me first' rules.[20] (This problem has already been encountered from an option theory viewpoint in section 5.12.)

The problem will be examined along the lines provided by Chen and Kim.[21] If a multiperiod approach is adopted within the framework of perfect capital markets, then security values will depend upon the distribution of future returns that they promise to owners. Assume that at time t the firm has fixed its value maximizing investment strategy for all future periods. The value of the firm V at time $t + 1$ is $\bar{V}_{t+1}$, the expected value of a random variable. This is made up of income generated between t and $t + 1$, termed $\bar{X}_t$, plus the discounted value of all future earnings $\bar{W}_{t+1}$. Thus:

$$\bar{V}_{t+1} = \bar{X}_t + \bar{W}_{t+1} \tag{8.18}$$

where $\bar{V}_{t+1}$ is the expected value of the company at time $t + 1$, $\bar{X}_t$ is the expected value of net operating income between time t and $t + 1$, and $\bar{W}_{t+1}$ is the expected value of future net operating income: $\bar{X}_{t+1}$, $\bar{X}_{t+2}$, ...

Suppose that the company has shares and debentures outstanding from $t - 1$ with its debentures maturing at $t + 1$. The total liability to debenture holders at $t + 1$ is $\tilde{Y}_{t+1}$. If bankruptcy occurs at $t + 1$, ownership of the company transfers without cost to the debenture holders. Given these assumptions, Chen and Kim define the gross returns to shareholders and debenture holders at $t + 1$ as follows:

$$\bar{Y}^{s}_{t+1} = \begin{cases} \bar{V}_{t+1} - \tilde{Y}_{t+1} & \text{if} \quad \bar{V}_{t+1} \geq \tilde{Y}_{t+1} \\ 0 & \text{if} \quad \bar{V}_{t+1} \leq \tilde{Y}_{t+1} \end{cases} \tag{8.19}$$

$$\bar{Y}^{B}_{t+1} = \begin{cases} \tilde{Y}_{t+1} & \text{if} \quad \bar{V}_{t+1} \geq \tilde{Y}_{t+1} \\ \bar{V}_{t+1} & \text{if} \quad \bar{V}_{t+1} \leq \tilde{Y}_{t+1} \end{cases} \tag{8.20}$$

where $\bar{Y}^{s}_{t+1}$ is the expected value of the shareholder 'interest' at $t + 1$, and $\bar{Y}^{B}_{t+1}$ is the expected value of the debenture holder's 'interest' at $t + 1$.

The addition of (8.19) and (8.20) gives the following expression:

$$\bar{Y}^s_{t+1} + \bar{Y}^B_{t+1} = \bar{V}_{t+1}. \tag{8.21}$$

If, as previously, the equilibrium market values of the shares and debentures of the company at time t are represented by S_t and B_t, then (8.21) implies that in equilibrium:

$$S_t + B_t = V_t. \tag{8.1b}$$

This is precisely what would be expected as this is a restatement of (8.1a).

The implications of 'me first' rules can now be examined in more detail. What happens if the company, at time t, issues new debentures which promise a payment of $\bar{Y}^n_{t+1}$ at time $t+1$ and have a market value of B^n_t, and the company pays out the proceeds as dividends to shareholders? If the company's investment decisions are assumed to be unchanged, its net operating income at $t+1$, $\bar{X}_{t+1}$, will remain the same, as will its overall value $\bar{V}_{t+1}$. After this change in financing arrangement the shareholders' wealth will be equal to the new value of their shares plus the extra dividend distribution, that is, $S'_t + B^n_t$, and the value of previously existing debentures will be B'_t.

Therefore if the value of the company is unchanged its value must be determined from (8.1b):

$$V_t = S_t + B_t.$$

But although its overall value has not changed, following the change in its financing arrangements, the constituents of this overall value have changed, as shown in the following expression:

$$V'_t = S'_t + B^n_t + B'_t. \tag{8.22}$$

A comparison of these two expressions for V_t and V'_t shows clearly that any change in the value of the equity interest, following this financial restructuring, will be matched by a change in the value of the original debenture interest of equal and opposite sign. This is shown in the following expression:

$$S'_t + B^n_t - S_t = B_t - B'_t. \tag{8.23}$$

This means that some changes in a company's capital structure could conceivably be detrimental to either the shareholder or debenture interests without altering overall company value. In the example given, if $S'_t + B^n_t > S_t$ then the shareholder's wealth has increased at the expense of the original debenture holder's wealth, for it follows that $B'_t < B_t$. It was to avoid these possible ambiguities that Fama and Miller suggested 'me first' rules. In the example this would entail shareholders compensating original debenture holders for their loss of wealth.

However, Fama has subsequently demonstrated that these 'me first' rules are not strictly nesessary.[22] Within the context of a pervect market he demonstrates that two distinct approaches can prove the irrelevance of a company's financing decisions without resort to 'me first' provisos. One approach involves the assumption that both investors and firms have 'equal access' to capital markets. In essence this ensures that in equilibrium 'arbitrage' forces company values to be unaffected by capital structure. This is because investors can replicate company gearing with their own gearing which enjoys a similar attribute of limited liability. It is achieved, perhaps, by pledging their security holdings as collateral for loans. This leads to a stronger proposition about the general equilibrium in financial markets in which company financial decisions are irrelevant.

The second approach involves the assumption that no firm issues securities for which there are not perfect substitutes in the form of other firms' securities on the market. In practice it involves a concept similar to Modigliani–Miller's original 'equivalent return' classes. As only firms can issue these securities, Fama points out that this leads to a weaker, partial equilibrium statement that the financing decisions of any one particular firm are irrelevant.

He also demonstrates that the difficulties cited at the beginning of this section concerning the maximization of either combined debenture and shareholder wealth, or one at the expense of the other, can be avoided. He suggests that in a perfect market there is a clear stimulus to maximize combined shareholder and debenture holder wealth. If this policy is not followed, outsiders have an incentive to take over the company and expropriate the one-off gain which would result from reversal to this policy. The fact that market values reflect current investor sentiment about company investment policies provides further stimulus to this.

8.12   LIMITATIONS ON THE 'ARBITRAGE' PROCESS AND BANKRUPTCY COSTS

The 'arbitrage' process, which is crucial to the 'irrelevance of capital structure' thesis, rests upon the substitution of home-made gearing for corporate gearing. A problem arises from the fact that corporations enjoy limited liability whereas individual investors normally do not. This means that home-made gearing is not a perfect substitute for company gearing, as it involves the possibility of a negative income, whereas company gearing, via limited liability, at worse involves a zero return. If an investor's holdings, partly financed by his own borrowings, do not yield a sufficient income to pay the interest on those borrowings, then he is liable for the difference. Admittedly some investors, such as the increasingly dominant financial institutions, do enjoy limited liability, but the only way an individual investor could get round this problem would be by seeking permission to pledge his shareholdings as security for the loan. It must be conceded that the 'arbitrage' process does not require all investors to engage in it, but merely sufficient to enforce the 'equilibrium' price, and how many make a sufficient number is very much a moot point.

The trade-off between the tax 'savings' and bankruptcy costs associated with gearing up have been employed by a number of authorities as a means of rehabilitating the traditional approach.[23] A major contribution towards the analysis of bankruptcy costs has been made by Stiglitz who has also provided further proof of the irrelevance of financing decisions in the context of a general equilibrium, state preference framework.[24] This proof requires much weaker assumptions than partial equilibrium proofs, but even so Stiglitz suggests there are three major assumptions which constrain the theory. First, changes in financial policy must have no effect on investor expectations. Second, individual investor borrowing must be a perfect substitute for company borrowing. Finally, and he regards this as the most onerous constraint, there must be no possibility of bankruptcy involved with gearing up, or, in other words, debt must be riskless. This means that the possibility of bankruptcy is ruled out. If debt is risky, then there is a possibility that net operating income will not be sufficient to cover interest charges, and, at the same time, company prospects will appear so bleak that the company will not be able to issue new securities to cover its liabilities. If this possibility exists, increased gearing could increase the probability of bankruptcy. The spectre of bankruptcy has a number of associated costs such as legal fees, lost production, the cost of having management tied up with the proceedings, lost tax credits, and so forth. As long as debt is risky, these expected costs will increase with gearing up.[25] If the framework for firm valuation, given the possibility of bankruptcy, as utilized in (8.19), (8.20), and (8.21), and if BC_t represents the expected value of bankruptcy costs and TG_t the expected value of tax gains from debt, then (8.1b) can be rewritten as follows:

$$\bar{S}_t + \bar{B}_t + \overline{TG_t} - \overline{BC_t} = \bar{V}_t$$
$$\bar{S}_t + \bar{B}_t \qquad\qquad = \bar{V}_t - (\overline{TG_t} - \overline{BC_t}). \qquad (8.24)$$

To optimize the value of the firm the term in (8.24) in parentheses is maximized, and thus the concept of an optimal capital structure can be reinstalled as trade-off between the tax-saving element of debt and the expected cost of bankruptcy.

However, this approach has been dismissed by Miller, basically on the grounds that bankruptcy costs are relatively insignificant.[25] As yet, there is little empirical evidence either way on this point. But before it is admitted that, as yet, there is no satisfactory explanation of observed capital structures, one further line of approach which has been developed in recent years will be considered which involves explicit consideration of managerial self-interest.

8.13   MANAGERIAL SELF-INTEREST AND THE
FINANCIAL SIGNALLING APPROACH

Ross has adopted the concept of signalling, developed originally by Akerlof and Arrow, and employed it in the context of financial markets.[27] This approach assumes the existence of uncertainty and an imperfect market incorporating information barriers. Managers are assumed to possess privileged inside information about the profitability and risk of a company's activities, which is signalled to the market via financing decisions. The managers are compensated by an incentive system of which outsiders have full knowledge. Ross assumes that they receive a payment that is proportional to the value of the company, and the managerial incentive compensation could be of the following type:

$$MI = (1 + r)\gamma_0 V_0 + \gamma_1 \begin{cases} V_1 & \text{if} \quad V_1 \geq H \\ V_1 - L & \text{if} \quad V_1 < H \end{cases} \qquad (8.25)$$

where MI is managerial incentive compensation, γ_0 and γ_1 are positive constants, V_0 and V_1 are the values of the company at periods 0 and 1, H is the face value of debentures, and L is the penalty associated with bankruptcy as experienced by managers (not to be confused with costs of bankruptcy to the firm). (NB: MI is valued from the point of view of time period 1 in two-period model.)

If increases in gearing are positively interpreted by investors in the market as signals of managerial confidence in the profitability of the company, then increases in gearing will lead to increases in company value and an increase in managerial compensation as long as bankruptcy is avoided. However, increases in gearing involve an increase in the probability of bankruptcy, $P\{V_1 < H\}$, and its associated expected costs, $P\{-L\}$. This means that a trade-off exists between these two factors from the manager's point of view, and therefore the optimum level of gearing is determined at the point where the marginal gain in managerial compensation, resulting from increased firm value, is just equivalent to the marginal cost of the bankruptcy penalty. This approach suggests, once again, that an optimal capital structure exists. It is admittedly still in its infancy, but has recently been further developed by Bhattacharya.[28]

8.14 AGENCY THEORY

Jensen and Meckling have developed a theory of agency costs which has interesting implications for capital structure theory.[29] They take as their starting-point the divorce of ownership from control, in the typical large corporation, and suggest that the employment by outside shareholders (the principals) of professional management (the agents) to run the corporation on their behalf leads to the development of agency costs. Their central arguments have extremely far-reaching implications, though the technicalities of the model they develop are somewhat limited in that they only apply to cases where management have a shareholding too. This being the case, they demonstrate that if it is assumed that both outside shareholders and the management (in their role as managers, as well as shareholders) are utility maximizers, then the following costs are likely to arise:

(a) Monitoring costs borne by the shareholders.
(b) Bonding costs incurred by the managers.
(c) Residual loss.

The analysis underlying this runs as follows. It is likely that there will be some divergence of interests between the management, who are likely to consume perquisites and the like, and the shareholders. The shareholders will therefore be prepared to incur monitoring costs so that they can 'keep an eye' on the activities of the management. These will typically take the form of payments to the company's auditors for the production of a set of annual accounts which will enable them to assess management performance.

If the managers have an interest in the ownership of the company, they will face a trade-off between increased consumption of 'on-the-job' perks and the decline in the market value of the firm, and in their shareholding, that is likely to result from such activities. The bonding costs might take the form of contractual guarantees, or limitations on the management's decision—making discretion in certain areas. These actions will cut possible 'perks' but will serve to reduce agency costs. Finally, there will be some residual loss, since when decisions are taken by proxy it is unlikely that they will be strictly optimal and identical to those desired by the shareholders.

There are a number of possible ways in which the preceding analysis is likely to influence capital structure decisions. If the controlling interest in a corporation is heavily weighted in favour of owner/managers with a small proportion of outside shareholders, then the capital structure of the corporation is unlikely to include a lot of debt. This follows from the analysis of the 'me first' rules considered in section 8.11. Under these circumstances there would be a strong temptation to take decisions which transfer wealth from the debt-holders to the shareholders. Various indentures, provisions, and covenants included in debt issues will guard against this but will increase the agency costs associated with a debt issue. At some stage a point will be reached where the marginal agency costs of a further debt issue outweigh the marginal agency costs of a further equity issue; depending on the scale of these relative costs it will pay to issue either debt or equity. Thus funding decisions are determined, but it is not simply a capital structure theory since it is also a function of ownership structure (given the proviso that the management are always assumed to have some shareholding in the company). Thus, the capital structure decision will be a function of how closely the company is held as well as of the related agency costs, all of which are ultimately borne by the owners.

8.15   CONCLUSION: WHAT CAN WE SAY ABOUT THE CAPITAL STRUCTURE DECISION?

There is no doubt that Modigliani and Miller's original proposition about the irrelevancy of capital structure decisions in perfect markets has been proven conclusively. Thus, in this context, the separation theorems hold, and financial decisions can be separated from real decisions. Indeed, in perfect markets all financial decisions are irrelevant, and both the dividend decision considered in the previous chapter, and the capital structure decision, are 'mere details'.

If this is the case, though, why is it that firms devote such time and expense to the consideration of these matters? Well, obviously financial markets are imperfect, and the exact status of company financial decisions in imperfect markets has yet to be determined. There has been a lot of empirical work undertaken but it is at best inconclusive. This is not surprising given the formidable difficulties likely to be encountered in statistical and econometric work in this area. The problem frequently encountered in empirical work related to company valuation is that of setting up the model and data in such a way that other factors which effect company valuation are 'screened'. Furthermore, if an attempt is made to compare the variations in company value associated with different capital structures in a cross-section of companies, then screening all the other factors which affect valuation is virtually impossible. On the other hand, if attention is focused on the effect of capital structure changes in individual companies then there are likely to be related costs and associated flows of funds, in or out, in conjunction with the 'pure effects' of capital structure change, which are likely to affect company value. Some of the major studies will be referred to briefly in the light of these difficulties.

An early classic study was undertaken by Miller and Modigliani who analysed the cost of capital to the electric utility industry in the period 1954–57. They claimed that evidence from their sample of 63 companies supported their theory and showed a contribution to corporate valuation from the tax subsidy available on corporate debt.[30] Hamada attempted a test of the Modigliani–Miller theorem by means of a CAPM methodology. (For a consideration of capital structure theory in the context of CAPM see appendix 8.1.) He interpreted evidence from his sample of 304 firms as being consistent with the Modigliani–Miller theorem.[31] However, there have been a large number of studies which support the traditional view, and thus the findings are mixed with no clear-cut answers.[32] In a sense, tests of CAPM are tests of capital structure propositions (see appendix 8.1), but given the formidable doubts about the adequacy of current tests, considered in section 4.15, there is not likely to be much consolation from this area of the literature.

Thus no definite conclusion can be reached about the existence or nature of an optimum capital structure. Yet this is not necessarily a cause for despondency. It is to be hoped that the material covered in chapters 7 and 8 has given an intimation of the tremendous advance in the understanding of financial decisions which has taken place in recent years, and which will continue in response to the increasing sophistication of the mathematical and econometric techniques applied within the field.

TEST QUESTIONS

1. With which of the following statements do you agree?
   (a) Risk and expected earnings per share are a positive function of gearing.
   (b) Optimal gearing is achieved at the level of gearing where expected earnings per share are maximized.
   (c) According to MM, the value of a geared company is a positive function of the amount of debt issued because of the tax treatment of debt interest.
   (d) In a MM world without taxes the weighted average cost of capital is constant irrespective of the level of gearing.
2. A firm's beta coefficient is 0.8, the risk-free rate is 10 per cent, and the market risk premium is 8 per cent. Assuming that the company is all equity financed, what is its cost of capital?
3. The capitalization rate for an all equity financed firm of comparable risk is 15 per cent. The rate of interest on debt is 10 per cent. The company in question has chosen to finance itself by 50 per cent debt and equity. According to MM's proposition 2, what is its implied cost of equity capital?
4. In a world of no taxes, company A has perpetual net operating income of £1,500, is financed by equity, and has a value of £15,000. Company B has the same net operating income subject to the same risk, and has £6,000 of 5 per cent debt issued, and a total market value (debt plus equity) of £18,000. Assume that you own 10 per cent of the equity of B and can borrow at 5 per cent.
   (a) What opportunity do you have to engage in arbitrage?
   (b) What is the equilibrium cost of the equity capital of company B?
   (c) What is the equilibrium value of company B?
5. Do you agree with the following statements?
   (a) Firms with stable sales and earnings should have higher gearing ratios.
   (b) Shareholders are better served by lower gearing since their dividends are 'safer'.

(c) Tax considerations should be paramount in determining company capital structure.
(d) The decision to issue debt has an information content which parallels that of the dividend decision.

CAPITAL STRUCTURE THEORY IN A CAPM CONTEXT

This appendix demonstrates the Modigliani–Miller theory of capital structure in a CAPM context, and draws on the treatment by Hamada.[33] The treatment which follows assumes the existence of a perfect capital market and the conditions required for the Sharpe–Lintner CAPM (as outlined in section 4.13). The equilibrium return on a share of a company entirely financed by equity can, according to CAPM (4.17), be written as:

$$E(r_{eu}) = RF + \frac{[E(R_M) - RF]}{\sigma_M^2} \text{ cov } r_{eu} R_M \tag{8.26}$$

where $E(r_{eu})$ is the expected return on a share of an all equity financed company, RF is the risk-free rate, $E(R_M)$ is the expected return on the market portfolio, σ_M^2 is the variance of returns on the market portfolio, and cov $r_{eu} R_M$ is the covariability between return on shares of the all equity financed company and returns on the market portfolio. For $[E(R_M) - RF]/\sigma_M^2$ will be written λ, commonly referred to as the market price of risk.

The equilibrium one-period expected return from the shares in the all equity financed company could be defined as follows:

$$E(r_{eu}) = \frac{E(X)}{S_{eu}} \tag{8.27}$$

where $E(X)$ is the expected value of the company's earnings in the next period, net of depreciation but prior to the deduction of interest and tax, and S_{eu} is the current equilibrium value of the company's shares. This could also be written according to CAPM and the previous simplification as:

$$E(r_{eu}) = RF + \lambda \text{ cov } r_{eu} R_M. \tag{8.28}$$

The return on the equity of a company completely identical to the all equity financed company, that is, of the same size, earnings, and operating risk (not financial risk) but with some debt in its capital structure, will be denoted $E(r_{eg})$, since this company is geared or levered. If it is assumed that the debt is financed at the risk-free rate RF, then the one-period return on the shares of this company to the equity holders can be written:

$$E(r_{eg}) = \frac{E(X) - RFB}{S_{eg}} \tag{8.29}$$

where $E(r_{eg})$ is the equilibrium return on the geared company's shares, RFB is the interest payments on the company's debt (B is the value of the debt), and S_{eg} is the equilibrium value of the geared company's shares.

From the equilibrium rates of return given by CAPM the following identities must hold:

$$RF + \lambda \operatorname{cov} r_{eu} R_M = \frac{E(X)}{S_{eu}} \tag{8.30}$$

and

$$RF + \lambda \operatorname{cov} r_{eg} R_M = \frac{E(X) - RFB}{S_{eg}}. \tag{8.31}$$

The risk of the geared equity would be expected to be greater than that of the ungeared equity because of the presence of financial risk; that is,

$$\operatorname{cov} r_{eg} R_M > \operatorname{cov} r_{eu} R_M.$$

From (8.30) it is known that:

$$E(X) = S_{eu}[RF + \lambda \operatorname{cov} r_{eu} R_M].$$

If this identity is substituted into (8.31):

$$RF + \lambda \operatorname{cov} r_{eg} R_M = \frac{S_{eu}[RF + \lambda \operatorname{cov} r_{eu} R_M] - RFB}{S_{eg}}$$

$$\therefore \quad S_{eg}\left[\lambda \operatorname{cov} r_{eg} R_M + RF\left(1 + \frac{B}{S_{eg}}\right)\right]$$

$$= S_{eu}[RF + \lambda \operatorname{cov} r_{eu} R_M]. \tag{8.32}$$

Hamada has noted that, from the definition of covariance:

$$\operatorname{cov} r_{eu} R_M = E\left\{\left[\frac{X}{S_{eu}} - E\left(\frac{X}{S_{eu}}\right)\right][R_M - E(R_M)]\right\}.$$

Since the current equilibrium value of the all equity financed company is given, then:

$$\text{cov } r_{\text{eu}} R_{\text{M}} = \frac{1}{S_{\text{eu}}} \text{cov } XR_{\text{M}}. \tag{8.33}$$

By the same token:

$$\text{cov } r_{\text{eg}} R_{\text{M}} = \frac{1}{S_{\text{eg}}} \text{cov } XR_{\text{M}}. \tag{8.34}$$

The substitution of (8.33) and (8.34) into (8.32) gives:

$$S_{\text{eg}} \left[\frac{\lambda}{S_{\text{eg}}} \text{cov } XR_{\text{M}} + RF \left(1 + \frac{B}{S_{\text{eg}}} \right) \right] = S_{\text{eu}} \left[RF + \frac{\lambda}{S_{\text{eu}}} \text{cov } XR_{\text{M}} \right]$$

Multiplying through the brackets:

$$\lambda \text{ cov } XR_{\text{M}} + RFS_{\text{eg}} + RFB = RFS_{\text{eu}} + \lambda \text{ cov } XR_{\text{M}}$$

$$\therefore \quad S_{\text{eg}} + B = S_{\text{eu}}. \tag{8.35}$$

Expression (8.35) shows that the total value of the geared company is equal to that of the all equity financed company. This is equivalent to Modigliani and Miller's proposition 1, previously met in (8.8), is repeated as follows:

$$V_j = (S_j + B_j) = \frac{\overline{X}_j}{K_n}.$$

In terms of the current example, from (8.27) and (8.35):

$$V = S_{\text{eg}} + B = S_{\text{eu}} = \frac{E(X)}{E(r_{\text{eu}})}. \tag{8.36}$$

This establishes that the financial package chosen by the firm to fund its assets has no effect on company valuation; but what about their proposition 2? What would be the equilibrium required rate of return on the equity of a geared company, and how would that change as a function of changes in the gearing ratio? Proposition 2 can be derived as follows. If the definition of covariance given in (8.33) and (8.34) is used, and substituted into (8.30) and (8.31), then:

$$E(R_{\text{eu}}) = RF + \frac{\lambda}{S_{\text{eu}}} \text{cov } XR_{\text{M}} \tag{8.37a}$$

$$E(r_{\text{eg}}) = RF + \frac{\lambda}{S_{\text{eg}}} \text{cov } XR_{\text{M}}. \tag{8.38}$$

If (8.37a) is subtracted from (8.38) then:

$$E(r_{eg}) - E(r_{eu}) = \frac{\lambda}{S_{eg}} \text{cov } XR_M - \frac{\lambda}{S_{eu}} \text{cov } XR_M$$

$$= \lambda \text{ cov } XR_M \left(\frac{S_{eu} - S_{eg}}{S_{eg} S_{eu}} \right).$$

But from (8.36), $S_{eu} - S_{eg} = B$; it follows therefore that:

$$E(r_{eg}) - E(r_{eu}) = \lambda \text{ cov } XR_M \left(\frac{B}{S_{eg} S_{eu}} \right). \tag{8.39}$$

From (8.37a) it is known that:

$$S_{eu}[E(R_{eu}) - RF] = \lambda \text{ cov } XR_M. \tag{8.37b}$$

The substitution of (8.37b) into (8.39) gives:

$$E(r_{eg}) - E(r_{eu}) = S_{eu}[E(r_{eu}) - RF] \left(\frac{B}{S_{eg} S_{eu}} \right).$$

$$\therefore \quad E(r_{eg}) = E(r_{eu}) + [E(r_{eu}) - RF] \left(\frac{B}{S_{eg}} \right). \tag{8.40}$$

Expression (8.40) is Modigliani and Miller's proposition 2 which shows how the premium or required rate of return on the geared company's equity increases as a linear function of the company's gearing, and is equal to the rate of return on an equivalent all equity financed company, plus a premium.

Hamada also demonstrates how the CAPM treatment can be modified to incorporate tax effects consistent with the Modigliani–Miller theorem.[34] He then employed this theoretical integration of the two models in an empirical test of capital structure propositions.[35]

NOTES AND REFERENCES

1. Smith, A. *The Wealth of Nations* (1776), Pelican, London, 1970, book one, chapter 10.
2. Stiglitz, J. E. 'On the irrelevance of corporate financial policy', *American Economic Review* **64**(6), December 1974, pp. 851–66.
3. An example of this is given by the original, classic article in the field; Modigliani, F. and Miller, M. H. 'The cost of capital, corporation finance, and the theory of investment', *American Economic Review* **48**(3), June 1958, pp. 261–97.

4. Stiglitz, J. E. 'On the irrelevance of corporate financial policy', *American Economic Review* **64**(6), December 1974, pp. 851–66.
5. For a discussion of the more common ones see: Briston, R. J. *The Stock Exchange and Investment Analysis*, Allen and Unwin, 1973, chapter II.
6. Solomon, E. *The Theory of Financial Management*, Columbia University Press, New York, 1963, chapters VI, VII, and VIII.
7. For example, see:
Solomon, E. *The Theory of Financial Management*, Columbia University Press, New York, 1963, chapter VII.
Van Horne, J. C. *Financial Management and Policy*, Prentice-Hall, Englewood Cliffs NJ, chapter IX.
Archer, S. H. and D'Ambrosio, C. A. *Business Finance Theory and Management*, Macmillan, New York, 1972, chapter VII.
8. Durand, D. 'Costs of debt and equity funds for business: trends and problems of measurement', National Bureau of Economic Research, 1952; reprinted in Solomon, E. (ed.) *The Management of Corporate Capital*, Free Press of Glencoe, New York, 1963.
9. Modigliani, F. and Miller, M. H. 'The cost of capital, corporation finance, and the theory of investment', *American Economic Review* **48**(3), June 1958, pp. 261–97.
10. Ibid.
11. Durand, D. 'The cost of capital, corporation finance, and the theory of investment: comment', *American Economic Review* **49**(3), September 1959, pp. 639–55.
12. Modigliani, F. and Miller, M. H. 'Corporate income taxes and the cost of capital: a correction', *American Economic Review* **53**(3), June 1963, pp. 433–43.
13. Ibid.
14. Van Horne, J. C. *Financial Management and Policy*, Prentice-Hall, Englewood Cliffs NJ, 1975, chapter IX.
15. Robichek and Myers argue that it is impossible in a perfect market for the marginal cost of debt to be greater than the marginal cost of equity, as the debt holders are always paid before the equity holders and are therefore subject to less risk. See: Robichek, A. A. and Myers, S. C. *Optimal Financing Decisions*, Prentice-Hall, Englewood Cliffs NJ, 1965, p. 35.
16. Ibid., pp. 42–44.
17. Miller, M. H. 'Debt and taxes', *The Journal of Finance* **32**(2), May 1977, pp. 261–75.
18. DeAngelo, H. and Masulis, R. W. 'Optimal capital structure under corporate and personal taxation', *Journal of Financial Economics* **8**(1), March 1980, pp. 3–29.
See also: Masulis, R. W. 'The effects of capital structure change on security prices: a study of exchange offers', *Journal of Financial Economics* **8**(2), June 1980, pp. 139–77.
19. Modigliani, F. 'Debt, dividend policy, taxes, inflation and market valuation', *The Journal of Finance* **37**(2), May 1982, pp. 255–73.
20. Fama, E. F. and Miller, M. H. *The Theory of Finance*, Dryden Press, 1972, chapter IV, section III.
21. Chen, A. H. and Han Kim, E. 'Theories of corporate debt policy: a synthesis', *The Journal of Finance* **34**(2), May 1979, pp. 371–87.
22. Fama, E. F. 'The effects of a firm's investment and financing decisions on the welfare of its security holders', *American Economic Review* **68**(3), June 1978, pp. 272–84.

292   *Corporate Investment and Financial Policy*

23. Robichek, A. A. and Myers, S. C. 'Problems in the theory of optimal capital structure', *Journal of Financial and Quantitative Analysis* **1**(1), June 1966, pp. 1–35.
24. Stiglitz, J. E. 'On the irrelevance of corporate financial policy', *American Economic Review* **64**(6), December 1974, pp. 851–66.
25. Han Kim, E. 'A mean variance theory of optimal capital structure and corporate debt capacity', *The Journal of Finance* **68**(2), March 1978.
26. Miller, M. H. 'Debt and taxes', *The Journal of Finance* **32**(2), May 1977, pp. 261–75.
    For a study of bankruptcy costs see: Warner, G. 'Bankruptcy costs: some evidence', *Journal of Finance* **32**(3), May 1977, pp. 337–48.
27. Ross, S. A. 'The determination of financial structure: the incentive signalling approach', *The Bell Journal of Economics* **8**(1), Spring 1977, pp. 23–40.
    Akerlof, G. 'The market for 'lemons': qualitative uncertainty and the market mechanism', *Quarterly Journal of Economics* **84**, August 1970, pp. 488–500.
    Arrow, K. J. 'Some models of racial discrimination in the labor market', in Pascal, A. H. (ed.) *Racial Discrimination in Economic Life*, Heath, Lexington, Mass., 1970.
28. Bhattacharya, S. 'Imperfect information, dividend policy, and "the bird in the hand" fallacy', *The Bell Journal of Economics* **10**(1), Spring 1979, p. 259–70.
29. Jensen, M. C. and Meckling, W. H. 'Theory of the firm; managerial behaviour, agency costs and ownership structure', *Journal of Financial Economics* **3**, October 1976, pp. 305–60.
    See also: Myers, S. C. 'Determinants of corporate borrowing', *Journal of Financial Economics* **5**, November 1977, pp. 147–75.
    These arguments are discussed in section 6.14.
30. Miller, M. H. and Modigliani, F. 'Some estimates of the cost of capital to the electric utility industry, 1954–57', *American Economic Review* **56**(3), June 1966, pp. 333–91.
31. Hamada, R. S. 'The effect of the firm's capital structure on the systematic risk of common stocks', *Journal of Finance* **27**(3), May 1972, pp. 435–52.
    See also: Kumar, P. 'Market equilibrium and corporation finance: some issues', *Journal of Finance* **29**(4), September 1974, pp. 1175–88.
32. See also the following, which are no more than a small sample from a vast empirical literature:
    Boness, A. J., Chen, A. K. and Jatusipitak, S. 'On relations among stock price behaviour and changes in the capital structure of the firm', *Journal of Financial and Quantitative Analysis* **7**(4), September 1972, pp. 1967–82.
    Robichek, A. A., Higgins, R. C. and Kinsman, M. 'The effect of leverage on the cost of equity capital to the electric utility firms', *Journal of Finance* **28**(2), May 1973, pp. 353–67.
    Nerlove, M. 'Factors affecting differences among rates of return on investment in individual common stocks', *Review of Economics and Statistics* **50**(3), August 1968, pp. 312–31.
    Shwartz, E. and Aronson, J. R. 'Some surrogate evidence in support of the concept of an optimal financial structure', *Journal of Finance*, **22**(1), March 1967, pp. 10–18.
    Weston, J. F. 'A test of cost of capital propositions', *Southern Economic Journal* **30**(2), October 1963, pp. 105–12.
    Wippern, R. F. 'Financial structure and the value of the firm', *Journal of Finance* **21**(5), December 1966, pp. 615–33.

33. Hamada, R. S. 'Portfolio analysis, market equilibrium and corporation finance', *Journal of Finance* **24**(1), March 1969, pp. 13–31.
34. Ibid., pp. 19–20.
35. Hamada, R. S. 'The effect of the firm's capital structure on the systematic risk of common stocks', *Journal of Finance* **27**(2), May 1972, pp. 435–52.

PART IV

Conclusion

CHAPTER 9

The current state of the
theory of finance

Expectation, time itself, is alien to reason, except in the perfect, void freedom of pure mathematics, where time is merely
an extensive variable, not the real, enigmatic, unarguable
reality.[1]

In this chapter will be encountered the weight of Shackle's telling
criticisms, as applied to the theory of finance in particular rather
than to economic theory in general. But first will be reviewed the
remarkable advances made in the theory of finance, most of which
have already been encountered in the course of this book. Some of
the more obvious structural defects should become apparent, and so
too should the fact that some of the foundations may be placed upon
shifting sands rather than bedrock.

9.1 THE THEORETICAL UNITY OF THE STRUCTURE

Chapter 2 began by considering the nature of uncertainty and the
various ways in which attempts may be made to appraise it. At the
core of this was the use of subjective probability distributions. The
various objections to this were considered, plus the further limiting
assumptions that the distributions of returns on financial assets were
usually viewed as being finite, stationary normal distributions.

The other twin pillar of the theoretical structure was met in
chapter 3, which introduced the hypothesis that investors or financial decision-takers seek to maximize the expected utility of the consequences of their decisions. Various forms of utility functions which
lend themselves to this, and their various merits and defects, were
reviewed. (They were subsequently seen to be consistent with an
objective function of maximizing shareholder wealth, in the case of
corporate equity investors.)

So armed, the reader could then confront one of the centre-pieces of the theory of finance: modern portfolio theory, first met in chapter 4. Markowitz's contribution lay in the rationalization and formal specification of the benefits to be obtained from risk diversification. His portfolio selection procedure, with its accent on portfolio efficiency, highlighted the primary trade-off characterizing financial markets – namely, the relationship between risk and expected returns, the two fundamental parameters employed in modern financial theory.

The generalization and extension of his work into the capital asset pricing model provided an equilibrium pricing model for valuing risky assets. Its linearity seemed to promise amenability to empirical verification and a means of measuring portfolio performance. Much empirical work followed, though as was seen in later sections of the chapter, serious doubts have been raised about its acceptability. The work on arbitrage pricing models avoids these pitfalls and will, perhaps, be the natural successor to CAPM. Major problems remained as a consequence of the single-period nature of the analysis, and it was demonstrated that it could only be extended to the multiperiod case by the addition or imposition of fairly restrictive assumptions. Nevertheless it remains a monumental piece of analysis.

On a theoretical level, equally imposing was the development of state preference theory, an extremely powerful theoretical tool for employment in the analysis of capital markets under conditions of uncertainty. The lack of market 'completeness' in practice seemed to present a barrier to empirical work in this area, but the recent integration of option pricing theory and state preference theory suggests that ways may yet be found round this problem.[2]

The most complete and successful marriage of theory and empirical work is without doubt to be found in the literature on market efficiency. The evidence for the weak and semi-strong forms of the efficient market hypothesis is very imposing. The strong form is, not surprisingly, much more problematic, and the economics of information and information processing will be returned to later in this chapter, as its treatment has far-reaching implications for the theory of finance.

Chapter 5 introduced option theory, the most exciting theoretical breakthrough of the last decade, with extraordinarily wide potential applications in the valuation of financial liabilities. The way in which it has ingeniously been extended, refined, and subjected to considerable empirical testing, all in the space of ten years, is truly remarkable.

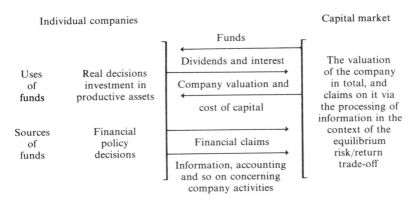

FIGURE 9.1   *The linkage between company decisions and capital market decisions via company valuations*

At first sight it might seem surprising that so much emphasis has been given to capital market and valuation theory, but this material now lies at the heart of corporate finance as well as financial theory in general. As long ago as 1966, Solomon pointed out that both sources and uses of funds could now be treated within a single theoretical framework, and that the traditional distinctions between the management of the two sides of the balance sheet no longer held.[3] Weston has suggested that 'the traditional trinity of money and capital markets, business finance, and investments is no longer meaningful'.[4] Rubinstein has gone even further and provided a mean–variance synthesis of corporate financial theory.[5]

The links between capital market and corporate theory can be considered in terms of figure 9.1.

Corporate decisions were introduced in Part III. In chapter 6 was considered the corporate investment decision. In perfect capital markets, under conditions of certainty, it was found that the net present value rule unequivocally served shareholder interests, but once realistic imperfections were admitted the rule became ambiguous. Under conditions of uncertainty, in perfect capital markets, the capital asset pricing model should apply, but even here serious difficulties were encountered. It was found that it could only be applied in a multiperiod context under very restrictive assumptions, and again the admittance of realistic imperfections, like non-homogeneous expectations and imperfect markets, rendered the whole approach unworkable.

Corporate financial decisions were introduced in chapter 7, in which valuation theories and corporate financial decisions were

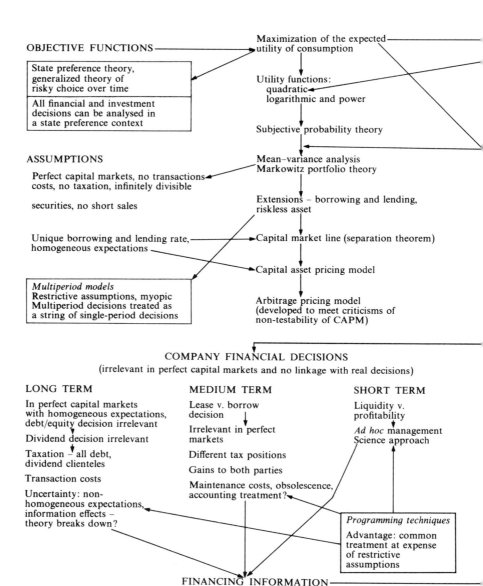

FIGURE 9.2 *A skeletal outline of the major theoretical areas and some of the linkages in the theory of finance. Obviously information generating and processing is central to the whole dynamic process.*

Basic assumptions of this type of approach
(1) Maximization of shareholder wealth – objective function
(2) Decision rules developed in perfect capital markets, idealized uncertainty

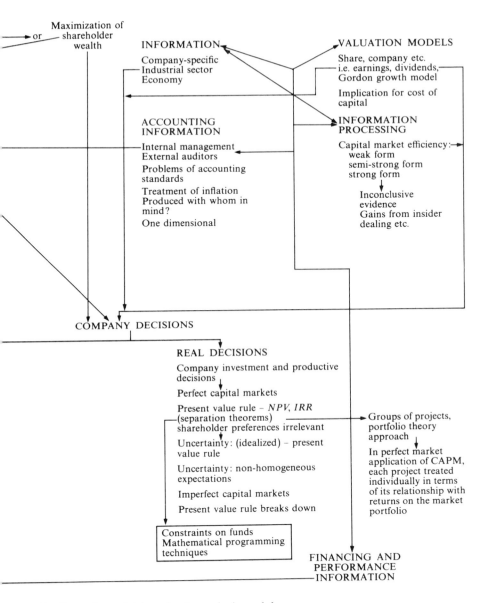

Maximization of
or — shareholder
wealth INFORMATION   VALUATION MODELS

Company-specific   Share, company etc.
Industrial sector   i.e. earnings, dividends,
Economy   Gordon growth model

            Implication for cost of
            capital

ACCOUNTING   INFORMATION
INFORMATION   PROCESSING

Internal management   Capital market efficiency:
External auditors   weak form
Problems of accounting   semi-strong form
standards   strong form
Treatment of inflation
Produced with whom in   Inconclusive
mind?   evidence
One dimensional   Gains from insider
            dealing etc.

COMPANY DECISIONS

   REAL DECISIONS

   Company investment and productive
   decisions
   Perfect capital markets

   Present value rule – *NPV, IRR*
   (separation theorems)   Groups of projects,
   shareholder preferences irrelevant portfolio theory
   Uncertainty: (idealized) – present approach
   value rule   In perfect market
   Uncertainty: non-homogeneous application of CAPM,
   expectations   each project treated
             individually in terms
   Imperfect capital markets   of its relationship with
   Present value rule breaks down returns on the market
             portfolio

   Constraints on funds
   Mathematical programming
   techniques   FINANCING AND
          PERFORMANCE
         INFORMATION

(3) Central model is a single-period model
(4) The rules tend to be rather shaky when faced with 'normal inperfec-
tions', that is, taxation, transaction costs, general disparity of expectations, information discrepancies
(5) There are still major questions or difficulties in the treatment of: multiperiod decisions; the nature of the return-generating process; liquidity;
behaviour of the term structure of interest rates, etc.

explicitly linked. It was seen that in the context of perfect capital markets, assuming a given investment policy, dividend policy is irrelevant, having no effect on company valuation or shareholder wealth. It was also seen that once realistic market imperfections were admitted to the scenario, it was difficult to decide what the outcome of the argument might be. The fiendish difficulties associated with any attempt to isolate dividend policy effects on corporate valuation mean that, at the moment, appeals to econometric tests are unlikely to resolve the arguments.

A similar situation was found to exist in the theory of capital structure decisions introduced in chapter 8. Once again the assumption of perfect capital markets relegated the capital structure decision to a position of complete insignificance. Given these conditions, 'real' decisions concerning investment and production could be separated from financial decisions; the latter need not be of concern anyway, as they are of no consequence. The paradox of a theory of finance which suggests that financial decisions are of little importance will not have been lost on the reader. Again the entry of market imperfections opened the argument and the existence of an optimum capital structure was found to be likely, though its exact specification remained elusive.

The adoption of an economic-theory-based approach, combined with an explicit treatment of uncertainty and a readiness to apply quantitative methods and techniques wherever appropriate, has given a remarkable strength and unity to the theory of finance. This unity can perhaps be best appreciated via consideration of the configuration of its outline, central elements, and linkages, all portrayed in figures 9.2 and 9.3. It is undoubtedly a remarkable theoretical achievement and has led to a revolution in the understanding of financial markets and corporate financial decisions.

However, it displays the hereditary defects associated with its parentage in 'contemporary' economic theory. It is essentially an 'equilibrium' theory developed in the context of perfect markets. Under these conditions it has to be admitted that the theory is exceedingly powerful. Fama has recently demonstrated that the 'irrelevance' of corporate financing decisions can be proven, in this context, either on the assumption that both companies and investors have 'equal access' to the capital markets, or on the assumption that no firm issues securities for which there are no perfect substitutes in the form of other firms' securities.[6] Ross has generalized his arbitrage pricing model to prove many of the basic financial theorems by assuming merely that there is 'open access' to capital markets, and

An option has a derived value dependent upon the value of the asset against which it is written

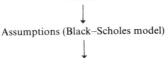

Assumptions (Black–Scholes model)

(1) No transactions costs or taxes
(2) A fixed short-term interest rate; it is possible to borrow any fraction of the price of a security at this price
(3) Options are only exercisable at maturity: 'European'
(4) No market imperfections or restrictions on short-selling stocks or options
(5) Stocks against which options are written pay no dividends
(6) The distribution of potential stock prices is log-normal. This is consistent with stock prices following a random walk in continuous time. The variance of the rate of return on the stock is constant

Subsequent work has shown that the model is quite robust and most of these assumptions may be relaxed. Even so they are remarkably few

Potential applications: Option theory as a means of valuing corporate liabilities

(1) Can provide useful insights into the valuation of the debt and equity of a geared company
(2) Can be employed as a tool for the valuation of warrants, convertible debt, rights issues, underwriting contracts, insurance contracts, to name a few areas.

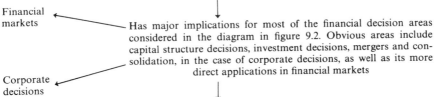

Financial markets

Has major implications for most of the financial decision areas considered in the diagram in figure 9.2. Obvious areas include capital structure decisions, investment decisions, mergers and consolidation, in the case of corporate decisions, as well as its more direct applications in financial markets

Corporate decisions

One of the most exciting theoretical developments of the last decade, the full potential of which is yet to be determined

FIGURE 9.3   *Option valuation: a theory of relative valuation*

therefore that no unexploited arbitrage opportunities exist.[7] Thus the generality is beyond dispute; but what are the drawbacks of such an approach?

9.2 SOME DIFFICULTIES ASSOCIATED WITH 'EQUILIBRIUM' ANALYSIS

Arrow and Hahn have suggested that there are two fundamental related concepts of equilibrium in economics.[8] The first rests on the idea of determinateness; the description and arguments of the vari-

ables employed to represent the economic system must be sufficient
to determine the values of the variables. Equilibrium could also be
viewed in terms of the relation between variables being represented
by a balance of forces with an in-built mechanism to absorb disturbances and move back to equilibrium. Hahn has also written
extensively on the deficiencies of such systems and these will be
considered in the next section.[4] Much of the work on the theory of
finance rests on equilibrium theory of this type, which has its roots
in the work of Arrow and Debreu.[10] It has been seen that this work
has led to the development of remarkable insights, including the
genesis of state preference theory which is an extremely versatile
analytical tool. But the very nature of the approach carries with it its
own constraints and limitations. Kaldor has gone so far as to suggest
that the approach is 'barren and irrelevant as an apparatus of
thought to deal with the manner of operation of economic forces'.[11]

In his penetrating criticisms of the nature of 'value' within the
context of general equilibrium systems, Shackle has suggested that,
'Value theory in its rigorous form requires that all choices be pre-
reconciled, that is, simultaneous. Thus, time is reduced to a single
moment.'[12] His criticism strikes at the very heart of modern financial
theory. If his view is accepted that time and reason are incompatible,
on the grounds that knowledge changes and grows as a function of
time, then a determinate system which encompasses the passage of
time in a realistic manner cannot be obtained. Indeed, he would
argue that the employment of subjective probability, as utilized in
mean–variance analysis, allows only a sterile treatment of time and
uncertainty.[13] The usual employment of subjective probability
attempts to distribute 'certainty' over the distribution of classes of
outcome, but prior expectations are not typically of this form. In the
language of thought it is perfectly possible to have mutually exclusive
yet coexistent future possibilities. That there is undoubtedly sub-
stance to these criticisms has been seen frequently in the course of
this book, whenever it has been necessary to maintain an equilibrium system and yet integrate uncertainty in a dynamic, multiperiod context. It was seen that there was no satisfactory solution to
the problem and recourse frequently had to be made to 'idealized'
uncertainty, in which expectations were homogeneous, and in the
multiperiod context further restrictions were usually required.

The equilibrium, comparative statics approach has to assume that
all the parameters of the system are known. If this is the case the
adjustment process from one point of equilibrium to another can be
investigated. But what guarantee is there that systems are ever in

equilibrium and that decision-taking agents have full knowledge of the consequences of their actions?

Most commentators seem to agree that Keynes was the first to fully address this problem, with his concept of 'effective demand' and his accenting of the effects of the revision of expectations.[14] The concept was formalized by Myrdal in his distinction between *ex ante* and *ex post*.[15] The problems involved in the confounding of expectations and their subsequent revision are absolutely central to financial economics, yet any treatment of the problem is essentially arbitrary. The problem was specifically encountered in consideration of the application of CAPM to capital budgeting, but it is extremely general. Brainard and Tobin have chronicled the difficulties of modelling adjustment processes in an equilibrium system, and these alone are formidable.[16] The problem of the revision of expectations is omitted at peril, yet the additional difficulties are extreme. But without it there is no role for money and liquidity within the theory.

9.3 THE ROLE OF MONEY AND LIQUIDITY
IN THE THEORY OF FINANCE

It is no accident that in the chapters completed so far there is no formal treatment of the demand for money in its own right or the value placed on liquidity. In figure 9.2 it is mentioned that the only framework available for managing liquidity and short-term assets is an *ad hoc* management science approach, and this is the reason why a formal treatment is omitted from this text. This obviously is a major omission from any theory of finance, yet why is this so?

The fact is that in the treatment of liquidity there has not been much progression beyond the 'transactions, precautionary, and speculative' reasons for holding cash, first suggested by Keynes in a characteristically prescient treatment of the difficulties.[17] Shackle regards Keynes's liquidity preference theory of interest as the 'greatest technical innovation' of his two major works on money, and regards the problem as a further aspect of the lack of a 'realistic' treatment of uncertainty.[18] He suggests that, 'Were it not for the problem of lack of knowledge, there could be no need for liquidity.'[19] The treatment of uncertainty in the theory of finance, as developed from the foundations provided by Arrow and Debreu mentioned previously, has room for one commodity to be used as a *numéraire* but none for a positive demand for money in its own right.

Hahn stressed the problems of integrating money into an equilibrium system.[20] A very difficult and extensive literature has developed with a view to providing a positive role for money. Only a very crude representation of it can be given, but essentially in a 'complete' market of the Arrow–Debreu sense, given a budget constraint on an individual agent's endowment of wealth, the present value rule holds, and this value of wealth can be frictionlessly reallocated through time. The division of its 'packaging' over time is of no consequence. In order to integrate money into the system, most authorities have postulated 'sequence' economies in which opportunities available to individual agents may depend upon the date of a transaction.[21] Hahn demonstrated that, with an inclusion of transaction costs, sequence economies are likely to be inefficient in a 'Pareto' sense.[22] Gale has integrated money into sequence economies via various routes, but basically they rely on the existence of market imperfections – either failure to conform to contracts, or information discrepancies and false signals to the market by individual agents.[23]

In general, imperfections involving information discrepancies are likely to be of singular importance to the theory of finance. There is a growing literature on the impact of information discrepancies on market processes.[24]

9.4   THE EFFECTS OF INFORMATION DISCREPANCIES

The processing of information is absolutely essential to the valuation of financial securities and the processes of financial markets. The complexities of the process were captured by Keynes in his celebrated metaphor, 'Professional investment may be likened to those newspaper competitions in which the competitors have to pick out the six prettiest faces from a hundred photographs, the prize being awarded to the competitor whose choice most nearly corresponds to the average preferences of the competitors as a whole. . . . We have reached the third degree where we devote our intelligences to anticipating what average opinion expects the average opinion to be.'[25] Yet the problems and complexities of information processing, and the effects of irregularities in the distribution of information, are, for the most part, assumed away in a theory of finance framed under the assumption of perfect markets. Even when uncertainty enters the analysis, it is frequently of the 'idealized' type which assumes homogeneity of expectations.

Akerlof has demonstrated that, in the face of information barriers and extreme difficulties in assessing the quality of a good offered for sale, the potential purchasers may prefer not to trade at all, and thus the entire market mechanism may break down.[26] Actual financial markets will be located somewhere in the continuum between Akerlof's extremity at one end and perfect competition at the other. Akerlof also points out that further implications of his linkage of quality and uncertainty are the existence of various 'institutions' which ensure trust, such as guarantees, brand names, and various licensing practices. This leads on to the next obvious question about the role of financial institutions in general in the theory of finance.

9.5 THE ROLE OF FINANCIAL INSTITUTIONS IN THE THEORY OF FINANCE

The usual explanation given for the existence of the various types of financial intermediary and the process of intermediation is the role they play in the smoothing over of the various types of market imperfections characteristic of financial markets.[27] Institutions can exploit various economies of scale in information gathering and processing, transactions and dealing costs, and sheer discrepancies attendant on size of dealings. They are in a position to provide insurance services via the matching of their assets and liabilities, and can also exploit and bridge any market asymmetries. If there is a preponderance of 'short' lenders and 'long' borrowers the institutions can reconcile the conflicting needs by accepting the appropriate type of liability and issuing or purchasing the required type of security.

The manifest irregularities and complexities and innumerable types of imperfections which have all served to stimulate the growth of the remarkably mature and sophisticated family of institutions within the UK financial system, for example, are not readily accommodated within the structure of the theory of finance as it stands at present. Some interesting attempts have been made to take some of these factors into account. Leland and Pyle have produced a theory of financial intermediation based upon informational asymmetries, and Hirst has produced a 'map' of the financial system which explores the topography of the system as a function of information appraisal costs as well as the more customary dimension of risk.[28] But by definition, any such approach starts from the premise of imperfect financial markets which, as has been seen, is not customary in the broad thrust of financial theory.

Imperfections and information effects are likely to be written large in the future development of financial theory. It can be seen in figure 9.2 that these effects are assumed away when theory is developed in a perfect market structure. In reality they are likely to be integral to the workings of both real and financial markets. When the existence of these effects is acknowledged, and attempts are made to integrate them into the analysis, then in the comparative statics framework frequently adopted they are likely to lead to 'extreme corner' solutions. One of the best examples of this is the introduction of corporate tax effects into the Modigliani–Miller analysis of capital structure.[29] Yet in practice companies do not finance themselves by the 100 per cent debt that this tax effect implies, and therefore recourse has to be made to other imperfections and restrictions which may be the explanation of this.

9.6 'POSITIVISM' AND THE THEORY OF FINANCE

A possible rebuttal of the criticism that a theory developed in the context of perfect market assumptions is severely restricted could be made via recourse to Friedman's dictum that, 'The relevant question to ask about the "assumptions" of a theory is not whether they are descriptively "realistic", for they never are, but whether they are sufficiently good approximations for the purpose in hand.'[30] Despite the existence of certain possible contradictions in the strict interpretation of this thesis, I think that it would be fair comment to state that its spirit has been embraced in the development of financial economics.[31] One of the apparent strengths of the development of financial theory is the mutual relation between the advance of the theory and its modification, refinement, and 'verification' via empirical testing. The amount of empirical 'support' for some of the central postulates of modern financial theory is truly remarkable.

However, in recent years some important doubts have been expressed. Some of the most celebrated were met in chapter 4 in which were encountered Roll's criticisms of the ability to effectively test the veracity of the capital asset pricing model.[32] At the heart of the matter is the movement from *ex ante* expected to *ex post* realized returns, a crucial dilemma in any theory of finance which incorporates an acknowledgment of the existence of uncertainty. Given the fact that the best that can be done is to test a proxy for the mean–variance efficient market portfolio, a proxy which is not likely to have these qualities, then as Roll demonstrates the resultant potential measurement errors undermine the whole analysis.

It seems likely that these doubts are reflected in many other areas of financial economics, despite the remarkably rapid advance and increasing sophistication of econometric techniques in recent years. The broad implication of a theory of finance based upon perfect market assumptions is that financing decisions are irrelevant. The central question is whether currently available econometric techniques are sufficiently powerful to detect significant deviations from the null hypothesis in such areas as capital structure or dividend policy. Thus, essential doubts remain despite the existence of a vast and impressive empirical literature. At the conclusion of a remarkably sophisticated empirical investigation of the impact of UK public policy upon UK corporations, King was prompted to state ruefully, 'In a world of uncertainty there is a great deal about the behaviour of companies and their response to public policy which we do not as yet understand.'[33]

9.7 THE 'NEO-CLASSICAL PARADIGM' CURRENTLY PREVALENT IN FINANCIAL ECONOMICS

The reader will have become aware, whilst progressing through the chapters of this book, that the theory of finance is currently very 'neo-classical' in spirit. The assumed objective of shareholder wealth maximization has the merit of being multidimensional in the sense that it encompasses, at least, expected returns and risk, but nevertheless it is close in essence to the profit maximizing theories central to neo-classical economics. Thus many of the more interesting recent developments in the theory of the firm, in particular the 'managerial' and 'behavioural' literature with its origins in the implications of the divorce of ownership from control, have, until recently, been neglected in the development of financial theory.[34] There are probably countless potential applications and extensions of this literature in the theory of finance.

Jensen and Meckling have made a notable start in their development of a capital structure on the basis of a consideration of 'agency costs' (as considered in section 8.14).[35] Fama has attacked this approach on a number of counts.[36] He suggests that the approach does not fully develop the distinction between the risk-bearing function, which takes place in the financial markets for securities, and management, which is a separate input or factor of production with its own separate markets. Fama suggests that the risk bearers are not the main monitors and disciplinary agents of managerial performance, but that competitive pressures within markets for managerial labour and competition between managers within a firm will serve this function. The key to the question lies in whether or not the managerial markets are sufficiently competitive and efficient to enforce *ex post* revision of contracts when a manager changes position, after excessively pursuing his own interests whilst with his previous firm. My own view would be that markets for managerial labour are likely to be grossly inefficient with the existence of considerable information barriers, when attempts are made to assess individual performance from a background of corporate collective effort.

Only a few other attempts to follow this approach have been made. Baker has made steps towards integrating a 'managerial' approach into corporate valuation and investment theory, and attention has been paid to some of these factors in the study by King mentioned previously.[37]

As a further corollary of the 'neo-classical' spirit of the adopted approach, finance is very much the province of the rational decision-taker as personified by 'economic man'. Simon has consistently argued that rationality is 'bounded', and that the expected utility/subjective probability approach to uncertainty, as it now stands, is unrealistic.[38] These sentiments are paralleled by those of Shackle.[39] Surely, before long, they must be reflected in the theory of finance?

9.8 CONCLUSION

In the course of this book have been covered, in outline at least, most of the developments that have taken place in the theory of finance over the last thirty years. The pace, scope, and sheer intellectual stature of these developments is breath-taking. There is no doubt that the theory now has a robust, unified, remarkably consistent structure, supported in varying measure by a vast empirical literature. But attached to these developments there is also a cost.

In this final chapter I have tried to indicate some of the aspects of this cost. These are necessarily a complement of the paradigm or 'world view' embedded in the theoretical structure. This view does not accommodate itself readily to disequilibrium situations, imperfections of all market types, whether concerned with information barriers, dealing costs, or heterogeneity of expectations, and indeed the role of money and institutions. Its apparatus for dealing with multiperiod decisions is also remarkably suspect.

Nevertheless it remains a considerable achievement, and the story is still only at its beginning. One thing is certain – the next decade of developments within financial economics will also be extremely exciting and will bring a further rich harvest of insights.

NOTES AND REFERENCES

1. Shackle, G. L. S. *Epistemics and Economics*, Cambridge University Press, Cambridge, 1972, preface, p. xi.
2. Breeden, T. and Litzenberger, R. H. 'Prices of state-contingent claims implicit in option prices', *Journal of Business* **51**(4), October 1978, pp. 621–51.
   Banz, R. W. and Miller, M. H. 'Prices for state-contingent claims: some estimates and applications', *Journal of Business* **51**(4), October 1978, pp. 653–72.
3. Solomon, E. 'What should we teach in a course in business finance?', *Journal of Finance* **21**(2), May 1966, pp. 411–15.
4. Weston, J. F. 'New themes in finance', *Journal of Finance* **29**(1), March 1974, pp. 237–43.
5. Rubinstein, M. E. 'A mean–variance synthesis of corporate financial theory', *Journal of Finance* **28**(1), March 1973, pp. 167–81.
   For a general survey of the unity of the field, see: Lister, R. J. 'Business finance – an evolving field of study', *Journal of Business Finance and Accounting* **5**(1), Spring 1978, pp. 1–26.
6. Fama, E. F. 'The effects of a firm's investment and financing decisions on the welfare of its security holders', *American Economic Review* **68**(3), June 1978, pp. 272–84.
7. Ross, S. A. 'A simple approach to the valuation of risky steams', *Journal of Business* **51**(3), June 1978, pp. 453–75.
8. Arrow, K. J. and Hahn, F. H. *General Competitive Analysis*, Oliver and Boyd, Edinburgh, 1971, p. 1.
9. See, for example: Hahn, F. H. 'On some problems of proving the existence of an equilibrium in a monetary economy', reading in Hahn, F. H. and Brechling, F. P. R. (eds). *The Theory of Interest Rates*, Macmillan, London, 1965, pp. 126–33.
10. Arrow, K. J. and Debreu, G. 'Existence of equilibrium for a competitive economy', *Econometrica* **22**(5), July 1954, pp. 265–90.
    Debreu, G. *Theory of Value*, Wiley, New York, 1959.
11. Kaldor, N. J. 'The irrelevance of equilibrium economies', *Economic Journal* **83**, December 1972, pp. 1237–255.
12. Shackle, G. L. S. *Epistemics and Economics*, Cambridge, 1972, p. 120.
13. Ibid., pp. 364–408.
14. Ibid., preface.
    Robinson, J. 'Time in economic theory', *Kyklos* **33**, part 2, 1980, pp. 219–29.
    Kregel, J. A. 'Economic methodology in the face of uncertainty', *Economic Journal* **86**, June 1976, pp. 209–25.
15. Myrdal, G. *Monetary Equilibrium*, Hodge, London, 1939.

16. Brainard, W. C. and Tobin, J. 'Pitfalls in financial model building', *American Economic Review*, **58**(2), May 1968, pp. 99–122.
For a discussion of the problems of modelling expectations revision, see: Klein, L. R. 'The treatment of expectations in econometrics', reading in Carter, C. F. and Ford, J. L. (eds). *Uncertainty and Expectations in Economics*, Basil Blackwell, Oxford, 1972, pp. 175–90.

17. Keynes, J. M. *The General Theory of Employment Interest and Money*, Macmillan, 1961, pp. 194–208.
The usual treatment in the literature is to employ the Keynesian transactions motive. See, for example: Baumol, W. J. 'The transactions demand for cash: an inventory theoretic approach', *Quarterly Journal of Economics* **65**, November 1952, pp. 545–56.
Miller, M. H. and Orr, D. 'A model of the demand for money by firms', *Quarterly Journal of Economics* **80**, August 1966, pp. 413–35.
Tobin has integrated the liquidity preference motive into a portfolio theory context for individual investors. See: Tobin, J. 'Liquidity preference as behaviour towards risk', *Review of Economic Studies* **26**(1), February 1958, pp. 65–86.
Tobin, J. 'The theory of portfolio selection', reading in Hahn, F. H. and Brechling, F. P. R. (eds). *The Theory of Interest Rates*, Macmillan, London, 1965, pp. 3–51.

18. Shackle, G. L. S. *Epistemics and Economics*, Cambridge, 1972, preface.

19. Ibid., p. 216.

20. Hahn, F. H. 'On some problems of proving the existence of equilibrium in a monetary economy', reading in Hahn, F. H. and Brechling, F. P. R. (eds). *The Theory of Interest Rates*, Macmillan, London, 1965, pp. 126–133.

21. Radner, R. 'Existence of equilibrium of plans, prices, and price expectations in a sequence of markets', *Econometrica* **40**(2), March 1972, pp. 289–303.

22. Hahn, F. H. 'On transaction costs, inessential sequence economies, and money', *Review of Economic Studies* **40**, 1973, pp. 449–61.

23. Gale, D. 'The core of a monetary economy without trust', *Journal of Economic Theory* **19**(2), December 1978, pp. 456–91.
Gale, D. 'Money, information and equilibrium in large economies', *Journal of Economic Theory* **23**, 1980, pp. 28–65.
For a review of the problems, see: Clower, R. W. 'The anatomy of monetary theory', *American Economic Review* **67**(1), June 1977, pp. 206–12.

24. See, for example: Rothschild, M. 'Models of market organization with imperfect information: a survey', *Journal of Political Economy* **81**(6), November/December 1973, pp. 1283–308.
Diamond, P. and Rothschild, M. *Uncertainty in Economics*, Academic Press, New York, 1978.

25. Keynes, J. M. *The General Theory of Employment Interest and Money*, Macmillan, London, 1961, p. 156.

26. Akerlof, C. A. 'The market for "lemons": quality, uncertainty and the market mechanism', *Quarterly Journal of Economics* **84**, 1970, pp. 488–500.

27. See, for example: Goodhart, C. A. *Money, Information and Uncertainty*, Macmillan, 1975, chapter 6, pp. 102–36.

28. Leland, H. E. and Pyle, D. H. 'Informational asymmetries, financial structure and financial intermediation', *Journal of Finance* **32**(2), May 1977, pp. 371–87.
Hirst, I. R. C. 'Mapping the financial system', unpublished discussion paper, Dept. Business Studies, University of Edinburgh, December 1979.

The current state of finance theory

See also: Campbell, T. S. and Kracaw, W. A. 'Information production, market signalling, and the theory of financial intermediation', *Journal of Finance* **35**(4), September 1980, pp. 863–82.
29. Modigliani, F. and Miller, M. H. 'Corporate income taxes and the cost of capital: a correction', *American Economic Review* **53**(3), June 1963, pp. 433–43.
30. Friedman, M. *Essays in Positive Economics*, Chicago, 1953, part 1, sections 1, 2, 3 and 6, reprinted in Hahn, F. H., and Hollis, M. (eds). *Philosophy and Economic Theory*, Oxford University Press, Oxford, 1979, p. 27.
31. For criticisms of the Friedman view, see: Rotwein, E. 'On the methodology of positive economics', *Quarterly Journal of Economics* **73**, 1959, pp. 554–75.
Nagel, E. 'Assumptions in economic theory', *American Economic Review* **53**(2), May 1963, pp. 211–19.
Hollis, M. and Nell, E. J. 'Two economists', chapter 3 in Hahn, F. H. and Hollis, M. (eds). *Philosophy and Economic Theory*, Oxford University Press, Oxford, 1979, pp. 47–56.
32. Roll, R. 'A critique of the asset pricing theory's tests', *Journal of Financial Economics* **4**, 1977, pp. 129–76.
33. King, M. *Public Policy and the Corporation*, Chapman and Hall, London, 1977, p. 252.
34. As representatives of this literature one might cite:
Marris, R. *The Economic Theory of Managerial Capitalism*, Macmillan, London, 1966.
Baumol, W. J. *Business Behaviour, Value and Growth*, Macmillan, New York, 1959.
Leibenstein, H. 'On the basic proposition of X-efficiency theory', *American Economic Review* **68**(2), May 1978, pp. 328–34.
Williamson, O. E. *The Economics of Discretionary Behaviour: Managerial Objectives in a Theory of the Firm*, Prentice-Hall, Englewood Cliffs NJ, 1964.
Cyert, R. M. and March, J. G. *A Behavioural Theory of the Firm*, Prentice-Hall, Englewood Cliffs NJ, 1963.
35. Jensen, M. C. and Meckling, W. H. 'Theory of the firm, managerial behaviour, agency costs and ownership structure', *Journal of Financial Economics* **3**, October 1976, pp. 305–60.
See also: Alchian, A. A. and Demsetz, H. 'Producation, information costs, and economic organization', *American Economic Review* **62**, December 1972, pp. 777–95.
36. Fama, E. F. 'Agency problems and the theory of the firm', *Journal of Political Economy* **88**(2), April 1980, pp. 288–307.
37. Baker, A. J. *Investment, Valuation, and the Managerial Theory of the Firm*, Saxon House, Farnborough, 1978.
King, M. *Public Policy and the Corporation*, Chapman and Hall, London, 1977.
38. Simon, H. A. 'Rationality as process and as product of thought', *American Economic Review* **68**(2), May 1978, pp. 1–16.
Simon, H. A. *Administrative Behaviour* (3rd ed), Macmillan, New York, 1976.
39. Shackle, G. L. S. *Imagination and the Nature of Choice*, University of Edinburgh Press, Edinburgh, 1979.

Answers to numerical questions

3. The present value of an annuity of £20 for five years given an interest rate of 10 per cent is £75.82.
4. (a) The *NPV* of project 1 is £109.07.
   The *NPV* of project 2 is £113.60.
   (b) The *IRR* of project 1 is approximately 90 per cent.
   The *IRR* of project 2 is approximately 104 per cent.
5. The implied forward rate one year hence is 9 per cent.
6. The market value of the bond is £93.93.
   The duration of the bond is 3.469 years.
7. The real rate of interest is 3.6 per cent.

4. The expected return of the investment is 2.67 per cent and the standard deviation of the rate of return is 39.2 per cent.
5. The expected return of security X is 3.2 per cent and its standard deviation is 0.75 per cent. The coefficient of variation of X is 0.234.
   The expected return of security Y is 0.7 per cent and the standard deviation is 0.71 per cent. The coefficient of variation of Y is 1.014.
   The covariance between the returns on X and Y is -0.14 and the correlation coefficient between the returns on X and Y is -0.26.

CHAPTER 3

3. The bet has an expected monetary value of 0. The certain money equivalent will be less than this in the case of a risk averter and therefore he will reject the bet.
4. (b) $U'(W) = 10 \, e^{2W}$.

This is positive and therefore the marginal utility of wealth is positive.

(c) The function displays diminishing marginal utility of wealth and is therefore consistent with risk aversion.

(d) $\dfrac{-U''(W)}{U'(W)} = \dfrac{10 \, e^{-2W}}{20 \, e^{-2W}} = 2.$

This is consistent with constant absolute risk aversion.

CHAPTER 4

2. (a) The expected return of an equally weighted portfolio is 10.56 per cent. The standard deviation of the return on an equally weighted portfolio is 3.1 per cent.

(b) The expected return of a portfolio composed of 50 per cent in security B and 25 per cent in A and C is 11.75 per cent. The standard deviation of this portfolio is 3.62 per cent.

(c) If the investor concentrated on securities A and B and put 0.71 of his portfolio in security A and 0.29 in security B, the expected return of such a portfolio would be 11.45 per cent and its standard deviation only 2.65 per cent.

3. (a) The expected return on security X is 3.25 per cent and its standard deviation is 6.38 per cent.

The expected return of security Y is 8.0 per cent and its standard deviation is 5.24 per cent.

The covariance between X and Y is 33.

(b) When $X_i = 1.25$ and $Y_i = -0.25$, $E(R_p) = 2.0625$ per cent and $\sigma_p = 6.68$ per cent.

When $X_i = 1$ and $Y_i = 0$, $E(R_p) = 3.25$ per cent and $\sigma_p = 6.38$ per cent.

When $X_i = 0.5$ and $Y_i = 0.5$, $E(R_p) = 5.625$ per cent and $\sigma_p = 5.79$ per cent.

When $X_i = 0.25$ and $Y_i = 0.75$, $E(R_p) = 6.81$ per cent and $\sigma_p = 5.51$ per cent.

4. (a) The expected return on the portfolio is 19.66 per cent.
The standard deviation of the return on the portfolio is 26.45 per cent.
   (b) 40.35 per cent of the total portfolio risk is unsystematic.

CHAPTER 5

1. (a) The value of the option to the holder is 0 in state 1 and 25p in state 2.
   (b) The hedge ratio is −1.4.
   (c) The option premium is 9.74p.
2. The value of the European call is 11.34p.
3. The value of the European put is 1.9p.
4. (a) The implied current value of the firm's equity is £0.92m. The value of the firm's debt is therefore £0.58m.
   (b) If the risk-free rate rises to 20 per cent the implied value of the firm's equity rises to £1.14m and the value of its debt is therefore £0.36m.
   (c) If the standard deviation of the rate of return rises to 50 per cent the implied value of the firms equity is £1.01m and the debt has a value of £0.49m. (This assumes the interest rate is 10 per cent.)

CHAPTER 6

1. (a) Machine X has an *NPV* of £143.85.
Machine Y has an *NPV* of £179.43.
   (b) As the machines have differing lives their cash flows have to be converted on to a common basis for a comparison to be made. The periodic rental of an annuity over two years at an interest rate of 15 per cent with a present value of £143.85 is £88.46. The periodic rental on a three-year annuity at 15 per cent with a present value of £179.43 is £78.59. Therefore machine X is to be preferred, since its current value is 'worth' more.
4. (a) The certainty equivalents of the two cash flows are £187.07 and £180.77 (using a 17.6 per cent discount factor).
   (b) The *NPV* of the project is £267.84.
5. Project A *PVI* is 1.865.   Project B *PVI* is 1.585.
Project C *PVI* is 2.603.   Project D *PVI* is 1.625.

Although project C has the highest *PVI*, project D would make the greatest contribution to shareholder wealth since its *NPV* is £1,876.

CHAPTER 7

1. (a) Share price is 250p if *b* is 0.
   (b) Share price is 230.77p if *b* is 25 per cent.
   (c) Share price is 200p if *b* is 50 per cent.
   (d) Share price is 157.89p if *b* is 70 per cent.

CHAPTER 8

2. The firm's cost of capital is 16.4 per cent.
3. The implied cost of equity capital for the geared firm, according to proposition 2, is 20 per cent.
4. (a) The original holding of 10 per cent of B would give you an income of £120 (10 per cent of B's income net of interest charges). If you sold your 10 per cent stake for £1,200 and borrowed £600 to maintain the same level of gearing, you would have £1,800 with which you could purchase 12 per cent of A. This would give you an income, net of your own interest payments, of £150. Clearly you are better off and this arbitrage is worth your while.
   (b) The equilibrium cost of the equity capital of company B is 13 per cent. (NB: remember the equilibrium value of the equity is £9,000.)
   (c) The equilibrium value of company B's equity is £9,000.

Index

FINANCE
A Theoretical Introduction